of the Silent Generation of the fifties, but a thoughtful, carefully documented expression of where the generation gap is really at. As such, this book is must reading for anyone in contact with today's youth.

ISRAEL, SPRING 1969: MARK GERZON AFTER WORK IN A KIBBUTZ MELON PATCH

MARK GERZON, a sophomore at Harvard College when he wrote *The Whole World Is Watching,* has just completed his junior year abroad on an International Honors Program, studying with American and local social scientists in nine countries. He grew up in the Midwest and has traveled throughout the United States, meeting and talking with the young people whose world he describes.

The Whole World Is Watching

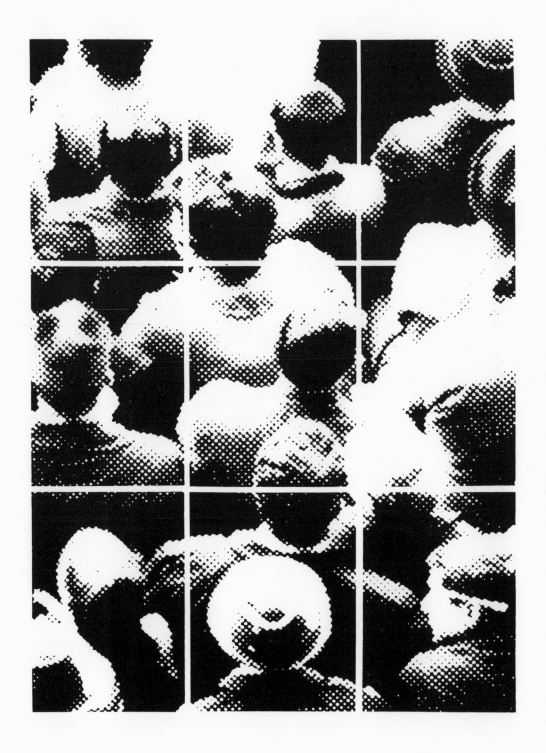

The Whole World Is Watching

A Young Man Looks at Youth's Dissent

by Mark Gerzon

NEW YORK / THE VIKING PRESS

Acknowledgments

Ahab Music Co.: From "Mr. Businessman" by Ray Stevens. Reprinted by permission.
Blackwood Music Inc.: From "Step Out of Your Mind." Words and music by Chip
Taylor and Al Gorgoni, © 1966 by Blackwood Music Inc. Used by permission. *Copper-
penny Music Publishing Company:* From "White Rabbit" by Grace Slick. Reprinted by
permission. *Dialogue Music, Inc.:* From "I'll Give You a Stone if You'll Throw It"
(Changing Times) by Janis Ian. Copyright 1967 by Dialogue Music, Inc. "Society's
Child" by Janis Ian. Copyright 1966 by Dialogue Music, Inc. Both used by permis-
sion. *Dunhill Records Inc.:* From "San Francisco Be Sure to Wear Some Flowers in
Your Hair" by John Phillips. Copyright 1967, published by Wingate Music Inc.
(ASCAP). Used by permission. *GNP Crescendo Records:* From "Now a Man" by the
Seeds. Used by permission. *Grass Roots Productions:* From "The Red Telephone."
Composer-lyricist, Arthur Lee. *Jefferson Airplane Music:* From "Plastic Fantastic Lover"
by Martyn Balin. Used by special permission of copyright owner, Jefferson Airplane
Music. *Stuart Scharf:* From "Give a Damn" by Scharf/Dorough. © Copyright 1968
by Takya Music, Inc. All rights reserved. Used by permission. *Schroder Music Com-
pany:* From "Little Boxes." Words and music by Malvina Reynolds. © Copyright 1962
by Schroder Music Co. (ASCAP). Used by permission. All rights reserved. *Vanguard
Record Society, Inc.:* From "Not So Sweet, Martha Lorraine" by Joe McDonald.
© Copyrighted 1967 Joyful Wisdom Enterprises, copyright permission granted.

For the members of my generation who, as an act of patriotism, went into the jungles of Vietnam, and to those who, as an act of conscience, went into the jails of America. May they unite and work together for a better society where future generations will not have to make either sacrifice.

ROSENCRANTZ: I remember when there were no questions.

GUILDENSTERN: There were always questions. To exchange one set for another is no great matter.

ROSENCRANTZ: Answers, yes. There were answers to everything.

GUILDENSTERN: You've forgotten.

ROSENCRANTZ (flaring): I haven't forgotten—how I used to remember my own name—and yours, oh *yes!* There were answers everywhere you *looked.* There was no question about it—people knew who I was and if they didn't they asked and I told them.

> —TOM STOPPARD, *Rosencrantz and Guildenstern Are Dead*

Foreword

This book is an attempt to describe part of the generation of young people who were born after the Second World War. I want to explain some of the reasons why many of them feel significantly different from the adult society of which they are expected to become a part.

The type of young man I describe is one who comes from a middle- or upper-class background; who is white; who attends college or is capable of doing so; and who would traditionally have become a leader in governmental, academic, scientific, or civic affairs. I am sure that what I have to say applies in different ways to some older men, to black men, to young men from lower-class backgrounds, or to those who do not go on to college. But the group which I am able to describe most accurately, and the group I think fits this description best, consists of the young men from relatively affluent backgrounds who attend college.

I cannot claim to represent the generation in its entirety. The aim of this work is to indicate some cultural forces that this part of the generation alone has had to cope with. Within the generation itself, many different reactions to these forces can be seen. When I use the terms "youth" or "this generation," they refer to those young people who perceive these new social circumstances and who recognize the new challenges, not those who continue to accept old values as if nothing had changed in the past quarter-century. Out of this group come most of the peace marchers, civil rights workers, Peace Corpsmen, the new rebel student leaders, the New Left, Vista workers, writers for the underground press, voluntary dropouts, draft-card burners, campus activists, and the hippies.

The alienated segment of the postwar generation is indeed still a minority. But, for many reasons, I think it is the most significant part. It is growing rapidly because more young people than ever before are from affluent backgrounds and are receiving college educations. And it contains the most articulate, energetic, educated members of the generation. I am no authority on these young people, but I think that much of my experience is representative of theirs.

This book is not itself a dialogue between the generations. It is merely one voice, a voice of youth, a voice which has been unheard in the discussion of the generation gap. The traditional adult viewpoint is largely omitted here because newspapers, magazines, television, books, schools, laws, churches, local and national politicians all so plainly expound it. This book is not balanced. *The balance,* if it is to be found at all, *is in the reader's mind,* where finally the already present voice of adult mass society may form a dialogue with a voice of youth culture.

Nothing in the book should be clearer than the fact that no single group can be blamed for the existence of the generation gap. The cause of the gap is social change, which is occurring at a rate which men could not before have imagined. There has always been some sort of gap between adult society and youth. But since changes which once happened over a forty-year period now come in four years, it is not surprising that the gap has widened. People grow up at the same rate, but modern society grows ever faster, and so social as well as family dynamics now divide the generations.

Speaking symbolically, the misunderstanding which fifty-year-olds have of twenty-year-olds indicates the kind of misunderstanding 1970 has of 2000. There is much more misunderstanding than there was twenty-five years ago because much more is happening. To prevent the continued growth of the generation gap is to contribute not only to the understanding between father and son, but also to the understanding of our society's future.

It is not the old conflict of, but the new gap between, the generations which is most to be feared. For I believe that, in this time of accelerated change, young people cannot know what to do in the present unless, through their parents, they understand the past. And, still more important, adults cannot know what to do in the present unless, through their children, they see what the future holds.

I have to talk about many things in order to talk about the postwar generation's experience: the draft, the media, the pill, the bomb; existentialism, acne, God, sex, marriage. All these topics, of course, cannot be discussed in depth in a single book. What I hope to contribute in this book is an idea of how these things *appear to*, and so how they *affect*, alienated youth today.

I must admit that what I say is happening to my generation is viewed through the lens of my own personal experience. I try to describe many different kinds of young people—traditional ones, hippie ones, radical ones—all of which no one person can be at the same time. My interpretation of these different groups is necessarily colored by my opinions at the moment. In this sense my personal involvement is a handicap. But in a much more important way, I believe, it is my greatest asset.

At different times I have identified with each of the various elements in this generation. So now I do not have to lift myself out of the older generation and try to imagine how it must feel to be a young man today. Nor do I have to consider only the externals—the clothes, the hair, the revolts—when I try to figure out what is happening. Rather I can look inside myself and inside the other young people I know and describe this generation on the basis of our collective impressions of ourselves and our society.

ACKNOWLEDGMENTS

Before I began this writing, a number of adults were of great help to me. I wish to thank Robert Archer, Thomas Wood, William Stark, Leonard Brisley, and Bruce Beck. In pursuing the writing to its conclusion, the encouragement and advice of certain adults in particular have been essential. I am indebted to George Goethals, Hans Hofmann, Dana Farnsworth, James (Jet) Thomas, David Riesman, Ann Orlov, Richard Todd, Cornelius Klein, and Bill Russell. My deepest thanks go to Alan Williams and Mary Chambers, who have made many valuable suggestions about the manuscript.

Many students have helped and encouraged my work. Without their conversations and friendships, the book would have been much less pleasant and much less accurate. For their openness and kindness, I am indebted to Hoppy Smith and Sally Thorpe Smith, Bart Casey, Rod Bernard, Dave Siktberg, Alan Robertson, Mike Bundy, Wizzer Short, James Sloan, Louis Sass, Jim Stuart, Michael Ferber, Henry Norr, Scott Carpenter, Chuck Peters, John Manners, George Mercer, and Brian who gave me a ride in Los Angeles. I especially appreciate the help of Jamey Smith.

I have to thank, without giving their names, all the people who gave me rides while I was hitchhiking throughout the country. Each of them left something important with me; collectively they helped me gain a special kind of optimism. I am very grateful.

My family has done a great deal for me during the time I have been working on this book. To each of them I say thanks a hundred times over for their help, their insight, and their patience.

I will always be grateful to Barbara Hancock, who fixed hot tea on cold nights—which made everything worth while.

Contents

House of
Mirrors: I

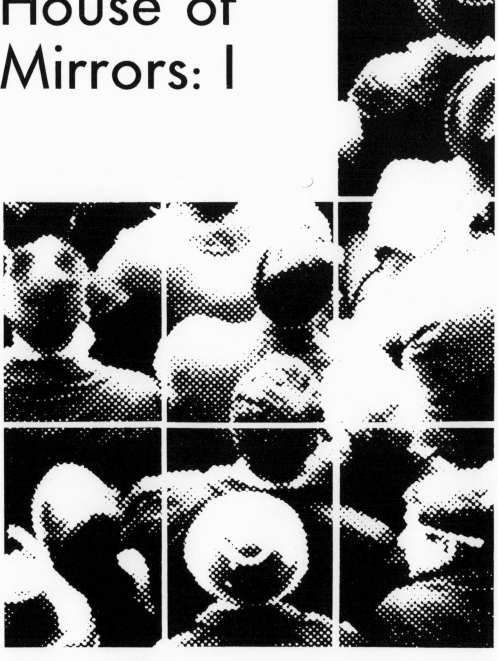

The postwar generation is the first to have faced manhood in a mass society.

The character of a young person is partly formed by his early relationships within his family. How mass society has affected these relationships is not the focus of this book, although the subject is touched upon quite often. The character of a young person is also greatly influenced by his relationship to adult society. This relationship is the focus of the following chapters, for the development of mass society has radically altered adult society, the traditional destination of the young generation. Because this destination seems unacceptable to many college youths, alienation has become widespread.

As the word "alienation" is used here, it represents something which is at the same time both good and bad. During the healing process, a wound often appears worse before it gets better. So, while alienation from society appears first as an affliction, with the pain of finding unacceptable the social values and character ideals that seem to satisfy others, it should at the same time be the beginning of the healing of the self. A wound is covered with an ugly scab. But it is that scab which protects it. So do young men try to protect themselves from those aspects of mass society which threaten to infect them with the germs of self-alienation.

The process of becoming alienated from society, then, is a process which must be completed: it makes the difference between a young man with a scar who can grow up to act with integrity and self-esteem, and one with a festering sore of self-alienation who is weak and conformist and never becomes a man. That is why it is so important that the reasons for and effects of alienation from society be analyzed and understood. It makes the difference between a generation which slides into an unacceptable adulthood and one which reaches for a meaningful manhood.

The postwar generation's alienation from society manifests itself in many different forms: historical, social, political, psychological, and cultural. Each should be examined in the context of an over-all pattern that is outlined in this chapter. These kinds of alienation are examined in this order because the culture of youth reveals that each is frequently a prerequisite for the next. A young man cannot become socially alienated until he has begun to feel a historical break between the conditions of his own life and those of the past. Nor can he become politically alienated until his social attitudes toward authority have changed. Nor does he feel psychologically alienated until economic and political activity have been recognized as being external to his personal problems. And he cannot become culturally alienated until he has explored the psychological dimension of society and of himself.

Distinct as these stages sometimes appear to be, a young person does not, of course, divide his life into different compartments of experience. Each man strives to experience his life as an integrated whole. Although for convenience writers discuss "economic man" or "psychological man" or "religious man," in the fabric of a man's individual life these threads of experience are interwoven into a complex pattern which leaves the specific threads virtually indistinguishable.

All too often in superficial analyses of the behavior of young people today, political attitudes or sexual activities, the use of drugs, or distinctive clothing have been examined as if each could be understood without knowing the over-all pattern of which it is a part. This makes criticism of the behavior much easier, of course, but it also makes understanding the reasons for this behavior much more difficult. Authors of such analyses, as well as their adult readers, have often failed to understand the complex experience of the postwar college generation.

They have seen only isolated threads and do not know how they fit into the life styles that characterize college youth today. By leaving the pattern as intact as possible, I hope to show that there is a logic to alienation, just as there is logic to conformity.

Without making distinctions between different kinds of alienation, a young person facing adult society can be represented as a person facing a mirror. Adult society has traditionally been the mirror of a young man's identity. The easiest thing for him to do is to look for his reflection in this mirror. It tells him how well dressed he is, how appropriately he acts, how well he learns—in short, it shows how effectively he measures up to the standards of adult society. But, as any little boy who has been in a "House of Mirrors" knows, what he looks like depends on the kind of mirror he is looking into.

For young men and women in earlier traditional societies, what kind of mirror they are looking in does not seem to have been a problem. They know of only one kind and assume that there are no others. Today's generation of young people, facing the mirror of mass society, cannot make this assumption. To a greater degree than any previous generation, modern youth can neither understand nor accept its reflection so easily.

This is true for three major reasons, the first of which I mention only briefly now. *Mass society provides its youth with the opportunity to gain a tremendous amount of knowledge about other cultures.* Because of both mass communication and mass education, young people know that societies which are less industrial, which have other economic systems, which are not Western, or which do not have mass media and mass culture are quite different from the industrial, capitalistic, Western, mass society in which they live. More mobile than any previous generation, young people today often have not only academic knowledge but personal experience of living in other cultures.

This generation has been forced to realize that the mirror of adult society is not a conventional one like the mirror that hangs above the bathroom sink. Adult society might be any one of the mirrors in a circus "House of Mirrors."

Second, *the uniformity of mass society has, paradoxically, caused each young man to receive multiple and conflicting reflections of his identity.* In traditional societies, both the wise men and the mentally ill were integrated into the culture. Today, neither group really is. Mass society's standards are so homogeneous and so pervasive that the mentally ill have been hidden from the public eye. Adult society has been taught that mental illness is descriptive only of "them"; it has nothing to do with "us."

As we shall see throughout the book, this generation has primarily a psychological critique of its society. The young have realized that those who do not fit the cultural mold reveal a great deal about those who do. In a sense, the mentally ill represent today another mirror adjacent to the mirror of mass society.

Just as Freud demonstrated that abnormality reflects the characteristics of normality, so is the mirror of deviancy in a position to reflect the characteristics of mass society. It is interesting to note that the patients through whom Freud became aware of this, who came to him with bizarre symptoms of hysteria, phobias, and even partial paralysis, were the cultural elite of turn-of-the-century Vienna. It is even clearer today than it was in Freud's time that a description of society in terms of those who do not fit is as important as a description of society in terms of those who fit the best.

Neither are today's "wise men" integrated into mass society. The intellectual social critics, those who are able but unwilling to accept mass society's standards, have become a separate part of society whose only function is to criticize it. The fantastic growth of higher education has increased the number of both these critical voices and of those they affect. Not only has the number of American academic critics skyrocketed, but, since the 1930s, America has acquired many outstanding European intellectuals. The American academic community has produced such varied critics as John Kenneth Galbraith, Paul Goodman, Margaret Mead, C. Wright Mills, and David Riesman, to name only a few. And to that group have been added the minds of European intellectuals such as Erik Erikson, Erich Fromm, Herbert Marcuse, Paul Tillich, and many others. Because over half of high-school graduates now go on to higher education, the work of these social critics becomes much more accessible to the young generation facing the mirror of mass society than to the members of mass society themselves.

These intellectual critics analyze different aspects of modern life and emphasize in one way or another that the mirror of mass society is a very peculiar mirror in the room full of historical and contemporary cultures—in the "House of Mirrors." In comparison to the situation even thirty years ago, there are so many more critics, and their criticisms are so much more incisive, that they have formed a mirror adjacent to that of mass society. It, too, reflects the nature of the mass society which the intellectuals were unable to accept.

Clearly, the members of the new generation cannot assume that the mirror of adult society provides them with an undistorted reflection of their identities. The mirror might best be compared to the kind of triple mirror found in clothing stores, and it no longer reflects a normal self-image to the young man facing adulthood. With mass society in front, the mentally ill on one side, and intellectual critics on the other, a young man receives different self-images, depending on which mirror he looks into. And each of them reflects the other two, so there is an endless array of reflections.

Like a customer in a clothing store trying on a new outfit, he receives many perspectives on his identity. His self-images do not define but confuse him, for they are often contradictory. Hesitant rather than challenged, unsure rather than enthusiastic, young men turn away from the mirror of adulthood and toward one another in order to discover who they are.

This brings us to the third reason for this generation's difficulty in accepting its social reflections of identity. *Mass society is characterized by extremely rapid change, which increases the distance between generations.* The experience, and therefore the accepted values and goals, of the older generation is grounded in a world which is quite different from the world the younger generation encounters. Although the distance in years between youth and adult society has remained roughly the same, the distance between them in social change is enormous. Most adults have either tried to rear their children for a world long past, or, in their own uncertainty, left child-rearing up to the school, the church, and the media of mass society.

The consequence is that the traditional values of adult society are now much less clear and much harder to accept. The ties to parents' attitudes are weaker. In its prolonged adolescence, modern youth is not swept up into adult society, as before, without ever looking into the mirrors of deviancy and social criticism. Today young people see themselves in all the mirrors. Some cannot make the leap into traditional adulthood, and many more do not want to. With multiple, fragmented, and often contradictory reflections of themselves from mass society, this generation finds it necessary to turn inward to find identity.

Standing before the closed door to manhood, the postwar generation also forms a mirror in which all society is reflected. Unlike the reflections of mass society from the mentally ill and the social critics, this reflection shows the parents' society head-on. There the dichotomy between those who are unwilling and those who are unable to gain manhood is less valid. The "best" and the "worst" are often intermixed: the young people who violate society's standards and reject society's norms are most often the most capable members of the generation. It is the mirror of youth itself that reflects the character of mass society most completely. And it is the alienation of youth that reveals the problems of living in mass society most clearly.

This, then, is the over-all pattern of alienation. Already it has become clear that the crucial problem is not "uptight" parents or "degenerate" youth, as each generation has suggested about the other. It is the rapidity of social change and its effects on youth ready to become men. In order to understand more precisely the specific social changes which have resulted in generational differences in values and attitudes, the different kinds of alienation must be examined separately. What should be kept in mind, though, is the over-all pattern of alienation among young people, and the consequent development of the young awareness.

Youth and History

I think everyone would agree that acne is an adolescent problem. Everybody knows that skin problems plague teen-agers. When the body is changing very rapidly, the skin acts up. Furthermore, everyone agrees that this has always been the situation, so it might be fair to call acne a "historical phenomenon."

Now later in this chapter I look at four major historical phenomena and try to show how they are different for this generation. But I think there are generational differences which apply equally well to this very small phenomenon that historians ignore, this phenomenon of acne.

Not too many years ago the majority of people lived on farms, or in small towns based on agricultural commerce. They had very little access to fancy food and restaurants, and, no matter where they lived, they had little money to buy special goods. Groceries carried farm produce and little else. Husbands and children ate their meals at home, and the food on the dinner table came either from their own farm or from a farm nearby. Also, not too many years ago a child's parents were almost the only people who taught him his eating habits. Radios did not advertise in every home, car, and store. Television commercials did not instruct him from crib to car what foods he should eat, and did not display cold Cokes or twirly cake frosting right before his eyes.

This generation, however, the "Pepsi generation," has had a very different childhood. Practically no one lives on a farm. Affluence has brought any candy, ice cream, or soft drink well within the means of today's youth. Mother today eats lunch alone: dad and the kids eat at the company or high-school cafeteria. Teen-agers also buzz the drive-in restaurant, where they eat food quite far removed from any farm. In general, food has become mass-produced and mass-distributed, and hundreds of ingredients have been added to it that no self-respecting farmer's wife would ever have dreamed of.

And as every mother knows when she packs Junior's lunch for school, parents are no longer the sole source of eating instructions. The menu for today's children is made up on Madison Avenue. If the cute freckled kid on television talks his mother into giving him a Super-Duper candy bar, then that's what Junior has to have. Advertising has told the young most explicitly what they should eat. The ads don't emphasize, of course, things like potatoes, vegetables, and fruit; farms had those things. Rather, they plug all the things that mother might quite naturally forget: the sugary breakfast cereal, the fizzy drink, or the new flavor of ice cream. The stuff that the advertisements which envelop teen-agers instruct them to eat doesn't come from any farm; it comes from the bright minds of advertisers working for food corporations.

So already it is not hard to see that this generation has a new kind of battle with good old acne. But the odds are stacked still higher against young complexions. For at the same time that television and radio push the products which help to cause acne, they have the audacity to offer cures for it. CBS, NBC, ABC—they all have something that will beat skin problems. With the number of products advertised on television and radio, kids have no doubt what to do about acne—buy something! (Besides, all the commercials make it quite clear that using their skin creams will improve one's love life.)

All too many young people continue eating and buying the way the mass media tell them. They are boxed in because the cure and the disease are recommended by the same source. All people who agree that acne is an adolescent problem must realize that it is not the same problem as it has been in the past. And when I turn to other, much broader historical phenomena—making a living, defending the country, communicating between cultures, and finding a challenge to manhood—

I am not at all saying that these issues never before existed. I am just saying that the problems they pose for this generation are radically different.

Another factor in the generation gap that must be kept in mind, in addition to specific social change, is the lapse of time between generations. Attitudes toward acne illustrate the first factor; attitudes toward Communist subversion can well illustrate the latter.

In the late 1940s Alger Hiss was tried and convicted for perjury in his testimony before a Senate investigating committee. He was suspected of having given government documents to the Communists in the 1930s. In the trial, Hiss's defense made it clear that the time of the alleged crime and the time of the trial were quite different: the 1930s were a time of disillusionment, poverty, and socialist thought, while the late 1940s were a period of victory, economic growth, and virulent anti-communism. To quote the opening sentence of a book on the trial: "We are about to look at the trials of a man who was tried in one decade for something he was said to have done in another."[1]*

Today another trial is going on, and the postwar generation is the accused. For when adults admonish young people for their ingratitude, lack of patriotism, immorality, disrespect for the law, and so forth by saying "Why, when I was your age I would have . . ." they are judging the young of this decade by the values of another. The problem is that more than two decades of unprecedented social change divide adults' adolescence from that of their sons, and so divide the judges from the accused.

I was still banging the bars of my crib at the time of the Hiss case, so I nave to piece together the effect that it must have had on people then. But as I see it, a generation of men had just returned from fighting a long and difficult war for their country. Trying to re-establish themselves, they realized how much had been lost in the war, but they considered it worth the price because the free world had been saved from the Nazi and Japanese onslaught. In this mood, they were told that a high government aide, a man who had been associated with President Roosevelt and part of a crucial Allied conference, had made photostats of important government documents and given them to Communist agents. The men who returned from the war felt that there were officials in the highest echelons of the government—which they had just risked their lives to defend—who apparently didn't give a damn about the security of the United States.

* Reference notes may be found at the back of the book.

American society was enraged at a possible traitor in its midst. Americans vowed to be on their guard against the insidious infiltration of subversive elements, and they became determined to expose those who were part of the "international Communist conspiracy." Still today, many Americans regard Communist infiltration as our greatest threat.

I wish to make only one point about what must have been a series of very interesting events. Whatever really happened, *half of America's citizens would have to read a history book to know about it*. Anyone born after the war might never know who Alger Hiss was. What young people today think about international issues is not affected in the least by Alger Hiss. Even if they have heard of him, the case cannot make the vivid impression on them that it made on their parents. In the experience of the postwar generation, there has been no incident comparable to Hiss's trial.

So we learn one thing about the young awareness: it is characterized by being uninvolved in many of the things that were of crucial importance for the old awareness. Adults, of course, use this as a basis for criticizing the young awareness. They say that young people have not "learned the lessons" that the Alger Hiss episode and other events of the past had to teach, and that young people are therefore less capable of dealing intelligently with present issues.

But young people are prepared with a defense. They agree that they are not so deeply affected by the past. But they feel that adults were so rigidly molded by past events that they have failed to respond to more important developments which have become crucial in the decades since the Alger Hiss case. In other words, while adults are stressing that youth hasn't learned the lessons of the first half of the century, young people are stressing that their parents' generation has failed to learn the much more important lessons which the events of the second half have to teach. And as the opponents in the generation gap polarize, the old deny any truth in the young awareness, and the young deny any truth in the old awareness, and truth itself has been the casualty.

Although truth is only wounded, communication is killed. Young people argue with their elders without realizing what a deep influence historical events such as the Alger Hiss case must have had. And parents, with equal blindness, fail to realize how remote such events must seem to their children. Although we need not now examine other specific incidents which divide the generations, some broad developments must be considered.

Between the time of our parents' childhood and our own, four spheres of life have witnessed great historical change. The most apparent is the economic sphere. Until after World War I there had always been economic hardship for most Americans. The sudden affluence of the Roaring Twenties was the only premonition of the 1960s: the young rebelled, spending was wild, new music and dances appeared. Deep generational differences could be seen for the first time in modern America.

But the generation gap never widened, for suddenly father and son were reduced to virtual poverty. They retained the economic bond that had united generations since time began. How can we feed ourselves and heat our homes? asked the generations in unison. The extended credit structure that had made the twenties roar collapsed beneath old and young alike. Security vanished. The traditionally close bond between father and oldest son remained intact because both had to apply their energies to caring for the younger children. Different generations and even different branches of families drew together, trying to find a semblance of security in an insecure time.

The son's circumstances remained quite similar to the circumstances of his father's childhood. Any gap in values was strictly limited by the generations' common economic situation. The social contexts of their lives were not radically different, and so neither were their values, attitudes, and beliefs.

The Depression years of the thirties and then the war postponed the revival of the economic conditions of the twenties until after midcentury. In the late fifties and into the sixties, continued economic expansion finally became reality for the majority of American families. More families had more money than ever before. At first there was a great deal of apprehension. Adults recognized prosperity and feared a crash like the one that hit them in their childhood. They had known poverty and could still feel it amidst affluence.

To the postwar generation, however, prosperity was the normal state of affairs. These young people had never experienced anything else. The economic conditions which their parents—the young people of the Depression—had to fight and work for were given to the next generation in childhood. Looking through the picture windows of their suburban homes, with Father's big car (and perhaps even Mother's compact car) sitting in the driveway, many members of this generation are clearly experiencing a world radically different from that of their parents. The traditional bond of material scarcity which formerly united generations has been severed. These young people not only do not have to concern themselves with their families' welfare, but really do not have to worry about eventually making a living themselves. They can concern themselves with *how*, not *whether*, they can make a living. Young men can earn at eighteen what their fathers only began to earn at thirty-five; they can earn after college, at twenty-three, a paycheck which their fathers, perhaps, earned only at fifty. In the span of one generation, the relationship of youth to adult society has been transformed by the beginning of the affluent age.

The second sphere of change is political. Before the late fifties there was, indisputably, somebody to fear and to fight. A scourge such as Nazi Germany was by any definition a formidable enemy. From the thirties to the end of the war, Hitler provided an ever-present threat to security. America and its allies could meaningfully engage in the effort to stop the Nazis and Japan; and, for a while after the war, they could meaningfully involve themselves in dealing with the aggressors and restoring the free world.

After the war, in Europe and the Middle East, communism had to be reckoned with—again a still credible enemy. Regarded as a force calculated to destroy the free countries with its inhuman, godless, socialist claws, it was seen as a world concern because of its triumph in China, the Berlin Airlift, the rape of Czechoslovakia, and the outbreak of the Korean War, and so a desperate rearmament began in the West. Americans who went home tiredly as victors after the war had to maintain a fully militant stance against the apparent Communist threat. That Joseph McCarthy could fan anti-Communist sentiments to white heat revealed that most Americans still felt they had a real enemy to hate and fight.

While this generation was still in nursery school, significant changes began to occur in the political sphere. Stalin died, and soon an unknown Khrushchev appeared. The American hydrogen bomb was followed by an equally powerful Russian weapon, and the nuclear arms race began. The McCarthy era was over, and more Americans perhaps became aware of the irrationality of the phobia of communism. But American society was slow to understand the difference between Stalinist Russia and Khrushchev's, slow to realize what the change from hot to cold war meant, and even slower to understand the difference between a world where the United States kept a superweapon on its hip, like the marshal of the town, and a world where no one would survive if a shot was fired in the saloon.

Today's generation became aware of the world situation only well after these changes had taken place. Young people of the 1960s did not have to modify past anti-Communist sentiments. They found themselves unable to define their ideology as anti-something, or define their nation as anti-someone. Well before this generation was born, Franklin Roosevelt told the nation, in his famous "Four Freedoms" speech, that one of America's goals was "freedom from fear." This goal has begun to be achieved. This generation cannot derive meaning by blindly hating another nation, because it cannot hate men with whom it shares the confines of a powder keg.

It became clear to this generation that adult society depended on a certain amount of fear. It was hatred for and fear of someone outside our country that often provided unity for disparate groups and interests within our own society. Adult society did not consider the decrease of fear and prejudice an indication that Franklin Roosevelt's goal was being achieved. Some adults took it rather as a sign that the young were irresponsible and lacking patriotism. But the young were responding to new political circumstances rather than old, and consequently the differences in political attitudes between generations became evident.

That a book entitled *The End of Ideology* could be written about American politics in the 1950s shows that something new was happening. Its author, journalist and scholar Daniel Bell, concluded that the old conservative-versus-liberal arguments had become meaningless; that the policies and programs had exhausted themselves. Of course politics itself doesn't look this way. Old conservatives and old liberals seem quite contented to continue using each other as targets. From all that can be seen in adult society, the old politics still seems pretty real. The young generation as a group is alone in realizing that the usefulness of the old political perspectives is gone. Or, as Bell says, "The new generation, with no meaningful memory of these old debates, and no secure tradition to build upon, finds itself seeking new purposes."[2]

Youth's political alienation is deep. Because the problems that face us today seem so much vaster than, and so different from, the problems of earlier times, neither the conservative nor the liberal alternative seems relevant to their solution. For the first time, consequently, a large part of the college generation was bored with the 1968 Presidential election (although many young people were involved with the conventions). Its members really did not care whether Nixon or Humphrey became President. With Eugene McCarthy as spokesman, they tried to fight the old political attitudes, but they were without support. Very few with political power seemed to have their young awareness.

The Republican and Democratic conventions were striking examples of the irrelevance of the old politics. I do not know of one New Leftist, radical, peacenik, yippie, hippie, or other young person who ever thought of planning any major action at the convention in Miami. Nixon had the convention completely under control, and the whole affair seemed so removed from the feelings of young people that no problems arose for the GOP. Nixon and the party powers successfully kept "law and order"; they kept it by appearing totally irrelevant to the aspirations of this generation.

The Democratic convention in Chicago, however, caused such a disruption of "law and order" that Walter Cronkite actually said Chicago appeared to be a "police state." The young people who caused the disturbances, and all those who identified with them, were there because that convention seemed to be potentially relevant. Maybe Edward Kennedy would be drafted; maybe Senator McCarthy would gain in the closing rounds, with George McGovern's help; maybe the platform would actually recommend that some money now allocated for destruction be designated for constructive purposes. Maybe traditional politics could still be relevant.

But these hopes were disappointed. It was Nixon against Humphrey, the cold-war lawyer against the politician of joy, mister black against mister gray. Young people, looking for someone who would light the world, had to turn elsewhere.

The third sphere of rapid change (and one which has influenced the generational differences in politics) is that of cultural communication. Our world, suddenly shrunk by mass-communication and transportation networks, no longer allows young Americans the luxury of ignorance. Situated like a giant fortress surrounded by its Atlantic–Pacific moat, America has been able to view the world in comfortable isolation. It has been able to cultivate an ethnocentricity unparalleled in most modern countries. The original ethnic diversity of its citizens helped create a willingness to conform to American culture. Mass education and mass communication have made this cultural narrow-mindedness a difficult attitude to maintain.

Furthermore, the economic hardship and the political threats to national security which necessitated much of the uniformity of American life have now been greatly lessened. As those spheres of life were transformed by technological change, the young generation's cultural blinders were removed. Economic and political necessities no longer demand exclusive allegiance to the set of social ethics and cultural ideals which they previously had molded.

Because of the beginning of the breakdown in our cultural isolation, today's young people have realized the relativity of cultural systems and have developed a receptivity to the values and character ideals of other cultures. They have a capacity to be involved with other societies that adult society as a whole lacks. The enthusiastic response of college students to the Peace Corps was a sign of this new perspective. Young men were not concerned, as were their parents, about "losing two years," or about having their fellow classmates get a "two-year jump" in the business hierarchy or professional world. The prospect of two years in an underdeveloped country excited the idealistic young people of the early sixties. Only when the advertising and Peace Corps rhetoric began, only when the Corps became an official bureaucratized organ for eulogizing the government's humanitarianism, only when its brochures began to point out that the Peace Corps was a smart step for businessmen of the future—only then did the appeal begin to diminish and the idealism of the original venture become tainted.

This generation finds it difficult to be satisfied with meaning derived from traditional cultural orientations and goals. The number of young men who are choosing jobs simply because of the size of the salary has diminished greatly. Young people today ask for some inherent value in their work, not just for monetary reimbursement. They know they personally can have enough money to live satisfactorily, and so they must find other criteria besides the size of the paycheck for selecting an occupation. Before, there was always a simple meaning to work: to eke out an existence, and then, if lucky, to achieve some level of luxury. It required time, energy, devotion, and sacrifice. It was a challenge, a test for manhood.

As these preoccupations diminished in importance, a broad segment of today's young people recognized the absence of, and the need for, a deeper meaning and a challenging goal. Without the canned meanings that satisfied previous generations, they felt an emptiness, an absence of purpose.

We now become aware of the fourth sphere of change, the intellectual and philosophical sphere. The minds of this generation are the first which are ready to listen to the message of philosophers who, writing during the last credible war, have been disregarded by most members of adult society. The message of these philosophers could be grasped only by people who found no absolute, set meaning in life. It is a philosophy for today's youth.

Amid the irrationality and cruelty apparent during World War II, some minds were led to emphasize an underlying futility and meaninglessness in life, but the books about absurdity that they produced had little impact on the postwar world. People's minds had been numbed. Those who had been involved in the war and its aftermath—those who had fought, whose brothers or sons had fought, or who were merely involved as aware adults or young people—could not listen to the voice of existentialism. Too much had been suffered, too much had been lost, to adopt a philosophy that spoke of life's meaninglessness.

But there has been a whole generation since the war that has never paid the price or felt the pathos that is war. The members of this generation, unlike their parents or the generation just ten years their senior, have lived only in a world where all-out war is futile.

Some parents, indeed, see this situation as the crux of the whole problem. One father, a medal-winning soldier in World War II, told me confidingly, "If there were another war, another *real* enemy, these kids today would realize what their duty was. They'd straighten up all right!" And a mother with two children in college explained to me, "Another depression—that would bring young people to their senses. Then a lot of this nonsense would stop."

Now these parents are right, I think. But their solutions to the generation gap are a coward's solutions. The situations that defined their youth —that were, to use Simon and Garfunkel's phrase, "the borders of their lives"—were military threats, economic hardship, and social climbing. These parents seem to be saying, "Let's turn back the clock so you can go through the same thing. Overcome the meaninglessness of life the same way we did. We grew up facing these challenges. They can be your challenges too!"

Fortunately, this generation has more guts than to fight in battles that have already been won. It realizes that the meaning of wars and the meaning of making a living can never be quite the same for American college students. The question is not, as parents ask, "How can we look at the new world so that the old meaning will fit?" The question is, as the young ask it, "How can we find new meaning in a new world?" This book is the story of young people trying to answer that question.

The goals of this generation could never have become so different from adult society's had it not been for the changes in these four historical spheres. For these changes, and all that accompanied them, created a world bearing little similarity to that of the older generation's adolescence. As Margaret Mead has said, the young people who were born after the war are natives to modern times, while the older people are like immigrants.[3] As natives, young people have no "old country" to break away from. Trying to find meaning that fits in modern times, they find themselves alone. Their parents are still pushing them to reach the old goals via the old values.

For alienated college students, economic success can no longer supply the needed challenge. Society has highly praised financial and occupational betterment as the main goal in life, but young people realize that the only valid purpose of striving for these goals would be to live a fuller life. And their parents' society seems to be enmeshed in materialistic, acquisitive values rather than liberated from them. Or, to put it bluntly, the older generation had to get uptight to get rich.

Today's college students have had to realize that for themselves the essential problem is not material but social and psychological. The problems they encountered in their lives of affluence could not be attributed to the fact that there was no fuel in the furnace, or no car in the driveway, or no money for education. The problems were not material, as previous generations could suppose, so they must be human. The problems must have to do not with one's money but with one's mind.

Yet adult society still encourages this generation to pursue the same goals, despite the fact that they have lost their challenge. These goals were challenges for today's adults when they were young. But if their sons are to become men, the same goals cannot be meaningful tests of manhood for them. Young people know that, to gain manhood in their own eyes, they've got to do their own thing.

The Dangling
Conversation

In their song "The Dangling Conversation," Simon and
Garfunkel describe the superficialities of life today, in
which meaningless dialogue and shallow reactions
are "the borders of our lives."*

Young people often approach existentialism with a personal intimacy and need which their parents do not share. All the changes
discussed in the previous chapter make this philosophy an understanding
of existence which they do not find only in the textbook. It is an understanding which they find by living daily in a mass society.

This is important. It is not necessary for today's youth to study (in
the academic sense) existentialism in order to come in contact with
the idea of the absurdity of life. As with other academic themes I discuss in this book, existentialism can be felt in the world this generation
experiences. It pervades modern life itself, and it is found in contemporary religion, literature, theater, and psychoanalysis.

Like T. S. Eliot's line "I have measured out my life with coffee
spoons,"[1] Paul Simon's "dangling conversation" leads us to the basic

* My intention was to reprint lyrics in their original form. The young poets who wrote
the songs I quote have stated their feelings so beautifully that their words should be
used. Unfortunately, for a number of lyrics I was unable to obtain reprint permission,
and paraphrasing became necessary. I can only suggest that readers listen to the songs
themselves.

question: "What kind of conversation with life can have meaning for me?" The challenge of overcoming the meaningless alternatives offered by adult society tends to lead the young to existentialism. Many young men come to Camus and Sartre trying to understand the absurdity of their experience. And of these, many leave existential philosophy with an idea of what their generation's challenge is.

With increased cultural communication, today's well-informed young people cannot accept canned meanings and opinions. They have access to too many thinkers and have too great a degree of mobility for the ethnocentric answers given them in childhood to remain satisfactory. Between the ages of eighteen and twenty-two, they are gaining an education which most of adult society has never had. And even those adults who went to college spent their years of study becoming aware of the world situation as it was during the 1920s or 1930s, not as it is today. The fact must be accepted: the young generation comes in contact with more information based on recent developments than its parents' generation does. This is the gift of the older to the younger today. While they work and earn, we study and learn.

One predictable reaction to this increase in available knowledge has been young people's unwillingness to commit themselves to anything whatsoever. This is the element of youth culture which Kenneth Keniston studied in *The Uncommitted*. These young men found that the way their parents chose their loyalties and their beliefs no longer worked, and so they decided to have *no* loyalties or beliefs. This extreme cautiousness, a fear of being fooled or "snowed," pervaded youth culture of the late 1950s almost to the point of passivity. The intellectual rootlessness in youth culture has changed this generation's outlooks more than is generally recognized.

For these young people facing adulthood, the question is not "What shall I believe?" but rather "Can I believe anything at all?" The past to them seems like a conflict between men believing in different and sometimes opposing systems of thought. They cannot feel involved in this historical conflict because they do not seem to have any system of thought to which they are committed.

The world may easily look absurd to those without traditional intellectual or social commitments. Jack Newfield, author of *The Prophetic Minority*, writes that the absurd pervades youth culture. This generation can find absurdity

> in the songs of [Bob] Dylan, the Beatles, the Mothers of Invention, and Phil Ochs; in the fiction of Joseph Heller, Thomas Pynchon, J. P.

Donleavy, Terry Southern, and Ken Kesey; in films like *Morgan* and *Dr. Strangelove*; in the poetry of Allen Ginsberg, and the comedy of Lenny Bruce; and the cartoons of Jules Feiffer.

These elements of youth culture all "mirror a generation's perception that logic, rules, and order explain less and less about a culture that puts Martin Luther King, Joan Baez, and Ken Kesey in jail—and Lester Maddox, General Hershey, and Ronald Reagan in power."[2]

The same idea of the absurd is what caused a Berkeley dropout to exclaim: "To have grown up among and amidst the cold war, the cold cities, the coldly intellectual existentialists, to have suffered the agonies of Hesse and Kafka, to have seen the terrifying visions of Camus and Sartre, and then to be told by adult society that things haven't changed!"

Art mirrors society in many ways, and the modern arts today reflect the violent break with traditional structure that has occurred in the rest of society. An editor of a collection of plays published in a volume entitled *Absurd Drama* described the work it contained: "By all the *traditional* standards of critical appreciation of the drama, these plays are not only abominably bad, they do not even deserve the name of drama."[3]

Why, then, adults might ask, have some of the plays he described had such wide acclaim and run very successfully on Broadway? It is because many people have realized that nothing can be judged by traditional standards, for we do not live any longer in a traditional society. How many parents have said about modern music and painting that they do not even deserve the name? The arts have broken with tradition because they found the limitations on style and structure unnecessary and artificial, i.e., absurd. Since today's young people are surrounded by these new forms of expression, it is not surprising that they find the themes of existentialism familiar before they have read any philosophy. For, as the title of Paul Goodman's book says, the postwar generation has been *Growing Up Absurd*.

It is the pervasiveness of the absurd that makes existentialism a significant influence on this generation. Certainly the roots of existentialism are deeply embedded in the philosophy of Heidegger and Nietzsche, and the beginnings of "modern" existentialist thought are over a quarter of a century old. But the intimacy between this generation's rootlessness and the themes of existentialism, and the consequent recurrence of those themes in other fields, provide contemporary existentialism with unique social relevancy.

Something can be learned about modern youth by understanding how

existentialism is misrepresented in youth culture.* Many young people
simply say that existentialism means that life is not worth living and that
it really doesn't matter what is done, since it's all futile anyway. And
isn't this the simplest, and today seemingly the most real, thing to conclude? It permits one to settle into a profound and stagnant apathy that
indeed affects a great number of this generation. The more hedonistic
members of this group combine sensualism with this apathy. They
attempt to deluge the senses with as much pleasurable sensation as possible in an attempt to milk life of all it can give. This reaction is of course
an undercurrent in many of the publicized happenings that so shock
the older generations, but it is also an element in "normal" college
behavior.

The more recent reaction to existentialism disagrees with the response
just described. This approach finds some validity in these attitudes but
concludes that, in their apathy and sensualism, young people have not
overcome the existential rootlessness of modern life but succumbed to it.
Perhaps the attitudes of this more recent, ever-growing group can best
be understood by examining one branch of existentialism itself, in the
context of Camus' *The Myth of Sisyphus*, which has been perhaps the
most popular book of philosophy in youth culture.

Those young people striving to overcome their rootlessness recognize
that some of the basic suppositions of the apathetic group are not valid.

> Hitherto . . . people have played on words and pretended to believe
> that refusing to grant a meaning to life necessarily leads to declaring
> that it is not worth living. In truth, there is no common measure between
> these two judgments.[4]

Since life is not automatically worthless, as the apathetic assume, the
question of why to live remains open. Camus goes on to tell his readers
that they cannot complacently blame the absurdity of their existence on
any "they"—whether it be society as a whole, or the evils of technology,
or the "nature of man," or just life in general.

> I said the world was absurd but I was too hasty. This world is not
> reasonable, that is all that can be said. But what is absurd is the
> confrontation of [the] irrational and the wild longing for clarity that
> echoes in the human heart. *The absurd depends as much upon the man*

* To say simply "existentialism" is, of course, incorrect, since there are many branches
of this philosophy. Were this a philosophical discussion of existentialism, not a sociological and psychological discussion of youth, they should be clarified. This is a discussion
of youth, however, and existentialism can safely be considered one body of thought in
terms of its social effect on this generation.

as on the world. . . . Man feels within him his longing for happiness and for reason. The absurd is born in this confrontation between the human need and the unreasonable silence of the world. [Italics mine.][5]

The reader must catch himself as did Camus, for it is quite easy to absolve oneself from any responsibility for the absurdity of life. The obstacles to finding meaning in life often seem so insurmountable that a man is pushed into a corner from which, to save his sanity, he opts for an apathetic, I-don't-give-a-damn attitude. Either that, or he becomes prey to one of the religious ethics that preach the irrevocability of man's original sin and the basic evilness of human beings without faith in the Calvinist God. Both escapes, the apathy ethic and the Calvinist dogma, enable those who use them to blame the world or "just the way man is" for their unfulfilled existence. By the Calvinist escape, by accepting the lack of fulfillment in mortal life and man's inability to change this, they absolve themselves of the blame for their own troubles, no matter how much they speak of original sin and guilt.

These escape patterns, and the remaining ghosts of traditional religions, are not merely inconsequential attitudes that remain vague in their adherents' minds. On the contrary, these attitudes toward the meaning of life determine the manner in which one loves, or raises children, or works at a job. Youth's rebellion against the Calvinist view of the basic evilness of man, similar in many ways to Camus' own rebellion, has been a crucial development, causing alienation from adult society, in which a secularized form of the Protestant ethic still prevails. Religious conviction remains in adult society in such a hypocritical form that the young have had to look beyond it.

If a young man has grown up to find that the thinking of Camus is much like his own, if he accepts the absurd as being caused by the individual himself, then he cannot consider himself a helpless form, tossed by the waves of the sea of life's irrationality. He must approach his life as a surfer, who can choose to ride a wave or to let it pass and wait for the next one; who can ride the crest or shoot the pipeline. He must approach his life as a man who can make choices and decisions and who can determine whether or not he will achieve a measure of self-fulfillment. He cannot absolve himself of the burden for the absurdity of his life as traditional believers in past generations could. If a young man today encounters a frustration, feels an inadequacy, discovers an alienation from society's goals, he may feel impelled to find and root out the cause. The emptiness he senses in his life is not cushioned by notions of immortality. He must strive for fulfillment or salvation through his capacity to reason.

The Myth of Sisyphus begins as a work of absolute reason. "I don't know whether this world has a meaning that transcends it," wrote Camus in the early 1940s, "but I know that I do not know that meaning and that it is impossible for me just now to know it. What can a meaning outside my condition mean to me?"[6] This extreme rationality confined Camus strictly to his own immediate circumstances; that he says "just now" it is impossible to find meaning is perhaps his acknowledgment of that.

It is interesting to wonder how Camus would have written this book in a situation other than the irrational and perplexing one of the French Resistance. For Camus defines his concept of absurdity once almost as a problem of probability:

> If I see a man armed with a sword attacking a group of machine guns, I shall consider his act to be absurd. But it is so solely by virtue of the disproportion between his intention and the reality he will encounter, of the contradiction I notice between his true strength and the aim he has in view.[7]

Because the lone man's chances are so small, practically nil, his actions are absurd.

But the very nature of Camus' illustration shows us the relativity of those odds. If the man with the sword faced a group of men with stones instead of machine guns, the odds might be nearer 50–50. And if he had a mere coat of armor, perhaps it would be the group of men with stones whose actions were absurd. The point is that *the confrontation of a man and his world is a constantly changing confrontation*. First, man brought nature to his bidding: there is abundance and overabundance instead of material scarcity; the forces of nature have become somewhat subject to man's control; labor is giving way to leisure. Second, man has begun to learn something about his own nature: Darwin explained the evolutionary process and allowed other men to realize that man has certain basic needs; Freud demonstrated that men could drift away from self-realization and then recover; modern psychology has explored the interaction of culture and personality and has helped modern man understand the way in which his culture limits or enhances his life. The constant change in confrontation between a man and his world has accelerated in this century at an unbelievable pace.

In particular, Camus' confrontation with his world in 1942 in the French Resistance was much harsher and bleaker than a young American's confrontation with his world today. Millions of innocent people were being killed because of a racist doctrine of Aryan supremacy. The pain and death went on needlessly because of the neurosis of one demagogic man with a funny mustache. In France, countryman fought against countryman.

Yet even with the "bad" odds of his condition during the war, despite its irrationality and absurdity, Camus found reasons to avoid suicide.

> Thus I draw from the absurd three consequences—which are my revolt, my freedom, and my passion. By the mere activity of consciousness I transform into a rule of life what was an invitation to death.[9]

He found reasons for living; yet he earlier stated that he knew of no meaning which transcends this world. We must conclude that Camus found his affirmation of life within the experience of living itself; that, like young people today, he rejected the religious codes which assume the worthlessness of life without faith in God.

Camus' reasons for living—revolt against traditional beliefs and meanings, freedom gained by losing these groundless ideologies, and renewed passion for "being aware of one's life, one's revolt, and one's freedom, and to the maximum"[8]—are also the characteristics of the young today who overcome their existential rootlessness. It becomes apparent throughout this book that no words better characterize the difference between this generation and those of the 1940s and 1950s than *revolt, freedom,* and *passion.*

Today youth is in revolt against the social creeds and practices which limit self-awareness. Because young people are unrelated to the past, they are gaining a freedom of action and thought that is the root of today's activism. And finally, through this freedom, they are developing a passion for being aware of and involved in life, which accounts in part for the hippie movement and for youth-culture behavior which is striving for a freer and deeper involvement with others and with oneself.

Some young people achieve only revolt; others, revolt and freedom; but today a significant number are also discovering passion. This passion is reflected in the upsurge of political activism. It is no coincidence that Kenneth Keniston's book representing the youth of the late 1950s and early 1960s was called *The Uncommitted,* and his book representing youth after 1964 was entitled *Young Radicals: Notes on Committed*

Youth. The change to passionate involvement was sudden and was reflected also in the popularity of the hippie ethic and the spread of psychedelic drugs on college campuses throughout the nation.

Their passion and involvement are what these young people feel differentiates them from their parents and from the beatniks of the 1950s. Their desire to live to the fullest by their definition, not society's, leads them away from adult society's logic and toward Camus'. For Camus points out that it is not only through man's capacity to reason that he may find fulfillment, but also through his capacity to love.

"There is but one luxury for [man]," Camus' absurd man tells us, "that of human relations. How can one fail to realize that in this vulnerable universe everything that is human and solely human assumes a more vivid meaning?"[10] Yet young people today know that adult society has indeed failed to realize this. Adults have tried to find meaning in the supernatural, and they have tried to find meaning in striving for ever greater wealth and social prestige and power. Because of the incompleteness of their beliefs, they have forgotten the only meaning their lives could have, that which rests in what is solely human: human relations.

This generation is becoming aware that the most significant part of man's world is other human beings; that each man faces the irrationality of existence; and that in this common bond one can find reasons for living. Relating to other people is not really a luxury, as the absurd man suggests, but the essence of human existence. To overlook the extraordinary emphasis placed on human relations in youth culture would be to sacrifice a crucial insight into the generation gap.

Whenever the rebelling members of this generation attach great importance to something, it is often because they feel that adult society has attached too little importance to it. They are concerning themselves less with the luxuries of adult society and more with the luxury it has forgotten—human relations. Consequently, they are also concerned with understanding their own personalities and the social system that has made interaction between people lose its spontaneity and wholeness. This attitude is a response to their most pressing challenge: overcoming the effects of the social pressures that divide the individual from others, and from himself. That young people are concentrating on meeting this challenge is evidenced by an already visible decline of college students' interest in finance and business, and a decline of interest in the physical sciences which has just appeared; and by a complementary increase of interest in psychology, sociology, and political science.

But this is only the academic reflection of the change that is occurring. One cannot prove historically an increased interest in human relations and in understanding one's own psyche and how society affects it. In finding their challenge beyond what the previous generation could achieve, young people have turned away from history, away from the mirror of mass society, and have turned toward themselves. Any further insight must come from examining contemporary youth culture and the attitudes of its members.

Youth and Mass Society

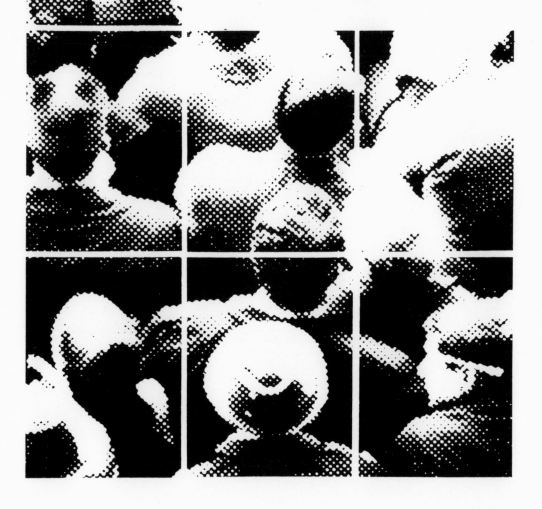

Both the political and economic changes discussed earlier, and the existentialist thought and interest in psychology that accompanied them, caused this generation to feel quite removed from history, both ancient and modern.* This unrelatedness to the past is accentuated by the nature of American society.

Most obviously, America is a land of immigrants and second-generation Americans. Because the citizens of other cultures are so quickly digested and given an American coating, their numbers are often not fully recognized. Second-generation Americans not only have to bridge the gap in time between themselves and their parents, a period full of truly radical changes in the world configuration, but also have to bridge the tremendous gap between European society and values and American ones.

Modern family structure, too, augments this unrelatedness to the past. Ever since the days when American family trees spread their

* The exception to this statement is to be discussed later, but it can be sufficiently summarized by the statement, "The past is okay if it's Oriental."

branches westward, our society has witnessed a great division in the traditional extended family pattern. Today in America, generations are more often than not spread across the country. Fathers follow job opportunities, wives follow husbands, and sons and daughters follow the college trail. Nor does the young man have the ever-present grandmother or friendly aunt who still exists in Europe and very rural America, and so he does not have the constant personal reminder of the past. The great mobility of the American people, which makes possible both freedom and rootlessness, gives a transience and fluidity to this generation's perspective on society.

Perhaps the most influential reason for this generation's unrelatedness to the past is the change in traditional authority. The home in American society has become a dormitory. The father does not work at home, and, especially if he travels or works long hours or has a difficult shift, there is less contact between father and son. For children, Father is someone who brings in money.

In less industrial societies, a father's work was a craft carried out in the shop that was part of the home. Or there was a privately owned small store next to the house. Or work was the tilling and harvesting of fields adjacent to the house. Children were as closely involved with their fathers' work as children can be.

Today American children have amazingly little understanding of what their fathers' work is all about. In working with ten- to twelve-year-old children from middle- and upper-class homes, I was intrigued by their lack of comprehension and (the more so, the older they were) lack of interest in their fathers' occupations.

> Where does your father work, Pete?
> —At Burns, Willoughby, and Fenster.
> What does he do?
> —Well, they give him papers which he brings home in his briefcase, and then sorts them. I think he adds up people's money, too.

More common is the child whose father works for a large corporation or for the government.

> John, what does your father do?
> —He works for the government.
> Yeah, but what does he do?
> —He takes care that their buildings here in the city are okay.
> I see. But does he do electrical stuff, or does he hire people to take care of buildings and grounds, or does he clean the buildings, or does he order equipment and supplies, or what?

—I don't know. But I know he's with the government [or with GE, or with DuPont, or with Ford, or . . .].

This situation is quite different from that of an earlier time, when a young boy would help his father in the fields or in the shop or in the store. Now, children not only do not help their fathers but understand so little about what the fathers do that their only relation to the work is that it "makes money." The father commands much less respect because of this, because children naturally find it difficult to appreciate Daddy's work when they do not know what it is.

The lack of relatedness to the father extends beyond his occupation. Parents, first of all, do not educate their own children. Education is all taken care of in the maternal world of the public school with mass-produced books and the "new" math, which even parents don't understand. It must be remembered, along with this, that a child is not necessarily learning what his parents already know. As social change accelerates, the school child often learns what his parents were never taught.

Chances are, too, that the father no longer teaches his son how to tie a tie: his son sees how one is *really* supposed to do it on television. The same with shaving: in fact, it is probably the son who is telling the father about the "new" razor or "better" shaving cream. And learning to drive is done in Driver's Ed or at a driving school or with high-school friends when nobody is looking. And, of course, sex: it is now assumed that the son or daughter knows the facts of life, although perhaps in a strange version, from friends, magazines, or "sex education" in school. In today's so-called sexual revolution, parents seem to entrust the media or the school with the job of telling their children what is accepted. Why hassle with it, parents must think, if somebody else will do it?

Since fathers no longer seem to have adequate answers for their children's questions, the rest of the relationships within the family have changed too. Most noticeably, the "older brother" takes on more importance. If an eighteen-year-old's big brother has just finished college, for example, and there are questions on the boy's mind, he turns not to his father but to his brother. The older brother, too, often feels a greater obligation to remain close to the younger children than he would have in the traditional family where the father was the absolute authority. Because conditions for growing up have changed so rapidly, older siblings have a *relevance* when they give advice or caution or criticism or praise that it is very hard for Dad to have. J. D. Salinger, who must be considered the literary godfather of the postwar college generation, foretold this beautifully in his writing. The central figure throughout a series of his stories dealing with a family of six children is not the father but the oldest brother.

The decline of the father's authority finds its academic reflection in David Riesman's explanation of the change from inner-direction to other-direction. A modern young man no longer accepts and incorporates the values of his authoritative, imposing father. He is brought up, rather, to be directed to others for instruction—to the school, to friends, to popular opinion, to the mass media. This other-direction, this preparedness to respond to other social authorities in place of the father, is the result of rapid social change. Young men cannot accept old values but are told to listen to the values of new, anonymous, and diffuse sources of leadership.

The father was once the tie to the past. Embodied in him were the values, the goals, the beliefs of an earlier period. If relatedness to the father is decreased, if his authority declines as the authority of more recent organs of opinion increases, it can logically be expected that the past will also seem more distant and irrelevant.

This unrelatedness to the time of their parents is certainly a major factor causing the individual lostness so characteristic of modern young people. But, at the same time, it also gives the generation a freedom of thought, a freedom from traditional controls, that earlier generations could not have had. It is this very lack of commitments to the past, whether political, religious, moral, or racial, that accounts for much of the freedom of action on these fronts (which in turn brings down the criticism of the older generation, still committed to previous attitudes).

This uncommitment and unrelatedness to tradition has created the reservoir of potential energy and enthusiasm necessary to meet the challenges facing the world community. But this reservoir, without a socially visible channel for expression, can also hold the vast amounts of energy seen in the cynicism and rebellion so often associated with the postwar generation. The dam of adult society can either let this energy flow constructively to fuel the generators of progress, or it can remain closed to this reservoir of power and let it build up until it floods the nation.

No generation can survive and develop completely unrelated: any remaining ties with history will consequently grow in importance. This has indeed been the case.

Youth today does not feel primarily related to the economic, political, and religious change of the past, but does feel a keen involvement with the psychological development of man through the centuries. Certainly, because of this generation's psychological interests, young people have to apply themselves to understanding other spheres of life and their contemporaneous development. But that this generation's avenue for historical inquiry is founded primarily on psychological dissatisfaction, rather than, as in the past, on economic or political dissatisfaction, is a change in approach that seriously affects its interpretation of the development of civilization and of the individual.

As evidence, it is interesting to note that, despite today's college students' unrelatedness to the past, the questions raised by anthropologists are being aired more frequently among them. In the study of people living untouched by modern civilization, the student feels he can at last witness the "basic" psychology of man by analyzing the primitive society it created. A sort of simple wisdom is sometimes expected to be found, for here are men untouched by the social pressures and technological invasions of modern mass society.

This change in perspective can be seen in many Peace Corps volunteers. Unlike the missionaries of the imperialist age, who were characterized by a desire to bring civilization to the primitives, most of the Peace Corps participants with whom I have spoken feel that they must hide from the Corps officials their feeling that they have more to learn from the society to which they are going than they have to teach it! Rather than bringing *the* answers, these young people are hoping to have some of their questions answered. We cannot fully understand this attitude so long as we are confined to the interest in anthropology, for it is but a small effect of a great cause. The cause was psychoanalytic psychology.

Freud's work met with tremendous opposition in American society during the first decades of this century. It was the parents of this generation's parents that provided this opposition, and so a dislike for psychology still rests deeply in most of today's adult society. The young reflected this dislike for psychoanalytic psychology: no generation before the 1950s read psychological literature extensively. But even the youth of the 1950s did not accord the study of psychology the welcome that the postwar generation gave it. There were not so many people in college then. Besides, psychology wasn't very practical. Steady economic growth had not yet begun, and so there was greater interest in business and other traditional occupations which would ensure a solid income. But most important, the college students of the 1950s had not grown up in the era during which the institutions of mass society more blatantly than ever before used psychological manipulation to achieve their ends. Consequently, it never appeared so necessary, to young men born before the war, to have a psychological understanding of themselves and their society.

Today it is hard to find a motivated liberal-arts student who has not read some of Freud's more popular works. Psychoanalytic terminology now pervades the language of young people. Some technical terms are used commonly in youth culture which a generation ago would have been only in the vocabulary of specialized psychologists. Post-Freudian psychologists find an unprecedented market for their writing in this college generation of the 1960s, and it will be still greater in the 1970s.

The impact of Freudian thought was so large that, although in youth culture we see its greatest influence, adult society has also been hit. But, as with existentialism, adult involvement for the most part is academic. Very rarely can a young man find a person who encountered psychoanalytic thought in adulthood and yet is able to apply it to himself and his own actions, as youth is attempting to do. It is difficult for the adult Western man to investigate psychoanalytic logic with an open mind because—capitalistic, business-oriented man that he is— he knows a lousy deal when he sees one. He is asked to trade in his concept of himself as a lofty man capable of objective, detached, rational choice for one that characterizes him as being composed of basic drives which, at least in part, control his supposed self-determination. For an American adult, trading his religious, nonpsychological self-concept for the concept of man in psychoanalytic psychology is "like trading a Cadillac for a VW," a salesman told me. "Although the trade'll save you on gas, it sure doesn't have the prestige." Most older people cannot even see that it saves on gas, and anyway, very few in status-symbol land decide to make the trade.

This generation has more than the tools for self-analysis. More important, it has the *need* to analyze behavior and social psychology. The culture's values appear so separated from their own that young men must question themselves as to the difference. They must question themselves to be sure they are right—right despite the criticism from adult society. Riesman makes a similar observation in his analysis of contemporary urban, middle-class America:

> A major difference between the problem of [John Stuart] Mill's day and ours is that somone today who refuses "to bend the knee to custom"

is tempted to ask himself: "Is this what I really want? Or do I only want it because . . ."

Today, Riesman continues, people "live in a milieu in which people systematically question themselves in anticipation of the questions of others." [1] This is self-analysis and demonstrates a personal if not academic interest in psychology, and it is much more visible in youth culture than in adult society.

The importance of psychology, both for its social use and as the remaining link to the past, necessarily prompts the young to question the traditional emphasis of the social sciences on economics and politics. Various scholars have helped bring this wave of questioning to a crest by their exciting psychoanalytic interpretations of history, a method of historical inquiry strangely neglected since the appearance of Freud's work.* Since the publication of these books, the further effects of this psychoanalytic method can be seen in similar psychological interpretations in sociology, anthropology, and media-study. The influence of these investigations has not yet been fully acknowledged by traditional historians, but the ever-growing number of analyses make interaction inevitable.

These books are an academic reaction similar to that of today's youth against the traditional historical approach to the development of civilized man. Historians seem to have grasped that the unfolding story of man is one in which the development of civilization has accelerated at an amazing pace. But nevertheless they strangely consider it a story in which the human psyche has remained immutable. Certainly the scientific revolution caused changes in man's concept of himself, they admit. Of course the industrial revolution altered man's relationship to his work and his society, they acknowledge. But they do not see—or perhaps it is just not their business to see—the vast influence these and other revolutions have had on human psychology.

This generation does not say that historians must be psychologists. It does say, however, that those who read traditional history should realize that they are getting only one part of the story of man.[2]

Electronic media have extended man's senses and nervous system throughout the world and transformed his perception and way of thought. Urban, technological life has accelerated and codified his every action. Economic expansion has revolutionized values and social stratification.

---

* Herbert Marcuse's *Eros and Civilization* and Norman O. Brown's *Life against Death* are the most popular in youth culture.

Science and mass communication have created brand-new mythologies for society.

Yet through all these vast transformations historians treat man's delicate mental balance, which psychologists touch with scrupulous care, as a standard and unchanging fixture in the whirling panorama of historical development. In the eyes of today's young generation, which feels this change, theirs is a one-dimensional view of man and society, and it is exacting its price. We are failing to understand ourselves and our changing motivations, and so will fail to understand this world, which is about to blow up under our feet.

The members of the older generations cannot feel this way so easily. They are too aware of and too involved in history. They remember too clearly the hardships of war and depression, or of fewer jobs and lower wages. They can see within the context of their lives that today is better than yesterday.

Their own sons talk to them of an inability to communicate or of alienation. But parents cannot help thinking that their sons are simply running away from the challenge of carrying on their tradition. Their sons talk to them of meaninglessness or of the absence of self-fulfillment in the lives of the people they see around them, but the parents cannot help feeling that their sons lack the gumption to face the challenges of manhood. They cannot help responding the way a young man's father, an insurance-company executive, responded to his son's psychological questioning. "There's entirely too much introspection going on these days," his father said, as if introspection were some sort of infectious disease that should be stamped out.

In a way, parents are right. If their son faced the same world and the same challenges that they themselves faced, then he would not be affronting them with these psychological dissatisfactions. But the fact is that he does *not* face the same world or the same challenges. No attempt to convince him that it is the same world, or that the same set of values still applies, will meet with success. Every aspect of his life feels the difference, and no appeal to parental or national loyalty will change those feelings.

Let the Hurt
Creep On Thru

Go on, let the hurt creep on thru, don't let it
Bother you, don't let it blow your mind, it's only
A sign of the changing times.

—Janis Ian

The older generation is searching far into the universe, striving to discover its secrets and extremities, struggling to gain an outpost, a station, a planet base. Man's imagination, his response to challenge, will lead him to the farthest star and to the most complex theories about its galaxy. And someday, given enough time, he will understand it.

Men are penetrating the most minute particles of our world, bisecting them and dissecting them and building more magnificent microscopes for exploring smaller and smaller particles. Each new division is subdivided, and new laws and theories arise, and man's science pursues and penetrates deeper. And someday, given enough time, he will understand it.

But there is an inside chance that he may not have enough time. One can reasonably fear that although the secrets of science will be the servants of man, man himself will still be the slave of his own nature. One rightly wonders, when the mechanics of the universe are understood and the power of the atom harnessed, whether there will still be hatred and prejudice, exploitation and inhumanity.

This generation manifests a lesser concern for technology and a greater concern for man, technology's inventor. The young today are not entranced by what technology does *for* man and so can better observe what it does *to* man. Just as learned men during the Renaissance had to inspect their society's assumptions about the nature of the world because of the discoveries of science, so today students are inspecting their society's assumptions about the inventions of science. Technological change has descended on us with such rapidity that even the most stubborn and conservative elements of adult society will soon have to acknowledge its pervasive social effects.

Yet youth's attitudes encounter animosity in an adult society in which established interests have a great stake in the maintenance of the values of a technological society. Even the scholars who point to the effects of new inventions are often severely criticized. Critics invariably conclude that the price of technological advance is the psychological sacrifice of individual independence. The older generations first failed to accept the full implications of Freudian thought for their supposed rational self-control, and now seem unwilling to acknowledge the growing power of mass society and its media over their lives. Perhaps this is because when they were children mass communications' influence was not so blatantly evident.

But if we are interested in the generation gap, we must look not only at the world of the older generation's childhood but at the world of their children. The mass media must be understood not only as they were but as they are. The most popular source we have for understanding contemporary mass media is the work of Marshall McLuhan.*

McLuhan's work is not necessarily a value judgment about print or mass media in general. Rather, what McLuhan stresses is that *unconsciousness of any forces upon the behavior of man is a potential danger, especially if those forces are controlled by other men.* When McLuhan says that the medium is the message, he means primarily that not only

---

* The typical reaction to McLuhan could be a very wasteful one in terms of ideas. One need not react to him in the same way that a friend of mine reacted to the Irish Catholic teachings with which he was raised. "If there really is no life after death," he said to his priest at confession, "then this is the biggest snow job that's ever been pulled off." The reader of McLuhan's *Understanding Media* should not feel forced to choose between accepting it as the gospel of media-study or rejecting it *in toto.* Like other initial forays into an uncharted field, McLuhan's work appears to contain many dubious conclusions. But that should not be reason enough to make the reader overlook the numerous and valuable insights he provides concerning the effects of the electronic media on human behavior and psychology.

what is communicated but also *how* it is communicated is important. Until McLuhan, we have been grossly ignorant about the "how," about the psychological dimension of the media. If the individual, especially the young individual, is not aware of the psychological influences of the media, this vast societal power is left to the manipulation of any organization with money that wishes to influence the thinking of millions.

McLuhan thinks that some generation differences have been caused by the development of the mass media. "Every technology creates new stresses and needs in the human beings who have engendered it," he writes. Because of the pervasiveness of the new electronic media in the lives of the postwar generation, reactions to these new stresses are part of this generation but not of the last one.

The fact that young singers have described social change in terms of media imagery suggests that they have a special awareness of the effects of the new communications technology. One psychedelic group (Love) sings that "the news of today will be the movies of tomorrow." Another group (the Lovin' Spoonful) explains that the deepest worries of one generation are the next generation's cartoons. Because media experience has been a greater part of this generation's childhood than of any before, young people have come to see social change not just in terms of history books but in terms of media imagery.

Television is the most powerful medium of communication differentiating this generation from preceding ones. In sheer numbers, the rapidity of change is breathtaking. At the end of World War II there were 7000 television sets in the United States. Twenty years later there were 60 million in active use; today there are a few million more. In less than a generation, television became the main transmitter of information.

Only the postwar generation has *grown up* in a world where human eyes could see the experience of men everywhere. Not only is it true, as young demonstrators in Chicago during the Democratic convention shouted, that "the whole world is watching" certain events; it is also true that the whole world is being watched. Just as optic nerves run from the eye to the brain, the electrical nerves of the new mass media carry messages from throughout the world to the eye.

According to McLuhan, because the electric technology—television, radio, telephone—extends the central nervous system and changes the type of experience it has to deal with, the technology has altered the values of the young who have grown up with its inventions as everyday household appliances.

The young people who have experienced a decade of TV have naturally imbibed an urge toward involvement in depth that makes all the remote visualized goals of usual culture seem not only unreal but irrelevant, and not only irrelevant but anemic. . . . The TV child expects involvement and doesn't want a specialized *job* in the future. He does want a *role* and a deep commitment to his society. . . .

The TV child cannot see ahead because he wants involvement and he cannot accept a fragmentary and merely visualized goal or destiny in learning or in life.[1]

Here we hit upon a major cause for the generation gap and the inability of young people to define their values in relation to those of their parents. McLuhan points primarily to television to explain the new urge for deep involvement, but, as I think most parents with children between the ages of thirteen and twenty would agree, electronic stereo equipment and musical instruments are also worth mentioning. In the sphere of electronic music the striving for all-inclusive participation is most obvious. It manifests itself in young people by the unprecedented form of new dances, and in adults by the order "Turn the stereo down over there!"

McLuhan says that this generation's fathers have specialized *jobs*, in which one has to remove one's emotions from one's work. Young people, on the other hand, are searching for involving *roles*, a full commitment to their occupation and, through their occupation, a full commitment to society. A role means an occupation that is rewarding in the activity itself, not only in the financial results of the labor. This generation feels a need for something more than the fragmentary or visualized goals in life with which its parents' generation was satisfied.

This attitude is reflected, on one hand, by the rejection of the typical businessman image and of the specialized scientific man by many members of this generation, and, on the other hand, by this generation's enthusiastic response to the civil rights movements, the anti-war cause, and the Peace Corps. Embracing these movements allowed the young to commit themselves ideologically and emotionally to their work, something which the necessities of detachment and traditional structure in their school work did not permit.

McLuhan also elaborates his concept of the "global village," which is closely related to many of youth's attitudes. The electric media, says McLuhan, involve modern man in everything and everyone. Man's awareness is extended far beyond his original physical capacities. Because of the psychic effects of the new communications, "we everywhere resume person-to-person relations as if on the smallest village scale. It is a relation in depth."[2] Youth culture as a whole is oriented toward relations in depth. Combined with an existential emphasis on human relations and a preoccupation with psychology, the modern age has caused young men to become concerned with the openness and completeness of interpersonal communication.

The increased effectiveness of our bodies because of the technology of tools and transportation is accepted by everyone. It is equally clear, too, that our minds and their outposts which take in and relay data—our eyes, our ears, and our voices—are also extended throughout the media which they use and become more effective. This extension of mental functions is the crucial development that has enabled us to be aware of other men and other places, as if the whole world had become the size of a traditional village.

Have we paid no price for this tremendous gain? We have indeed, McLuhan thinks. The amplification of mental processes "inspires the central nervous system to a self-protective gesture of numbing the extended area, at least as far as direct inspection and awareness are concerned."[3] The individual cannot control these mental media because he does not understand them. Unlike information received through interpersonal communication, information through the electronic media cannot be questioned. The source is anonymous and unapproachable. There can be no communication about the communication, since the information is unilaterally given by the media. A son can ask his father "Why?" or "What do you mean?" But he cannot ask a television set, much less a magazine advertisement, much less a book on sex education. The media speak brashly and ubiquitously but are silent when questioned.

McLuhan stresses one aspect of social change, the media, which other commentators mention only in passing. Keniston has remarked upon the slowness with which the public realizes that various kinds of social change might produce the "fringe" groups in youth culture.[4] Author and psychoanalyst Erik Erikson also emphasizes technological change and states quite directly that "today we face the question whether the prevalence of the machine will be solved by the mechanization of man or the humanization of industry."[5] McLuhan alone, however, is attempting to concentrate solely on the psychological effects of the media.

The values of this generation, gained from the new media, stress deep involvement and all-inclusive participation and are a distinct break from the values of the pre-electronic age. McLuhan feels that the printed media which prevailed up through the first third of this century engendered an urge for detachment and noninvolvement. He concludes that this generation, whose heritage of Western values is based on specialized jobs and detached, noninvolved lives, is challenging the society with the values of the "electric age," which emphasize all-inclusive participation and the involvement of the whole self. "Science since the Renaissance has exalted this gift [of detachment and noninvolvement] which has become an embarrassment in the electric age,"[6] he says, and he finds ample evidence of the effects of this clash of values, this embarrassment, in our generation.

Both in their personal and in their academic lives, Western young people have felt the impact of the age of analysis. In college, cold, academic, and critical rationality is demanded of students. The more often I encounter this clash in the lives of other students, the more often I witness this conflict between wanting to be involved and committed and the cultural priorities placed on detachment and dispassion, the more forceful it becomes. Take a friend of mine, a business-school graduate student, for example, who is personally deeply committed to alleviating poverty and hiring the unemployed. He told me one day that his professors tell him not to be *too involved*: poverty and unemployment are just factors in your analysis, they tell him, like any other economic variables. Don't be so emotionally concerned, they tell him, or your business analysis won't be efficient. This student sat in his room, talking of this clash of values, wondering if *he* had something wrong with *him*. He wondered if it was a personal weakness to be involved emotionally.

Countless times have I run into a student despairing over a paper that had just been returned, into which he had poured an inordinate amount of energy and thought. Something in the subject had made him personally involved, and he put twice the amount of work into the assignment that he normally did. But he gets it back with the comment: "You are too involved personally in this subject. Try to give a more dispassionate analysis." So he goes back to writing the old, unconcerned way, and often, ironically, gets better grades. Or, if he won't sacrifice involvement, he drops out.

Except for the now precious fields of drama, music, and creative writing and art, all fields require an ability to dissociate oneself from one's feelings. The priority is placed on logic, not feeling. A San Francisco College senior expresses this attitude toward school but realizes that it does not apply only to the academic community: "Too great a portion of the energies of colleges and universities is still devoted to the expansion of the intellect, at the expense of the emotions." *And the reason that today's young people are trained in this manner is because that is the way their society has become.* "Everywhere I look," he continues, "I see people of all age levels and groups being afraid of their feelings, of love, of their common humanity."[7]

Even in its personal lives this generation has felt the necessity for emotional noninvolvement. We can see throughout this book that society's demand on the personal lives of the young has required a limitation of emotional expression, substituted for by an increase in logical appraisal of social priorities and their fluctuations. This generation, which has accepted the new values of the "electric age" of involvement and participation, is still facing an adult society that demands detached observation.

Those who strive for emotional involvement in personal life are exposed to the same kind of criticisms to which students are exposed in the academic sphere. I heard a high-school senior, one of the most popular in her urban middle-class neighborhood, advise a friend who was somewhat less popular on the shortcomings of her social behavior. "You're *too involved*, too intent, in trying to share your feelings with people," she explained carefully to her less popular friend. "Don't you see? People don't want to be known. You've got to act like you don't give a damn; then you'll do okay."

The first girl had been rewarded in popularity for her acceptance of the cultural limitation on emotional involvement. We witness in her division of self the failure to realize that "the essence of life is human relations." The natural, spontaneous desire is to make oneself known and to communicate with another person deeply. But rather than do so, one is culturally patterned to act disinterested and self-contained. The spontaneous action must be curbed and another, thought-out set of detached actions substituted for it.

The modern man who accepts socially patterned behavior learns to approach his life as if it were a scientific experiment—to remain detached and analytical. He removes his inner feelings as fully as he can from the activities of life, and he sacrifices his capacity for spontaneous involvement. He reconciles himself to an unreasonable existence because the part of his being capable of deep communication is kept behind walls. He accepts what psychologist Erikson has called "the mechanization of man."

McLuhan's analysis is brilliant, but almost too brilliant for us to be able to accept all that his conclusions claim. That they are a factor to be included in the study of the bases of the generation gap, however, cannot be denied. What I would stress again is that this generation, whether the topic is psychology or existentialism or McLuhan's media-study, does not become aware of these outgrowths of social change through academic channels. What McLuhan needs great insight to grasp, a young man recognizes readily because it is the only world he has ever experienced. He becomes aware of the effects of the media through his life. He is aware of the effects these changes have on him and, if he can see beyond his own concerns, on his whole generation.

While I was still in high school, I first became aware of the social strain between the involvement a young man needs in order to grow up and the noninvolvement that this society encourages. I went to a public high school, but in a sense it was more "preparatory" than a prep school. One was perhaps not quite as well prepared academically, but socially the preparation was unsurpassed. For in today's public high school all the patterns of behavior corresponding to social mores in adult society are quite convincingly ingrained in the majority of adolescents. One learns how to present the self in public; how and to what to conform; the social utility of group membership; the limitations on personal relationships necessary for public prestige; and, the *summum bonum*, how to avoid becoming emotionally involved with anything or anyone beyond yourself in order to avoid being hurt, i.e., losing your cool. In high school, a microcosm of social pressures, individuals are made to develop with the uniformity of a well-clipped suburban lawn.

I was not aware of all this so clearly at the time. But in retrospect I realize that one of the few friends I had who fascinated me was, to use my analogy, a weed in the front lawn. He didn't fit.

Hal read voraciously about almost everything, but he ignored his classes because he said the information was "spoon-fed." He refused to accept the penny-loafer, leather-belt conformity and came to school in boots and jeans with empty loops. He ridiculed the mock shaving cuts and bimonthly haircuts and came to school wth a few days' stubble and unruly hair. Hal's attitudes, too, set him apart: he was not interested in subjects that are socially useful, and was intrigued by subjects about which, in high school, one is supposed to be ignorant. He was not satisfied with being (a) fashionably indignant, (b) unconcerned, or (c) mildly bigoted, which were the acceptable attitudes toward civil rights, but took a bus and went to march in Selma. Rather than involve himself in the restricted and socially patterned behavior of the dating system, he involved himself deeply and emotionally in relationships outside the dating games of high school. Myriad social conventions, which are conscientiously respected by all those who endeavor to be "in," he violated with abandon but with reason.

A good example was his language. Everybody but Hal upheld the adolescent's unwritten law of limiting obscenities in mixed company to expressions blaspheming God, while properly excluding sexual obscenities when girls were present. (Girls would smile admiringly at "Goddammit" but be appalled at "Fuck!") Hal decided to reverse the linguistic law and so revere God rather than intercourse.

He had read more about more religions than any of us and refused to give the token respect to a deity which the rest of us gave weekly. While the patterned topics of conversation were traditionally sports, cars, sex, and clothes, Hal—troublemaker that he was—talked about imagination and conformity, or social justice and discrimination. He would take opposing views just to make people think, because it seemed to him we didn't. He wanted to know people and to know life completely. He wanted more than the artificial interaction with both that our high-school society was satisfied with on grounds of "respectability."

As one could guess, Hal was alone. The rest of us were busy growing up as we were meant to. We wanted to be liked, to be included at all costs, to be successful. Whether we now admit it to ourselves or not, we excluded him. We knew how to act and what to do, learn, and wear. We knew how to keep our emotions, our selves, inside an outer social shell. We knew who our friends should be. We knew most explicitly who *we* were supposed to be.

Hal's "problem" was that he wanted to show he was serious and involved with life and the living of it—with becoming a man. He wanted to show he was concerned—about Negroes in Selma, about peasants in Vietnam, and about the people at our high school, regardless of whether or not they were "big men on campus."

No wonder we excluded him. The last thing we wanted to be was concerned, or open, or involved, or serious. We wanted to be cool, detached—and successful. We wanted to be tough—which we thought meant *not caring*. We had not learned, as he had, that real toughness is *being able to care*. The Beatles began singing in 1968 that "It's a fool who plays it cool by making his world a little colder." The thought is beautiful, but it came too late for Hal.

Failing to communicate to us through his life, he tried to communicate through his death. All we heard in the halls at school that morning was something about Russian roulette, a gun, late at night. By the time our class decided to collect money for flowers, the tragic irony had already struck me.

I realized that, to the dead living, living death is mute. The flowers we bought could not mark his grave, for no one knew him, and of the few of us who, disappointed in ourselves, made Hal our friend *post mortem*, so few realized what his death meant: that in mass society the flowers, as well as the weeds, are indiscriminately cut to keep the social lawn well trimmed.

Since knowing this high-school friend, I have seen countless college students, myself included, who have felt the strain of wanting to be involved and committed and serious in our approach to life but finding that the social pattern favors being detached, cool, and buried within ourselves. Clearly, young men who accept this socially patterned attitude toward life have not made the revolt, nor gained the freedom, nor found the passion, that Camus states are his reasons for living.

My friend had passion but found it alone, and so he killed himself with the same passion with which he had lived. In colleges today, the people with freedom and passion are finding others to share it with. (As one popular song repeats again and again, "I think it's so groovy now that people are finally getting together.") And it is these young people, on and off campuses, who set the tone of the generation. For they will not accept the detached, noninvolved way of life that modern American society has tried to prepare them for. They reach out, as my friend did, and get hurt and feel alone. So they take refuge in those communities, communities of ill fame in adult society, where they may share their passion and involvement in life.

We who make them run away should ask ourselves: from what kind of society are they trying to escape?

Mechanical Rape

All the red tape is mechanical
Rape of the TV program waste
Data control and IBM
Science is mankind's brother
But all I see it's draining me
                    —Jefferson Airplane

Concerning youth, we must realize that we are at the end of an era in America. Throughout the history of the country, until after the end of the Second World War, the development of science and technology on one hand, and the development of business, industry, and finance on the other hand, made those fields appear the most wide open to upcoming generations. They were the endeavors of the future, where a young man could hope to make his mark.

To many young people those fields today appear to have been pushed to the limits. All that can be done now seems to be fill-in. These fields are highly specialized endeavors—the ones that differentiate our nation from the rest of the world. To youth it seems often that they can absorb new people only into specialized niches. One cannot be fully involved in a role, because the work is merely part of a vast, highly developed, and impersonally run machine. It requires analytic detachment and emotional noninvolvement—what McLuhan calls "a mind of specialist action in which there is little opportunity or call for reaction," "considerable detachment from the feelings of emotional involvement,"[1] and observation of matters at a dispassionate distance. In other words, what is called for is an inner division between subject and object, between action and reaction, between emotion and labor.* It is this type of occupational niche into which this society is trying to fit today's young people—its young people who are looking for involving roles.

The young generation is reacting to the occupations that require this self-division by turning away from them. Not only is the percentage of students going into science and business declining, but the type of person going into these fields is changing. When they were the most exciting and new fields on the job horizon, they attracted the most capable and least bound by tradition of the upcoming generation. Young men today who accept the traditional high-prestige fields of science and business, the bastions of conservatism, comprise statistically the most traditional, least alienated group in liberal-arts colleges.

A survey at Harvard correlated a student's field of academic interest with his attitude toward the Vietnam war, with his use of marijuana, and with other activities likely to demonstrate the degree to which he was critical of adult society's values. The results were startling. In the sciences and mathematics, the cornerstones of our technological society, were by far the most conservative elements of the student population. And expectedly, at the other extreme, in the fields associated with psychology, sociology, and political science, were by far the most anti-traditional elements.[3]

The implication of these statistics is important when seen in the context of the social pressures that affect a young man growing up today. Uncommittedness, unsureness about values, unrelatedness to the past, widely diverging behavior in youth culture, unacceptable impressions of adult society's manhood—all this leaves a young man with very little to hang on to. He is not given acceptable answers by his elders, and he is not sure that what he figures out for himself is right.

* Psychologically oriented young people perceive in the extremes of this detachment and noninvolvement a form of mental illness. One becomes so detached that one becomes isolated; one becomes so isolated that one becomes sick. Conclusions of work on the schizophrenic condition by a British psychoanalyst describe this form of mental illness in the following words: "You may catch a glimpse of intense activity in the [patient's] inner world through dreams and phantasies, but the patient's conscious ego merely reports them as if he were a neutral observer not personally involved. . . . The attitude towards the outer world is the same; noninvolvement and observation at a distance without any feeling."[2] The words describing a form of mental illness are the words which McLuhan uses to characterize the type of personality cultivated by an entire historical period. In its less extreme form, this detachment is of course not considered mental illness. But what young people say is that it limits one's enjoyment of life because the depth of one's involvement in life has been diminished.

The hard sciences offer an alternative to this absence of permanence and absoluteness. In science and math, in fact in any field in which human beings and their social life are excluded from consideration, it is possible for the young student to gain expertise and sureness in an objective world of theorems and laws and corollaries. In quantum mechanics, or biophysics, or calculus, the student can become familiar with a scientific, structured world of logical relationships which provides his intellect with a realm where he can know *the* answer.

The subject matter of these pursuits does not change in substance; only man's knowledge and understanding of the subject change. The explanation of physical and mathematical relationships for which scientists are finding evidence would have been the same two thousand years ago, had men then been able to figure it all out. What is known about what is being studied is changing very rapidly, but what is being studied remains the same.

To become rooted in these disciplines where sureness, where *one* right answer is possible, is enticing to a young man floating in a cloudy world of unsureness and relativity. His scientific pursuits are separated from the psychological and the social fields, where quantification, objectification, and structure, if present at all, are much less precise and much more relative. This is because the natural sciences and the human or social sciences have one basic difference, a difference that will remain, no matter how hard social scientists try to make the study of man scientific and absolute.

In the social sciences, not only what is known about what is being studied, but also what is being studied, is changing. Man and society change right under the social scientist's nose. Why a man works, how a man decides who he is, what a man feels are the necessities of life, when a man is considered fully grown, what type of personality society needs—all the basic components of life are affected in varying degrees by the evolution of man's environment, by the evolution of human society. With the acceleration of social change, the nature of social man also changes faster. No matter how accurate or how scientific the social researcher's study, the truth he finds is evanescent and relative. Atoms are atoms and always will be; it is only a question of finding *the* accurate description. But modern societies, from one period of development to another, are always different. There is no single or absolute answer.

The social sciences, especially sociology and psychology, are anything but a haven of absoluteness. The student cannot leave the ambiguities of personal problems and human values to become involved in another, unrelated academic life, because action-oriented sociology and psychology are subject to the same questions of values, biases, and goals that perplex the student in personal life. If a young man is concerned about poverty, or about war and the draft, or about being isolated and depressed, there is no escape from the uncertainties of his worries if he studies human psychology and social behavior. He is merely returned to those problems in another context.

The function of a scientific pursuit for someone involved in personal questioning is illustrated well by one college graduate. He went through Princeton with straight A's in chemical engineering, but continued on as a Rhodes Scholar to Oxford not as a scientist but as a social scientist. "I needed science when I came to college," he told me. "I was unsure about so much that the sureness of science gave me something to stand on. Solving a chemistry problem made me feel I knew something. I knew something all right, but not about myself or my society. Now I'm ready to spend a few years learning about just that."

The college students of today, despite the cultural emphasis on science (and business), are turning away from the natural sciences to the social sciences.[4] This is in part a response to affluence, which lessens the priority of increased production and technological innovation in the outlooks of young men. But even more, this turn to the social sciences demonstrates this generation's emphasis on improving the social and psychological aspects of man's life, not merely the material. The consequent psychological orientation of members of this generation makes it increasingly difficult for them to occupy themselves with academic material totally unrelated to their personal situation. They are trying to find sureness in life itself and the study of it, because, in the lostness that characterizes this generation, sureness in the academic fields is not enough.

Of course, self-division and detachment are part of this generation as well as part of adult society. The difference is that the older generations, having grown up well before this period of clashing values, do not seem to recognize their noninvolved, detached way of life because they are not so greatly affected by the new values of involvement and all-inclusive participation. The decades of their youth were still almost totally structured on the values of fragmentation and specialization. Even in the generation of the 1950s, little visible reaction against enforced self-division could be witnessed.

Members of today's generation can see this rift within themselves because they are feeling the clash of two worlds. And as this generation looks at the still younger one, it sees that the new values of participation and involvement have had a yet greater influence. Whereas the grade-school years of the still younger generation were spent in the fully electronic, televised, Beatlemanic culture of the 1960s, today's college generation spent its childhood in the calmer, "silent-generation" culture of the 1950s, in which people were too conscious of the insecurity of war and the McCarthy era to do anything but plan for the "school, college, career, insurance, funeral, good-by" pattern. So whatever makes this generation anti-traditional will make the next one even more so.

This turn to the younger generation is a product of the same feeling that made today's college students turn away from the older ones. Just as they feel that previous generations cannot understand how technological society's high valuation of a detached, divided personality affected their lives, they feel that the next generation will be able to understand even better than themselves.

Today's youth, the pre-adolescents of the 1950s, had to switch horses in midstream—from Connie Francis and the Hit Parade to the Psychedelic Lollipop and Hullaballoo, from Superman and Dell comics to Dr. Strange and Marvel comics, from fragmentation and noninvolvement to all-inclusive participation and psychedelic involvement. The younger set has grown up with all these latter from the start. It is strange indeed to see a generation that begins to look more to little brothers or sisters ten years younger than to parents twenty years older, for guidance and companionship.

But this is an age conducive to strangeness. Erikson, who recognizes the influence of technology with such clarity, considers the modern age a time

> when man turns other men and himself into tools and the machines he runs into machinery which runs him. Here, obviously, man reaches the impasse of his existence as a species. . . . Now, somewhere between the exploitation of nature and the self-exploitation of mercantile and mechanized man, a gigantic transformation has taken place . . . and it dawns on us that the technological world of today is about to create kinds of alienation too strange to be imagined.[5]

But for young people who have recognized the division within themselves and the lack of fulfillment in the detached lives of those within our society, alienated behavior does not seem as strange as it does to "straight" society. For they have made the self-discovery and begun the self-therapy they equate with adulthood. Their actions are either a product of self-realization or a product of their attempts to prove this self-realization to the adult world, which refuses to recognize it. Indeed, why should today's adults recognize it? It challenges their mental health!

It is this very concern for one's own psychology that is more often than not scoffed at by older people, who feel very little in common with those on this quest for self-knowledge. (Remember the man who told his son, "There's entirely too much introspection going on these days.") But the young man of today urges himself on because he is aware of the human toll of living in a world that all too well fits Erikson's description. He can see it in the adult generation, from whose eyes it is hidden, and he can see it in himself. He can do nothing but travel further along the road of self-questioning in order to root out the psychological limitations on his enjoyment of life—limitations adult society does not recognize.

Those who engage in this socially unrecognized venture are at first alone or isolated because of it. They are finding out something important for themselves and they want to share it. So much of the behavior of alienated young people is an attempt to get across to adult society not that they are different, but that they want to be.

I was walking in Golden Gate Park in San Francisco, around the museums and aquariums which form the borders of an ornate square. In the middle of the square is a fancy fountain encircled by a small wall. The summer's tourists—in golf-hat, sun-visor, camera-and-light-meter uniform—were taking in the sights. Suddenly three figures jumped up on the wall of the fountain and began to dance rhythmically around it in time to the melody played by one of the members of the troupe on his flute. The tourists tried to figure out the sexes of the three minstrels. Their children pointed out that the one in jeans with shoulder-length hair was a girl, while the one with hair down to his waist, and the flutist with a water gourd around *his* waist, were boys. The cameras, which had been mostly idle before, started clicking—not at the edifices, not at the alligator holes or porpoises and turtles in the aquarium, but at the weird kids around the fountain. Now there was really something to show the folks back home! The younger generation was a more exotic subject than the animal world.

In an admittedly inarticulate way, the minstrels, like the generation of which they are a part, are trying to show the adult generation that the price paid for material overabundance and social prestige is a psychological limitation on the enjoyment of life; that the fragmented, specialized way of living was perhaps necessary for gaining the industrial and technological capacity of today but that it is not a way of life that will be accepted by a generation that doesn't have to accept it. In the eyes of today's youth, the goals of affluence and security and of social prestige and respectability were carried too far—too far because the sacrifice that was made was the human capacity for deep involvement with other people and with life. The socially successful man is respectable, secure, and affluent. But he is also too often detached and emotionally alone.

Detachment, or "coolness," when it becomes extreme, leads to a feeling of missing out on life. Adults who feel this look outside themselves for the way to overcome their separateness from life. If only they could earn more, or know more, or buy more, or travel more, or know more important people, they think, then at last they would be involved with living and living fully. But young men are becoming aware that, because society ingrains this feeling of missing out on life within the individual, the individual must look within himself to be able to overcome the socially patterned detachment from life.

I have come in contact with no more eloquent expression of this feeling of emptiness toward life than the following poem by Chris Hart, a young man of college age from New York City.

EPITAPH

A blade of grass
Tall and slender
Lives only to be walked upon,
And bends.
A dog, with a face that never smiles,
Lives only for the caress of a hand.
A tree
With limbs only a boy can climb,
Lifts his laughing face
Through the leaves.
And I,
A fool,
Who watched them all,
And died one day
Without living at all
Like grass, a tree, or a dog.

No Satisfaction

The Rolling Stones have rocked the generation with hit
after hit, and "[I Can't Get No] Satisfaction" was one of
the most successful. The Stones criticize the advertising
media for bombarding them with "useless information
supposed to buy my imagination." They look at mass
society and its media and conclude that they
"can't get no satisfaction."

The phrase today is "where the action is." That's the set of places in
each community where one is assured of living life to the fullest. But
wherever one is, one always fears another place or another group is
really "where it's at." Advertisers play on this theme continually: If
you're a young executive, they boom from the radio, and are not living
in such-and-such apartments, then you're not living. And they go on from
there: If you're not drinking such-and-such beer, says the TV sports-
caster, then you're not drinking beer. If you're not driving a certain car,
or wearing a certain shirt, or joining certain clubs, or attending a certain show, then, mass society says, you're missing *the* essential experience
of living.

This attitude is not confined to advertising: otherwise it would not be
so effective. The whole game of social prestige revolves around this
principle. Although the colloquialisms "in" and "out" have only fairly
recently been coined, the same psychological theme has long been part
of modern American society. There is an explicitly defined set of events

to attend, possessions to have, attitudes to support, colleges to attend, or companies to work for. There is a specific range of personality types to which one is supposed to conform in order to live to the maximum. To put it bluntly, there is an external set of characteristics and possessions which signifies membership in the modern American equivalent of Calvin's "elect."

For those who are unable or unwilling to conform to this rigid definition of life, to feel that they are "out of it" or "on the outside looking in" is a quite logical result of their individuality. But even for those who try to conform to the prevailing personality pattern, the end result is still a feeling of missing out on life. For one is asked not just to conform to an identity but to epitomize it. And so the conformist always feels he is not playing the part well enough.

In adult society we see everyone trying to keep up with the Joneses; but the sad thing is that the Joneses themselves are trying to keep up with the Smiths, and the Smiths with the Johnsons, et cetera. Like lemmings, many adults seem to be following the image of the socially ideal personality. The tragedy which this generation is becoming aware of is that *the image is based less and less on the real desires of men themselves, and more and more on a personality stereotype created by the media.* Young people realize that this stereotype is not made to develop individual happiness or fulfillment, but structured to reinforce the patterns of behavior which support industrial, technological values. Those who try to capture for themselves the evasive socially ideal personality are destined to psychological failure, even if they achieve social success.

The mass media manipulate the socially prevalent frustrations more openly and callously than other institutions do, and so they reflect those frustrations most near the surface. Young people realized they must cultivate mistrust, or else the media would callously manipulate them. What is there, young people wonder, that can be taken at face value? Is there anything that need not be first analyzed to find its real aim? Salinger's chronicle of alienation, *The Catcher in the Rye*, is the narrative of a young man who finds sham or two-facedness in everything. His struggle is to find something or someone that is direct and honest, and this is one of the major themes of youth's alienation today.

The members of this generation are aware of how different their everyday world is from that of their parents' childhood. They have been raised in an age when everything conveys a first impression and, also, an underlying and more revealing psychological message. Often the first front on which young people become aware of this is in the advertisements which permeate modern life.

To understand that television is an involving media, we have only to witness the effect of commercials on the very young. Children are told what personal qualities are desirable not only by parents and teachers but also by ever more frequent sales pitches. The child soon becomes aware that the goal is to be "the first kid on the block" with a particular gadget; but he learns, too, that this is a social achievement only if the other children follow his lead. Here is perhaps the earliest training ground for those special traits of other-directedness which sociologist Riesman described. The child is taught to be a leader, but only in those areas in which popular opinion is likely to follow.

This method, of course, is addressed to adults on a higher plane so as not to insult the "mature" mind. No longer is the individual's world the small, circumscribed area of the neighborhood block. The adult's world is that hazy realm known as "popular opinion," and fortunately advertising is constantly defining exactly what it is.

Parents, like their children, are shown the value of a product by being assured that it is to the mass taste. Whether it is that 1.5 million have taken the Mustang Pledge or that 2 million dogs wear Sentry Flea Collars, the message is the same: *it is good because it is everywhere.* Young people realize that no longer are the thousands of dollars for a full-page magazine ad spent primarily to inform the consumer about the particular merits of a product, but rather to use one of the same psychological themes that have inundated their minds since childhood. In this case, if the image of a product can be given the characteristic of popularity, whether or not the product is the best becomes secondary.

A similar approach to showing the consumer that he is "on the right track" is endorsement. The child is told what to buy by Captain Kangaroo or Roy Rogers, the adolescent by the Young Starlet or by the Rock-and-Roll Group, and the adult is informed by everyone from the Big (virile) Athlete, to the Successful (big desk, three phones) Businessman, to the Unbiased (white coat, test tube) Scientist. Depending on the product, whatever type of socially ideal personality best epitomizes the consumers' image of authority gives the plug.

Adults must have a measure of disdain for these messages, but they are different from young people in that they grew up with the change in advertising. Advertising grew with prosperity. Unlike their sons, adults were brought to the stage where they could accept that the media could tell them how they *really* thought and what they *really* wanted.

This metamorphosis can be seen in another omnipresent psychological theme of advertising: sex. After the army of virile men and sensuous women have endorsed everything from hair lotion to automobiles, in front of stampeding horses or falling parachutists or whatever makes them look Cool, Sexy, and Popular (the modern Trinity), some advertisers have finally taken the last step. They have come out and said quite straightforwardly that their product (toothpaste, for instance) gives the user sex appeal. One needs no perceptive cynicism to recognize what these ads are implying. "You're not sexy enough!" they tell the public. It is a message from the impersonal public media, but it functions successfully because of its use of personal, private frustrations. It makes continuous implications about the audience, but the audience can only listen, not speak.

This underlying theme of sexual or social inadequacy wreaks havoc in the lives of young teen-agers before they have rebelled against society's values. Vitally concerned about being accepted, they respond anxiously to the message "Don't be left out. Buy the new ——— now!" They implore their parents for transportation to the place where it's happening, in response to the Word from the media: "All your friends are going to be there. Don't miss it!" Concerned about fitting in and being part of a group, they respond frantically to the booming announcer's voice that tells them: "Don't be the only one without a ———. Buy one today!"

By playing the same game but with a higher level of sophistication, advertisers can manipulate adult consumers. They have managed to make it a standard cultural belief that the car a man drives, the clothes a man wears, and even the toiletries a man uses are reflections of his personality. Once upon a time, perhaps they were. But now the media have assigned their own meanings to every external characteristic. Just as advertisers tell young men that they'll never catch a girl without using a face soap to beat acne, they tell the adult that he'll never make it in "a man's world" without a certain kind of suit. A suit, they tell the worried executive in a high-class magazine, is "the measure of the man."

For young people, disregard for clothing, not only among hippies but also on many campuses, is a refusal to be measured by current social standards, by the money they have, or by the money they are willing to spend chasing the socially ideal personality.

Combined with modern science, the media have even got the jump on the two main reactions against their continuous manipulation. The first reaction is anxiety, more commonly called "nervous tension." Because the media helped create it, it is not too surprising that they should be prepared with a countermeasure. First, they made people think that nervous tension was natural. "The one thing you know never to kid someone about," an advertisement for a relaxant counsels, "is occasional nervous tension." The media have managed to make the taking of relaxants (and sleeping pills, pep pills, and so on) as culturally patterned as cigarette-smoking. Tension, to the magnitude that medicaments are necessary, is so accepted as a natural condition that one can frequently hear it mentioned as the *cause* of certain behavior rather than as the effect of deeper psychological circumstances. As Jacques Ellul says pointedly in *The Technological Society*, "One cannot but marvel at an organization which provides the antidote as it distills the poison."[1] If people accept recurrent tension and anxiety as natural, the media will have won their game.

The second reaction is a demand to be treated as individuals who can think for themselves. And advertising got the jump on this reaction too. Today one can see magazine advertisements in which the biggest print says, "It's for real!" or, "No kidding . . ." These are, of course, the more simplistic attempts at telling the reading public that advertisers are being sincere, that the psychological manipulation is over. The most succesful use of this approach appeared in the early 1960s with the Volkswagen advertisements. All of a sudden there was no big print, no glaring obnoxious statement, no psychological ruse, no flashy big-band-sounding ending. Rather, there was a quiet and straightforward, one-sentence-to-a-paragraph style of approach. It was, of course, well suited to its product, but its real success lay in the fact that once again the reader was treated as if he could reason independently of mass tastes. People did not feel their psyches were being manipulated, for they could find no sneaky psychological game beneath the first impression of the ad. Response was so favorable that the approach of the Volkswagen advertisements spread to many other products.

After a young man makes the initial discovery by which he learns to question the media systematically, he naturally responds to their messages in a more detached way. He loosens their control on his behavior. But, in retrospect, he realizes how totally involved he was (and how totally involved his little brother and sister are) with electronic media such as television. He resents the manner in which these media have been able to invade his mind and form his attitudes. Unlike parents, whose attempts to mold behavior and interests young people could question and differentiate between, the television "spoke" in images and words that could not be questioned. No motives, no personality factors, no circumstances could be applied to discriminate between messages. The voice of the medium was not only involving, but absolute.

McLuhan is not alone in concluding that the medium of television is highly emotionally involving, that it draws the viewer into all-inclusive participation. As a former newsboy who had to try to collect at houses out of which emanated that gray, shimmering light, I know that the chances of getting anyone's attention were slim, unless I synchronized my knock on the door with the traditional excursion to the kitchen during commercials.

A Little Insane

You gotta get out of your head,
You gotta step out of your mind,
Gotta be able to bend your brain
If you wanna get along on this world,
Gotta be just a little insane
If you wanna get along on this world. . . .
Do your living in a crazy dream
Keep your hero on a movie screen.

—The American Breed

I have belabored the pathology of the media because it is often the first means by which a young person becomes aware that what is considered normal in our society has various abnormal qualities. Young people are then just one step away from realizing the converse: that many aspects of what is considered abnormal in our society are, in fact, more normal than the society that condemns them.

What has become clear to young people is that the media reflect the expected social frustrations of the public to whom they are directed. For perhaps the first time in their lives, these members of a psychologically oriented generation become aware that there is some sort of accepted social frustration on which many of the basic functioning units of society depend. If the frustrations were to be diminished, the foundation of those basic functioning units would be undermined. Advertisers are merely the most obvious example of business interests which know and exploit the self-doubts that characterize the members of both adult and young societies. That such interests are effective and perpetuate themselves only proves to this generation that the individual in mass society is not aware of himself and his own psychology.

This rejection of the façade of society and the desire to understand what psychological and social frustrations prop it up are the characteristic responses of this generation to the adult environment. They are the first step which leads young people to self-analysis, to an investigation which they hope will help them be the product less of their society and more of the natural development of their own individuality. In liberating themselves from the unfulfilling goal of the socially ideal personality, they want to evade also the "natural" tension that characterizes the society that bred them.

The crucial point about this self-analysis which should be understood is that it comes as a result of recognizing the ambivalence, the hypocrisy, of adult society. It is the need to stop, to mistrust, and to analyze their society which causes young men to examine themselves. For the reflections from adult society that define a young man's identity are confusing and conflicting. He must look within himself.

A final example of the insight that this generation gains by analyzing the media from a psychological perspective will illustrate how young people may gain an understanding of the cultural façade they are attempting to penetrate. When a young man looks at the type of movies that have been extremely popular in recent years, for example, he cannot fail to notice the striking addition to the regular movie themes popular in youth-oriented areas. This same addition could be found in magazines and in books, but movies reveal it most plainly.

Before the 1960s, there were generally two kinds of heroes: the bad guys who exploited women and the good guys who passionately and successfully loved women. In a good-guy movie there was always a solid romance, even if only to reinforce a weak plot. But with the fantastic success of the James Bond movies, one can discern another type of hero. The series of movies based on Ian Fleming's novels had many obvious appeals: attractive women, virile Sean Connery, good scenery, complex gadgetry, world-scale plots, and thoroughly despicable villains. But they also epitomized a new trend: there was plenty of unabashed sex, but any romance or emotional involvement was purely incidental to the plot, if present at all. Emotional involvement was made to seem almost like a weakness in character.

Bond was fantastically successful with and fantastically attractive to women, both characteristics which men are socially patterned to feel that they lack. But Bond's magic quality was not only physical but psychological: he managed never to become emotionally involved with any woman. He would seduce one for his daily exercise, take on another to foil the villain's plans, and get a third just out of spite. Here was the ideal personality in all its unreality: he could get others involved but he could stay detached; he could see through others, but they could not penetrate him. He successfully applied capitalism to his emotions: maximum profit with minimum investment. He perspired once in five movies.

Bond was the social ideal incarnate, the man whose feelings are separated from his actions. He epitomized emotional noninvolvement and detachment once again. He had achieved the traditional behavior which the young people of McLuhan's electric age had found so difficult to master.

A whole barrage of similar characters followed Bond, both in the movies and on television, all of whom had the same "Don't get involved!" capacities that the young had tried unsuccessfully to cultivate. The demand for the "hard" character is what caused the fantastic Humphrey Bogart revival in college areas throughout the country. Young people could identify with Bogey because he was emotional and sentimental (and so, human) on the inside, but all this was buried deep within an outer, unfeeling shell that had been built for self-preservation. Both Bogart and Bond epitomized the successful achievement of a personality type which this generation had been unable—quite humanly—to achieve. Bond and Bogart only had to act that way between cuts on the movie set. But young men were asked to live that way.

Depending on one's level of analysis, one can draw entirely different conclusions from the evidence of this new movie trend (or from the new acceptable nudie magazines or sex paperbacks). Youth's level of analysis is an example of the significant difference that the psychological perspective of this generation makes.

If an adult examines the Bond movies from the traditional moral-religious outlook, he most likely concludes that we are in the throes of a sexual revolution. He sees naked women, and he sees naked Bond, and he sees them both in bed. And there are children in the audience. The movie would have been considered scandalous a few decades ago. It would not have been accepted with tolerance by millions of Americans when he was a young man. And so, the adult concludes, we must be in the midst of a sexual revolution.

Examined psychologically, however, the appeal of the Bond movies is rooted in a quite different explanation. This generation has faced an analytic, detached society that values emotional noninvolvement. Yet in order to grow up, a young man needs commitment and involvement. From this generation's psychological viewpoint, Bond indicates not sexual revolution but sexual inhibition. He indicates that, in order to function in this society, emotions must be turned inward. He indicates that external success may enclose internal failure. Along with acceptable nudie magazines and acceptable pornographic paperbacks, sexual openness in movies is accompanied by emotional closedness. All that the so-called sexual revolution in mass society indicates is that the division between emotional commitment and sexual involvement has become so socially patterned that it can be broadcast through the media and accepted.

In advertising, in movies, in magazines, on television, in everyday speech, and in sex education, there has been what seems to be a liberalization of sexual ethics. The culturally "in" attitude in adult society is one of apparent openness and frankness. Adults speak with enlightenment about contraceptives and about the trend on campuses toward more liberal dormitory regulations. They favor the liberalization of divorce and abortion legislation, and earlier sex education (limited to warnings about the peril of venereal disease and "getting involved"). On all these controversial issues, many adults are progressive. They follow the gradual trend that has been visibly growing since Victorian moral standards began to decline. But, as far as their own individual freedom and wholeness of sexual expression is concerned, relative to previous generations, they are no less repressed, no less frustrated, and certainly no less concerned about being man or woman "enough."

Consequently, even these liberal adults are critical of the real sexual revolution in the younger generation, which has discarded their values. The clearest evidence in youth culture is the free-love societies that have appeared not only at Berkeley and other college areas in America, but also as part of the *Kulturkrankheit* movement in Berlin and in the affluent Scandinavian youth cultures. They are but the extreme illustrations of the equally deep convictions of many young men who have realized that sexual openness and happiness have increased only in theory. The pressures of modern life have invaded man's private existence so that the "successful" executive or the "happily" married man or the Hollywood beauty queen is often as emotionally inhibited or incomplete as is the type of person one would normally associate with sexual unhappiness.

Young people have clearly begun to disdain the external image and to be concerned about the inner man. They are interested not in where a man got his degree or in what his income is, but in whether he is fulfilled in his marriage and if he can feel and love. The dress and behavior of the hippies, which (it is easy to remark) tends to obscure sexual differences or at least make them less "attractive," is an unmistakable outgrowth of this genuine sexual revolution. They refuse to be forced into the socially patterned sexual syndrome of having to prove their sexuality, or of having to glorify and magnify their sexual attractiveness.

These iconoclastic attitudes are part of a framework. There is a vital consciousness in youth about the discrepancy between external appearance and inner reality. The social-prestige aspect of a man has some meaning, but loses even that for young people if he has not been able to find himself and put other goals above the obvious prestige-oriented ones. In short, the young want to know what is beneath the civilized veneer. Does the tough businessman take two pills for his ulcer before each board meeting? Has the funny, funny comedian who is on television every night been divorced four times? Does James Bond really subscribe to *Playboy*?

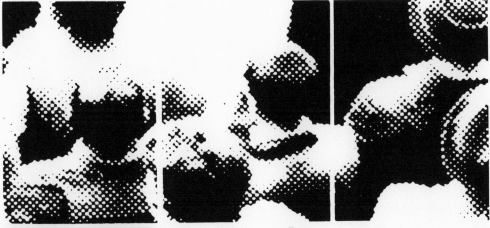

Youth
and Politics

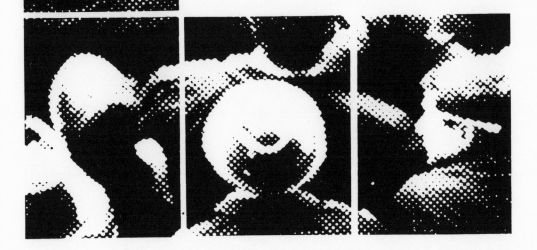

This generation of psychologically oriented young people first questions itself to find the source of the incompleteness and estrangement from life which is the result of living in a mass society. Because of its awareness of the psychological sacrifice that accompanied technology, its initial question is not "How can I find involvement in life?" but "How did I lose it?"

Like no previous generation, today's young people are aware both of the pervasiveness of the influences of mechanized mass society, and of the influence of childhood experience on "final" personality. They realize how the child is hammered by social pressures and parental directions designed to structure, to homogenize, and so to confine the manner in which his mind develops. Their rebellion against the socially ideal personality is the visible sign that their potential individuality is being confined. The quite rational distrust they have for mass society is supported by an intrinsic emotional dislike for the conformity which it demands.

At first, young people react against only specific aspects of society that impinge most directly on their freedom of development: the computerized, bureaucratized system of education; the outmoded and hypocritical function of most churches; the inequity and anachronism of Selective Service regulations; and so on. But soon they realize that in order to root out the alienation "too strange to be imagined" they must first systematically examine the forces that continually molded them throughout childhood into a specific and acceptable form.

"As far as the opinions I have been receiving since my birth are concerned," wrote questioning young Descartes long ago, "I could do no better than to reject them completely for once in my lifetime, and to resume them afterwards, or accept better ones in their place, when I had determined how they fit into a rational scheme." Now, much as adult society likes to harp on obedience, it must accept that it is the young men today who are questioning accepted opinion, as Descartes did, who furnish the fuel for social progress. Old conclusions cannot just be reapplied in a new world but must be re-examined and replaced by new conclusions.

Because of the rapidity of social change and the growth of higher education, young men are less and less resuming old opinions and more and more trying to "accept better ones in their place." What happens to these young people with new ideas is of crucial importance.

The political process is the means for social change in America. People with new ideas, i.e., people who dissent from old ideas, direct their energy into the political process with the aim of bringing about the desired change. For this process of change to function properly, it seems to me that two conditions must be met. First, the political process must retain its flexibility to respond to changing times and growing dissent. Second, the nature of the dissent must be in such a form that it can be digested by the political system. In other words, change must remain a *process*, and dissent must remain *political*.

As to the first condition, many scholars have written that the political process has lost its flexibility, that the maintenance of the *status quo* is deeply entrenched in the process itself, and that the power to bring about change is centered in a power elite which does not want to change. But then, of course, there are also writers who conclude the opposite. This question cannot be resolved in a study of youth and politics. Whether or not change in America can remain a gradual process can be left to political scientists, whose job it is to find the answer.

But if we look for the answer to that question in the response of the postwar generation, the answer must be an emphatic "No!" For the second condition for the functioning of the political process is that dissent remain political. Clearly this generation has gone beyond the political. The hippies have unmistakably rejected the political process as a means for making society the way they want it. Their dissent has not remained political but has become psychological.

Even the activists in youth culture demonstrate that dissent no longer falls within the traditional political dialogue. As they have shown in uprisings throughout the country, they are turning to violent as well as nonviolent extralegal demonstrations and sit-ins. Even the young people who backed McCarthy realized in the latter stages of the campaign that the political system of delegates, state and national conventions, and so on, had to be the eventual target of their activism, for they saw established political power crush the chances of an anti-war candidate.

Both hippies and activists share the feeling that mere political change is somehow not enough. Politically minded young people use the language of New Politics and the New Left, while apolitical dissenters use explicitly psychological terms. But, as my later discussion of civil rights and Vietnam shows, the same psychological dissatisfaction that visibly characterizes the hippies also underlies the activists' dissent. Many young radicals today, according to Kenneth Keniston, feel that psychological change must precede or accompany political change. Activists' psychological demands reflect what Keniston has called their "psychological-mindedness," their "habit of self-analysis," which has confirmed their radicalism.[1]*

This is not psychological reductivism by any means. For when political conformity is ensured not by legal coercion but by social pressure and psychological manipulation, then it is to be expected that social and psychological inquiry will be a focal part of becoming politically aware. The process by which young men become dissenters begins when they realize how deeply they distrust the symbols of authority in mass society —in other words, the credibility gap. If a young man realizes that he cannot accept his reflection in the mirror of mass society's political beliefs, then he turns to himself to analyze his political feelings.

* Keniston's comments imply that to become an active dissenter from the war (after coming from a family with middle-class, traditional political opinions) requires considerable questioning of self, as well as political questioning of society. The data I obtained on Harvard undergraduates would tend to confirm this. In correlating a student's academic major with his feelings about the war, I found that those majoring in political science, economics, and history were not as a group the most dissident. Significantly more against the war, in both number and degree, were those students in the Department of Social Relations, which consists of psychology, social psychology, sociology, and cultural anthropology.

It is no accident that the credibility gap, alleged to exist not only by the young but also by a large segment of the academic community, became a crucial issue in the mid-1960s. As the term is popularly used, it refers to the lack of political communication that can be trusted as valid and complete. In youth culture, this lack of credibility applies to almost all aspects of society, but let us first understand it in its political context. Riesman and his associates, in the introduction to their analysis of American society *The Lonely Crowd*, explain that their

> gravest concern about the media, however, is not their long-run impact on culture, but the fact that the press, the news magazines, and particularly the newsreels have become far more ethnocentric . . . than in 1948; they "cover" somewhat more foreign news, if only to smother it in the self-serving slogans and misleading rhetoric of the Cold War.[2]

This is the basic attitude of today's young people: most do not immediately consider the media in McLuhan's terms but are mistrustful because the media try to paint everything in American colors. At first, their criticisms were of sins of omission: the press would cover events or aspects of incidents that were favorable to the American image, but would leave out or play down occurrences that were critical or disconcerting. But now, since the Vietnam war has become the most unpopular war in our country's history, young people find sins of commission: instances where events are not treated with journalistic integrity, concerning both domestic dissent and international affairs.

Thus many young people who participated in the march on the Pentagon of October 1967, to protest the war, were amazed that the number and nature of the demonstrators could be so completely distorted by press reports. For students who wanted to register deep opposition to recent escalation, it was a dismal experience. First of all, they discovered that maybe half the people they had marched with did not exist: the press took the extremely low Pentagon estimate of the number of marchers at face value. That number was lower than the Washington Police Department's count. And it was extremely low compared to the estimates of independent observers. In other words, thousands of concerned people who came to the march did not exist in the minds of newspaper readers and television viewers across the country.

(A friend told me a few months later how all those "uncounted" people had disappeared. They had been magically transported by the mass media to *pro-war* marches in New York and Boston, for which the count of marchers was given as double the true number, rather than half.)

Certainly, by some stretch of the imagination, this can still be called honest reporting. At least no outright lies were told. If the American Legion has a pro-war march, the reporters ask the American Legion commander for the number of participants. But when the Mobilization Committee against the War in Vietnam holds an anti-war march, the reporters simply ask the Pentagon.

As soon as I saw the morning papers, I realized that not only did half the people that marched not exist, but the half that existed were no longer themselves. Mothers, veterans, high-schoolers, college students from across the country, professors, parents of GIs, people who just plain cared about their country—they all found out by reading the papers and watching the newsreels that they were bearded hippie kooks or Commies waving red flags. They also found out that they marched not because it was the only way they felt they could register their genuine opposition to our foreign policy, but because they were inspired by Communist agitators. By changing the numbers and changing the people, mass-media coverage helped most Americans dismiss the event with a yawn or perhaps a snarl of anger at those stupid kids littering the Lincoln Memorial.

When I got back to campus I heard student after student express this thought: *If a real event right here in the nation's capital can be so effectively distorted by the press, what must the news media be able to do with events that happen halfway around the world in the jungles of Vietnam?*

My disillusionment with the press was not yet complete. I caught a plane after the cold night at the Pentagon, for I was in a hurry to return to school to finish a paper that was due the next day. The plane was filled mostly with prosperous-looking businessmen, but the back ten or fifteen seats were occupied by some members of a professional football team. The husky players were raising a ruckus and flirting with a pretty stewardess by obstructing the path between the seats. There were only a few marchers on the plane.

After we took off, the stewardess served a snack. Without even looking up, I said, "Thanks," as she put the tray in front of me. "You know, you're the first person on this entire plane that has said thank you," she told me, smiling. "A few years ago," she went on, "flying was so special that just about everybody said thanks. But now they treat us sort of like waitresses, ignoring us unless they have complaints. Virtually nobody says thank you any more; that's why I noticed it."

She was worried that I might think she had been surprised at my politeness just because she knew I was a marcher. For by this time, of course, the football players had noticed that "their" stewardess was talking to a marcher. (I was dressed in such a way, after sleeping on the Pentagon parking lot, that it was not difficult to figure out that I had been demonstrating.) They were yelling the obvious questions as to why she talked to a stupid peacenik and not to them. Embarrassed, I suggested she might leave for a while and come back when she was finished serving.

When she returned, her mood seemed to have changed. She said she couldn't understand why a nice young man like me was marching against the war; did I want all the boys in Vietnam to have died for nothing? I told her that I just didn't want any *more* boys to die for nothing. After a few minutes she finally got down to her real gripe. She asked me if I knew that the march was "Communist-inspired," that the leader of the march was "a real card-carrying Communist."

When I told her that I had no idea who organized the march but that I went simply because it seemed the only way to let the President know a lot of people were against the war, she told me that the newspaper had said that the organizer had been a member of the Communist party during the 1930s. I realized after talking a few more minutes that that was all she really knew about the march. What else was there to know?

As I left the plane, she told me that she was glad we had talked, but she added, "I don't think I'll ever be against the war; my brother's over there. But a lot you said made me think."

I was troubled. People who read the same paper must figure that if one of the leaders was a Communist, the marchers must be Communist, and so no "real Americans" are against the war. They wouldn't realize that young Americans had grown desperate in searching for ways to express their opposition to a war that was doing nobody any good. The writer of the newspaper article, very easily and very honestly, maligned all the marchers by referring to one man's political affiliations during the Depression.

As if I hadn't had enough disillusionment about the coverage of the march, I was sent some clippings from my hometown newspaper. One columnist described how hippie girls at the Pentagon had lifted their ankle-length skirts and tossed them over the rifles of the soldiers who were guarding the building. Now, that might well have happened. I didn't see it, but an old columnist with an eye for pretty young legs might well have. It does indeed sound like a more effective tactic than placards. But seriously, it seems clear that the truth was distorted once again. By stressing that incident, as well as the pot-smoking in the ranks of youth, newspapers give the impression that *only* promiscuous girls and zany drug-users are against the war. The columnist must know, too, that many historians and Senators and professors and scientists and retired generals are against the war. But to destroy views that differ from his own, he undermined the character of those who opposed him. In this insidious way, anyone who stands in opposition to the war policy automatically has his character tainted. While old liberals are still breathing sighs of relief that the Joseph McCarthy era is over, many young radicals are gasping at how close we have come to a rerun.

The function of these essentially undemocratic actions is simple: the more people are made by the media to want and think the same things, the more efficiently they can be controlled within the framework of the established political system. In an age of experts and of classified information, the individual can no longer make decisions for himself on the basis of his own knowledge. He must get his information through the eyes and ears of hundreds of different organizations. He must learn to let external authority make his decisions for him. Young men who react against this concept share the conviction of American educator John Dewey that "the serious threat to our democracy is not the existence of foreign totalitarian states. It is the existence, within our own personal attitudes and within our own institutions, of conditions which have given a victory to external authority."[3]

The issue of external authority seems to be a focal one for the group of young men which receives the most criticism from adult society: draft-resisters. Students who turn in draft cards have often listened to speakers running the gamut from anarchists to former Secretary of Defense McNamara. They have read as much as they could and shared ideas with as many people as they could. And they have concluded that, on the basis of what they know, they would not kill another person in the context of the Vietnam war. Like Camus, they do "not want to do anything but what [they] fully understand . . . hence, what [they] demand of themselves is to live solely with what [they] know." Here the vital issue of external authority is raised.

For young people of the 1960s, two ways of thinking present themselves. They may realize that many adults, in the Pentagon and in the White House and in the news services and in universities, probably have more information and more direct experience with the issues concerning the Vietnam war than they do. They may realize also that these men have more authority than they do, since, after all, they are experts. So young people may conclude that the experts are closer to the truth, and that, *despite the fact that they themselves do not think the war is just, despite the fact that they themselves think it is undermining rather than strengthening their country's future*, they should go ahead and believe the authorities and fight. They should go ahead and obey.

In so doing, these young men will be called "loyal," "patriotic," and "brave."

The second option is quite different. Young men may conclude that above all they should listen to their own moral sensibility. To determine the morality of our behavior not by our own conscience but by the exhortations of external authority would be a dangerous step, they feel, as history has shown quite convincingly. They can decide that to act on the basis of what they are told is true, rather than what they feel is true, is to open the door for manipulation. To accept the decisions of experts and to deny the dictates of conscience would be equivalent to accepting external authority and denying the self. If they do this, young men think, the unit of construction in the ramparts of democracy—the individual—will become obsolete.

The young men who choose the second way of thinking about external authority are likely to become draft-resisters. They are called "disloyal," "unpatriotic," and "cowards."

Of course the issue is not as clear-cut as these two extremes indicate. On one hand, some authority is necessary for any social organization; but on the other hand, authority must be responsive to the people and must successfully convince them of its legitimacy. As more and more young people receive longer and longer educations, the answers authority gives must get better and better. Instead, during the Vietnam war, they have gotten worse. Throughout everything, the young were told to obey—not to think and decide, but to obey. But the young decided not to be sheep but citizens, for they agreed with Erik Erikson that "a democracy cannot afford to let matters develop to a point where intelligent youth, proud in its independence, and burning with initiative, must leave matters of legislation, law, and international affairs, not to mention war and peace, to 'insiders' and 'bosses.' "[4]

That respect for authority has radically changed in this generation was demonstrated in an extreme form by one encounter between draft-resisters and the press. The Boston draft-resistance movement had gained permission from a minister to harbor a deserter from the armed forces in his church and so offer the AWOL the right of sanctuary. The leaders of the resistance were announcing their move in a press conference in the basement of the church. One reporter asked what the resistance would do if the congregation, which had not yet confirmed the minister's permission, decided not to permit its premises to be used to help an AWOL escape the police.

It was a tough question, but the resistance leaders were tough young men. They had all openly disobeyed the country's draft regulations because they thought they were being used for an unjust war. One of them took the microphone. "We think that the tradition of this church is such that they will support us," the spokesman declared, as the reporters scribbled furiously. He took a puff of his cigarette in order to have some more time to think. "This church helped slaves escape the South. It disobeyed the law passed by Congress forbidding anyone to aid a runaway slave. This church has a tradition of loyalty to higher morality than the morality of this government. We think they will continue in this tradition and—" He never finished.

A very old Negro woman stepped toward the resisters from the side of the room. "It's also against the tradition of this church to smoke in the building," she said. "No smoking," she repeated. After a moment of stunned silence, the four resistance leaders crushed out their cigarettes. The reporters went on smoking. The guy at the microphone looked as if he wanted to say something more, but he sat down. He was finished.

It struck me immediately how different the alienated young men were from the reporters. It was unlikely that the newspapermen would ever have the freedom of action to disobey seriously the great authority of the American government and its legal system. But hell if they were going to obey some little old black lady telling them to stop smoking in a church! The resisters, having found the courage and self-reliance to stick up for their beliefs even to the point of going to jail for them, resisted the authority of the government but immediately obeyed the old woman's command. In a way, they recognized more legitimacy in her voice than in their President's.

Members of adult society would like to think that the only rebels against authority are the few thousand draft-resisters. But the truth is that the rebellion pervades youth culture. As Michael Ferber, the Phi Beta Kappa graduate student who was found guilty with Dr. Spock and two others of conspiring to counsel young men to evade the draft, said to the court after being sentenced to two years in prison, "I have not been part of a conspiracy but of a movement led by my generation born out of horror at what our country is doing overseas and at home."

Most young people, not yet affected by the draft, direct their criticism at other institutions. They react categorically against traditional figures of authority—the mass media, the educational institutions, the draft. Anything that is mass-oriented, not individual, anything that is rigid, not flexible, anything that is uniform and dogmatic, anything that is out of touch with the young awareness, has a strike against it from the start. This is another reason for the "be-ins" or celebrations held near college campuses from Boston to Bloomington to Boulder to Berkeley; for the attraction of a lapel button that reads I AM A HUMAN BEING: DO NOT FOLD, SPINDLE, OR MUTILATE; and for the growth of psychedelia, which promises experiences that seem highly individual.

Certainly these initially spontaneous youth-culture elements become habits, the images stereotyped. But the habits and stereotypes are directed against those of adult society. All human beings must form groups with similar behavior, but youth's behavior, unlike adult society's, has as its goal the supremacy of the individual rather than the supremacy of external authority.

This emphasis on the preservation of the individual in the age of his obsolescence is fortunately not confined to youth. John W. Gardner, Secretary of Health, Education, and Welfare until the Johnson administration became too distasteful to him, first probed this problem in his brilliant book *Excellence*. Later, in 1967, in the most succinct summary of the problems facing America I have read, Gardner saves the relationship of the individual to mass society for his final consideration. "Everything that we do, all that we achieve," he concludes, "must be measured in terms of its effects on the individual."[5]

The young today regretfully find all the country's overriding concerns being pursued not in terms of the individual, but in terms of national prestige, or of the GNP, or of the statistics which the press displays to praise the American system. Once again, the Peace Corps alone is the advocate of youth's attitudes. Director Jack Vaughn has said that we cannot confront the world with economic graphs or GNP figures. He feels that the job of communicating between cultures must be done person-to-person, and that the people with the flexibility to do this most successfully are of the college generation. "We can't have peace if we do it by computers," Vaughn says when he speaks to college audiences. "The GNP—that's our fixation here in America. But it is not the Peace Corps'. The Peace Corps' fixation is people." This attitude, which strikes a responsive chord in young people, is rarely heard in the bureaucracy we call government.

The Vietnam situation symbolizes the national concern for other interests besides the individual's, and so the feelings of young people are concentrated on that aspect of the generation gap. For a dubious commitment fifteen years ago, the country is compelling this generation to witness not only the sacrifice of our fighting men but, equally tragic, the loss of the lives of Vietnamese. The latter loss is unusually close to the hearts of young people because they find it easy to see, in the simple, peasant way of life, elements of individuality, independence, and autonomy that are the very characteristics they consider missing in modern America.

The young seem to have a measure of empathy for the Vietnamese that many adults do not share. Just as this generation feels controlled and circumscribed by the vastness of American mass society, so does it see the Vietnamese being subdued. Their society is being destroyed not because of racism, not because they are pawns of communism, and certainly not because they are apathetic or lacking in determination, but because they typify a way of life that is being crushed by the technological culture of the West.

The young see mass society's effects not only in the Vietnamese war; the effects are equally clear in the influence of the American dollar throughout the rest of the world. This generation does not applaud such Westernization in the manner that an earlier one was stirred by Rudyard Kipling's "white man's burden." Young people today resent the homogenization of other cultures into a form increasingly resembling the American one they reject. This viewpoint is reflected in the questions of a young researcher at Harvard's East Asian Research Center. "Is it right to expose a society . . . to the trauma of adaptation when we have seen so many unhappy results? Should we relentlessly eliminate differences until mankind is reduced to an ultimate dull uniformity from pole to pole?"[6]

The young think expressly in terms of the individual, not of the GNP or power politics. They say that all too often we are so aware of the materialistic merits of our system and the vestiges of actual freedoms that exist along with it that we do not perceive the system's more subtle shortcomings as it affects the individual. Americans consider their culture, therefore, with the attitude of a brand manufacturer who cannot admit that other brands have their own particular merits. They consider their culture so exportable that they cannot understand those who approach it with less than wholehearted enthusiasm. Because American society cannot accept cultural diversity, it often equates the power faction of a country which most readily accepts American influence with the one most able to run that country.

Young people refuse to be part of this. They are able to identify psychologically with the underdeveloped nations. Both young people and young nations are trying to grow and achieve autonomy, despite the pervasive power of the American system. Young people in America have in common with the young people in underdeveloped countries their lack of historical relatedness. Both care about the next twenty years, not the gains of the last twenty. American young people cannot help thinking that if we had talked to the young in Vietnam, for example, if we had worried more about poverty than about Peking, if we had cared more about land reform than about supporting an aristocratic puppet under whom social change stagnated, if we had applied ourselves with one-tenth the money and ingenuity that we now use to pursue the war, it is doubtful that we would be facing the military stalemate or world-wide criticism that we do today.

America needs the attitudes of its youth. So many of adult society's attitudes are still based on the early concept of communism as a united, aggressive world force rather than the present polycentric collection of Communist nations. Adults' attitudes are directed against communism but actually further it, for the United States channels funds and personnel into achieving the goals of the Cold War rather than the goals of the underdeveloped nations themselves. A cogent analysis of the situation by Irving Louis Horowitz in his book *Three Worlds of Development* makes precisely this point. He explains that the political literature of the underdeveloped countries generally shows more pointed *social* criticism of the Soviet Union than of the United States. But *political* criticism is another story; for the Soviet Union has an economic policy toward and political identification with the underdeveloped world which makes the United States look "imperialistic" by comparison.

Horowitz sums up the crucial difference between the images of the two world powers quite bluntly:

> The United States defines justice in terms of political liberty. The Soviet Union defines justice in terms of economic welfare. The latter best suits the needs of the [underdeveloped] world.[7]

The United States woos South Vietnamese peasants with promises of free elections (which they have never been accustomed to and which they know nothing about); North Vietnam promises them that land will be taken from the wealthy aristocracy and distributed to the peasants. As Horowitz says, the latter does indeed find greater support.

This is one specific example of how young people's attitudes are a response to the future. In their alienation they quite painfully see how an affluent politician of their parents' generation is unable to realize how different the experience of a poor Asian peasant is from his own.

There is in this "global village" generation a source of empathy and identification with the real needs of the underdeveloped countries that is hardly visible in adult society. The enthusiasm and idealism of youth, which were but glimpsed during the Kennedy years, could be the source of energy that enables the rich countries to help the poor stave off the disaster of starvation and revolt which now looms imminent on the horizon.

It would be a tragic loss if the potential for progress found in today's youth were to continue to be dissipated in cynicism, picketing, and—worst of all—apathy. Today these are the frustrated responses to present policies. Young people cannot make the political decisions. They can only furnish the enthusiasm, manpower, and idealism that could mean the difference between a cooperative free world and disaster.

In tangible resources, America lost $70 billion in 1968 for destruction. How much America has lost in its greatest resource—the faith of its college youth—history will have to tell us.

The Old Road Is Aging

In his song "The Times They Are A-Changin'," Bob Dylan
tells the older generation not to criticize what is
beyond them—the young awareness. He tells them that
their children are no longer under their control
because the way of life they represent—"your old road"—
no longer leads to meaning.

Given this mood of youth—angry, disappointed in foreign policy,
alienated from American rhetoric—it is not surprising that striking
new developments have appeared in the political sphere. College students and graduates emigrate to Montreal and Quebec. Thousands of
draft cards are turned into the Justice Department. Campuses are rocked
by demonstrations and violence. Tens and tens of thousands of people
have marched on the Pentagon, and many have suffered crushed heads
and tear-gassed lungs. Desertions of American servicemen are mounting.
Convention sites have been besieged by angry young people. And there
have been campus sit-ins by the dozens, and picketing and disruption
of Selective Service induction centers.

The immediately visible reason for this is, of course, the war. But
even without the war, much of this dissent would exist, directed against
other targets. What underlies it, as I have pointed out, is this generation's
psychologically oriented concern for the individual in mass society.
Young people would concur with former Secretary Gardner and Jack
Vaughn and would disagree entirely with the prevalent attitude of those
in the national government.

Rather than thinking in terms of the individual good, older generations function in terms of a highly defined concept of "national interest" to which individual good is subordinated. They assume that what the nation needs, what technology and industry need, must always be what the individual needs. Fewer and fewer college students accept this assumption today.

On many fronts, young people are realizing that it is what the individual needs that industry should need. Industry does not need unpolluted air; but people do. Industry does not need fresh rivers; but people do. Industry needs people who work like machines, efficiently and predictably; but people need spontaneity and feeling. But it is not in these general questions that young people first realize that individual autonomy is in jeopardy. Like all people, they learn from what concerns them personally. Fathers complain about taxes, and sons complain about the draft.

Criticism of the draft, like criticism of domestic problems and international issues, demonstrates that young people have psychological concerns that conflict with adult society's strictly political perspective. At first glance, Selective Service appears to have given students a good deal. While the less educated half of the generation serves in the armed forces, students are allowed to remain in civilian life, preparing themselves for occupations of their own choice. Some students, of course, have to serve after graduation, but until recently most continued their education or went into occupations that enabled them to avoid military service altogether. This is the surface appearance of the effect of the draft, and this political dimension of Selective Service is all adult society sees.

But the appearance is misleading. Selective Service is most explicit in its devotion to the "national interest" at the expense of individual freedom. In one of its own publications, it states that "the [Selective Service] System is heavily occupied developing more effective human beings in the national interest." Its goal, according to this document, is to make the individual feel as if he is "standing in a room which is uncomfortably warm. Several doors are open, but they all lead to various forms of recognized, patriotic service to the Nation." It refers to the "club of induction," which "has been used to drive out of areas considered to be less important to the areas of greater importance . . . those individuals who did not . . . participate in activities which are considered essential" to the nation.[1]

Although this sounds patriotic and good for the nation, it sounds idiotic for the young men who are affected by it. *Psychological manipulation in the draft, as in advertising, is not an accident but a goal.* Loss of deferment, to many, means having to kill in a war with which one is in complete disagreement. Selective Service aims to capitalize on this, too. "Throughout his career as a student," explains a document in the organization's "Orientation Kit," "the pressure continues. It continues with equal intensity after graduation. . . . He is impelled to pursue his skill rather than embark upon some less important [*sic*] enterprise. . . . The loss of deferred status is the consequence for the individual who has acquired the skill and either does not use it or uses it in a *nonessential* activity" (italics mine).

The unpopularity of the war is only one reason why there is so much dislike for Selective Service. The Service considers essential activities to be military service, work in defense industries, and education in the technological sciences. Until recently it granted deferments to graduate students in the technological sciences, but not to graduate students in the social sciences or the humanities. The priority Selective Service places on science is part of a culturally patterned attitude that is present also in the public schools.

This deferential treatment has influenced many young men in the past to choose careers in scientific fields when they might have preferred, say, social work or academic careers. Until now, channeling has been smooth because in our industrialized modern society the need for technically trained people is great, and so the rewards have been great in terms of money and social prestige. Technological science as a professional career has been held out to young men as an occupation of the greatest merit.

This generation, however, feels the challenge of science with much less intensity. The statistics on choice of major in many American colleges show that more young men are entering the social sciences or are planning academic careers, and fewer are turning to the technological sciences. But while the supply has been decreasing in terms of percentages from the outstanding colleges, the demand for highly qualified scientists has been steadily increasing. Advertisements exclaim that the need for engineers is doubling; that a shortage of industrial scientists is anticipated in the tens of thousands; that trained computer programmers are in great demand; and so on. And of course, recruiting of scientists on campuses by industry has become ever more extensive and systematic.

The necessity of channeling young people into these fields—implicitly by using educational priorities, social prestige, and recruitment procedures, but explicitly and even coercively by the Selective Service—should have been expected. For the nature of youth is that it must prove itself by meeting its own challenges, not merely pursuing the challenges of the older generation. Young men in the 1920s and 1930s, scanning the horizon of the job world, saw a wide-open field in technology and its industrial applications. All around them they heard about awesome figures of self-made men who had made fortunes through industrial breakthroughs. The men at the heads of the sprawling industries, as John Kenneth Galbraith has explained, were known by name. They were inspiring figures, what psychologists might call "role models," for a generation of young men bred in the Depression. Today there are no names. There are no legends equal to the Ford, Montgomery Ward, Carnegie, Procter & Gamble legends. The heads of these firms today are unknown.

The individuality of science, too, has disappeared. The brilliant figures of the late nineteenth and early twentieth centuries, whose renowned discoveries had dramatic effects on industry, transportation, and business, are gone. In their places have appeared research teams working as appendages to massive corporations where the researcher is asked to fit into a niche in a corporate effort.

The charisma of progress and scientific discovery no longer lures as many capable young men. Progress, this generation has been told not only by General Electric but by science in general, has become America's most important product. William H. Whyte's now famous book *The Organization Man* documents the change in technological scientific endeavors. Fewer and fewer individuals may choose the problems with which they want to work. The vast majority of scientific professionals are assigned by superiors to specific projects designed to be useful to the corporation. The scientific establishment has become a bureaucracy, an organ of industry set up to produce progress. Youth today can understand what Einstein meant when he said that he would now become a plumber, not a scientist, in order to have some independence.

The horizon of the job world has changed, but Selective Service's ideas have not. It seems to today's critical young people that the need for studying the human sciences is greater than that for studying the natural sciences. But Selective Service's concept of the "national interest" is still the same.

In addition to its disproportionate emphasis on technological science, Selective Service also has an overtly military interpretation of "national interest." Young men encounter the outmoded attitudes of the older generation, whose members adopted a once necessary, primarily militaristic stance toward the world. This attitude has been institutionalized in many arms of the government and now it is the younger generation that is affected through the draft and channeling powers of the Selective Service.

Draft regulations have interpreted service in the "national interest" to include only military service and related "defense" endeavors. For example, linemen for civilian telephone companies who work at bonus salary for the benefit of foreign-based military installations are often permanently deferred afterward. Selective Service considers their work to have somehow furthered the "national interest." On the other hand, a college student who works on a volunteer economic-development program in South America is not considered to have performed any service to the nation.

Criticism of this aspect of the draft regulations was not widespread prior to the war in Vietnam because nonmilitary work was still allowed to continue. But now the issue has become crucial. College students and graduates wishing to work in nonmilitary international service have been unable to do so for fear of being drafted for the war. As one college graduate said, after being told he would not be given a deferment to work on a literacy program in Africa, "The damn draft board will let me kill for peace, but it won't let me work for it!"

Countless individuals have been refused deferments for educational, agricultural, or technical work in underdeveloped countries, and so returned to the once-safe haven of academia. By default, we are leaving leadership to others. And, as in Vietnam, those who take the relinquished leadership may well be considered "enemies" in the future.

Vietnam itself is not the subject here. Because of the immediacy and atrocity of the war, this generation often directs its criticism exclusively against it rather than against its long-range effects. Even when young people defer to the opinion that our Vietnam policy is not in itself a tragic mistake in foreign policy, it is nevertheless clear to them that the war is causing a frightening series of mistakes. By its power to channel young men into the "essential" industries, Selective Service is compelling this generation to continue lopsided manpower emphasis on technological science at the expense of social science, and on the military-industrial complex as opposed to peaceful, humanistic endeavors.

It is perfectly clear to the postwar generation that technological science and the industrial-military complex have accomplished amazing things. They have propelled America to the position of power it now holds, and have enabled it to be a potential force for world peace and progress. But it is equally clear to the young that a forced overemphasis on those endeavors is not going to solve the problems that will beset us in the future.

When adults cite statistics that show that the percentage of men America channels into science far exceeds that of any other country, they automatically think these figures are wonderful. Only young people seem to ask: Are you sure that scientists, engineers, and mathematicians are what we need most of all? Only young people seem to realize with enough horror that, even with millions of scientists and engineers, we will still have rioting in Watts, death in Vietnam, starvation in Africa, riots in colleges, poor education in the cities, and many other problems. The young realize that those disciplines will not solve such problems. Yes, these fields improve the efficiency of our war in Vietnam; *but they do not provide men with the cultural and political knowledge to decide whether we should be there in the first place.*

Technological science and military-industrial interests have protected and preserved the values of our country. But now they seem to *determine* those values—and, more immediately, the careers of this generation. Of course, the adults who administer Selective Service do not recognize these facts. I had the chance to talk to one important Selective Service official who illustrated how deep the gap between us was. "I can understand why some young fellas are acting up because of this war," he began. "I was sort of radical too, when I was young. But what you kids don't understand is that the Selective Service does much more than just send fellas to Vietnam." I know it all too well. "We also make sure that young people do what the nation needs. Do you know that the nation was short thousands of engineers, and that without our help not half as many fellas would have gone into the field?" I didn't seem too impressed, I guess, so he repeated the point. "Don't you see? Somebody has to see to it that the nation gets the kind of people it needs. You young fellas shouldn't rebel against us. Just look what we do for the nation!" But I still couldn't accept his point.

I knew that this generation could see that there were plenty of engineers in Vietnam designing bombs and barracks and bridges. What the young wanted was to get an education that would help them convince others that Vietnam was wrong. Engineering wouldn't be their bag unless someone forced them into it. And the Selective Service tried to. This process of coercive channeling is a self-fulfilling process. Our funds and personnel are directed toward war efforts and science and away from economics, political science, psychology, history, and cultural study. The potential role of this generation as a knowledgeable force, backed by wealth and proper training, which could be devoted to aiding the independent, nationalist development of the poor countries, appears to be a role that *is not* being fulfilled. But even more tragically, it does not seem that the role *will be* fulfilled in the next decades, because this college generation is not able to develop academically the methods to meet the problems of the future, but is being forced to orient itself towards methods of the past. This is not the result of relinquished leadership but of bad leadership.

Young people are thus in an awkward position that can best be expressed by analogy. If a mother teaches her daughter a strict moral code and yet encourages her to walk in a miniskirt and tight sweater downtown at night on Saturday, she is likely to have trouble with her. In a similar way, adult society informs its sons of American values, of their obligation to help the poor both inside and outside America's borders. At the same time, however, Selective Service encourages this generation to pursue methods that can no longer support those values or fulfill that obligation, and actually prevents them from developing methods that can better achieve these ends. Young people cannot reject the ideal of helping the poor, and so must reject the regulations that prevent them from doing so in the best way possible. Thus it is not surprising that this society is having trouble with its youth.

The opposition to the draft is growing because the concerned members of this generation are beginning to realize that the effects of Selective Service's anachronistic definition of "national interest" are not to be limited to the present. Quite the opposite. When a young man computes the cost of the Vietnam war, he must calculate as sacrificed much more than American dead, South and North Vietnamese dead, billions spent for destruction, and the dissipated energy of dissent. To find the real sum, he must wait to compute the cost for a few decades to come—the cost of decades provided with men who were forced to learn to approach the world in terms of their parents' past rather than their own future.

I am afraid that more is going to have to be done than simply making the draft a lottery system. To date, that has been the only solution offered by political leaders. But that suggestion misses the point: it is not only how young people are chosen to serve that is wrong, but what they are chosen to serve for.

What college students resent is that they have to serve their country in terms of the priorities of adult society, with which they are in such heated disagreement. If a young man, for example, is sure that the war in Vietnam is undermining America's future, then he can hardly feel that he is serving his country by fighting in the war. Nor can he feel he is serving his country by studying to become a scientist, if he thinks that what his country needs most is not scientists but city planners or social workers.

I don't think many young men would fight the draft if they were asked to serve what *they* saw as the national interest. For instance, if college graduates were drafted to serve in a teachers' corps and to spend two years teaching in an urban ghetto, they wouldn't run away to Canada. They would be the first to enlist. But for this to happen, for fighting illiteracy and poverty and unemployment to be considered just as much in the national interest as killing Vietnamese or becoming an engineer, adults would have to admit that the world is changing. They would have to admit, with Bob Dylan, that the old road is getting older. And perhaps, rather than simply get out of the new road, they might even lend a hand.

As it stands today, the draft still leaves college students alone for four years. But even their deferment is objectionable. They feel guilty that other young men, just because they are poorer and have less education, must fight and risk their lives while the more fortunate sit and study. College students are caught in a vise: on one side, they of course don't want to fight in a war they think is unjust, but on the other side they also realize they don't want to be exempt because of—to put it bluntly—their social class.

Placed in this double bind, many young men have turned in their draft cards in an act of protest against the Selective Service and the war. Their friends and their parents cautioned them, saying that they would certainly lose their deferment if, indeed, they were not actually imprisoned. But draft-resisters reasoned about their deferments much as Camus must have reasoned when he was warned that, because of his stand on certain moral issues, he might lose his credit. "I hope so," he said, "if that's what it's made of."[2]

Mr. Businessman

Mr. Businessman . . .
The smiles are all synthetic
And the ulcers never stop
When they take that final inventory
Yours'll be the same sad story
Everywhere
No one will really care.

—Ray Stevens

W hat has occurred in the attitudes of young men toward technological science has also occurred concerning business. To say that
young men are confused as they face the job world would be an under-
statement, for youth culture and adult society have diametrically opposed
attitudes. An advertisement in college newspapers for a career in finance
asks assuredly in bold letters: WANT TO MAKE MONEY YOUR CAREER?
But the Beatles song to which a young man might be listening at the
same time instructs him to "keep all your money in a big brown bag
inside a zoo." To whom does a young man listen, his parents or his peers?

The age of affluence and subsequent mass education have weakened
the rationale for competitiveness and acquisitiveness for the members
of this generation. As William H. Whyte explains in *The Organization
Man*, the young men facing the business world in the decade after the
war "were somewhat nervous about the chances of a good life. They
seemed almost psychotic on the subject of a depression."[1] The next
generation, born after the war, knew the hardship of neither depression
or war. It is to be expected that their attitudes are different.

Commentators from many areas of adult society have noticed the
lack of interest and even the disdain of many young men for careers

in business. Well-qualified college graduates are increasingly turning away from business positions which, in terms of income or social prestige, would have been considered prize finds in the early postwar years. A survey taken recently in some large Eastern colleges and universities, according to W. H. Ferry, shows that only 30 per cent of undergraduates intend to go into business and industry. The proportion just a few years before for these colleges, which once were a main supply for corporate manpower, was 70 per cent.[2] As Paul Samuelson, professor of economics and author of widely used textbooks, has noted (in an article entitled "Business in a Doghouse"), "the declining fraction of the graduating classes at the Ivy League and prestige colleges testified to the reduced prestige of business as a profession." As today's students disregard "the most princely offers of the corporate recruiters who swarm to the campuses," Samuelson says, "how to be more loved has become a major preoccupation of the business establishment."[3]

The corporation has responded to this decline by trying to build up its image. But the businessmen themselves do not realize the full basis of the disaffection, as can be seen from their attempts to overcome it. Their advertisements appear in college newspapers and in big-name national newspapers. The tone of the message varies in the different media but the reasoning is much the same. The logic is directed at the students who seem to be most enchanted with business, a group consisting of graduates from the best colleges and outstanding students from good-to-average universities.

The format of the advertisement is often an "open letter," a direct approach designed to overcome the general mistrust of the media. It aims to destroy the impression bright young men have of business: that it is dull, unimaginative, gray-flanneled sameness. The businessman replies to the challenge by citing circumstantially different but thematically identical examples. The message always boils down to this: "To make a real good company we need imagination, not sameness." One letter, to take an example, explains how very necessary it is for a corporation always to be in the process of refounding, that is, of redirecting its production to additional consumer needs and consequently expanding the business (which equals progress). This advertisement cites the example of a lumber company that converts to manufacture facial tissue. The businessman writing the open letter concludes that businesses which cannot afford to fail cannot afford to be unimaginative, and so a business career is exciting and fulfilling.

What changes in adult society and youth culture have made it necessary for the business community, the cornerstone of adult society, to lure young people? There are four major changes, the first of which I have already mentioned. Affluence has given this generation not only Kleenexes but chiffons. It has made material necessities secondary considerations. No longer does a generation have to make money its goal. The more overloaded middle- and upper-class homes become, the greater the disaffection with traditional business enterprise will be.

Second, just as the changing attitudes of the young toward science were but a reflection of changes in the field itself, so too has the business community undergone quite radical changes. John Kenneth Galbraith's *The New Industrial State* is the most recent charting of the paths the American economy has followed. With an implicit psychological perspective, Galbraith discovers a feature of the economy which youth had already discerned in Selective Service: the organized and methodical attempts of established institutions to control the social thought and behavior of individuals.

Galbraith explains that the most important consequence for economics in increasing affluence is that "the further a man is removed from physical need the more open he is to persuasion—or management— as to what he buys."

> Goods that are related only to elementary physical sensation—that merely prevent hunger, protect against cold, provide shelter, suppress pain—have come to comprise a small and diminishing part of production. Most goods serve needs that are discovered to the individual not by the palpable discomfort which accompanies deprivation, but by some psychic response to their possession. They give him a sense of personal achievement, accord him a feeling of equality with his neighbors, divert his mind from thought, serve sexual aspiration . . . or are otherwise psychologically rewarding.[4]

In short, "in a society where wants are psychologically grounded, the instruments of access to the mind cannot be unimportant."[5] Much as the technological interests of industry control the occupational choices of men through Selective Service, so does business attempt, through advertising media, to control the quantity and direction of consumption.

It is Galbraith's and young people's psychological orientation which permits them to perceive this change. They realize that the once-upon-a-time economy—in which the almighty consumer by his autonomous choice determined what and how much was produced—is dead. Consumption is increasingly controlled by pervasive advertising and consequent social pressure. The industrial system creates the kind of man it needs, "one that reliably spends his income and works reliably because he is always in need of more."[6] It creates the market behavior and social attitudes of those whom it is supposedly serving.

With these tools for controlling the individual, the industrial system causes young people to adopt a cynically detached attitude in order to preserve their autonomy. It is not surprising that the "source" of these messages—business—has become less popular with those who have figured out its methods.

There is a third reason for the young's dislike for business, which also is bound up in their psychological orientation. This book stresses that this generation is concerned about the openness and fullness of interpersonal relations. A business occupation seems to be far from ideal for young people searching for such a way of life. Arthur Miller's play *Death of a Salesman* was conceived at the same time as the members of this generation. It portrays a casualty of the business world who "knows" he has many, many friends, but who toward the end of his life realizes he is desperately alone. He epitomizes for this generation the type of man whose relationships are many but shallow. He is the prototype member of adult society's "lonely crowd."

Businessmen are lauded if they are able to *handle* and *manage* people. They are praised if they use personnel with maximum efficiency. The relationships in business occupations appear to be the opposite of what young people are looking for. The psychological, interpersonal dimension of life stressed so heavily in youth culture seems to be most noticeably lacking in the endeavor of adult society which is given the most prestige.

The final reason explaining young people's rejection of business is the apparent opposition of business's conservatism in social equality to their own heightened social activism. Business appears to be the most lethargic section of adult society in ridding America of discrimination and exploitation. It seems to be concerned more for corporate profits than for social good, and concerned more for an active economy than for decreasing defense expenditures.

The activism of young people in civil rights and poverty projects reveals that one of their primary concerns is for economic equality. *Ramparts* magazine's scathing denunciation of the active role of American business in racist South Africa; the enthusiastic response to the Peace Corps' person-to-person rather than dollar-for-dollar approach to foreign aid; the outcries of young Americans denouncing the cold-war interventions in the Americas as actions taken on behalf of exploitative American business interests; the endorsement of political candidates from the professions or academia rather than of those from the business community; all these examples illustrate that young people's view of business as a force of progressive domestic leadership is diminishing if, indeed, it has not already disappeared. Consequently, the number of aspiring executives is in precipitous decline.

The modern business mind is hard for the "global village" generation to accept because it is fragmented and specialized. It is a thoroughly detached mind: it searches for a job, not a role. It is a product of the technological society because it is totally absorbed with the question of technique, of *how*. The modern business mind places less emphasis on the *why*, on the reasons for and goals of their activity.

I well remember reading the comments of an Army general when he was asked what was wrong with the United States military effort in Vietnam. We should either get out of there, he said, and let them deal with their own problems, or we should quit this limited warfare and use all the stuff we've got; it's just not practical this way. What was important to him was not *why* we were there, the question that has divided our nation, but *how* we should fight there. The ideological goals and human values for which we are fighting don't matter, he seemed to say, as long as we fight with maximum efficiency.

Once efficiency becomes the primary consideration, once the importance of the "how" has dwarfed the importance of the "why," the line between making a living and making war is very thin indeed. One adult, when asked by Dan Wakefield (author of *Supernation at Peace and War*) what he thought of the government's Vietnam policy, replied, "It's just like in business; once you've invested so much you can't back out." How many young Americans die, what alternatives develop, what the Vietnamese *themselves* want—none of this matters to this shrewd businessman. If he invests capital, he establishes "the business," even if he destroys a nation in the process.

When the "how" reigns supreme, the young have realized, to talk about the "why" is heretical—whether the subject is warfare or business. When I told a wealthy banker that it seemed that for this generation the excitement and challenge of business had diminished, he told me that kids were simply wrong. "There's a great challenge in business!" he exclaimed, anxious to set me and my generation back on the right track. "You know, I personally made $150,000 for my bank in bond deals because I played the market better than the next guy. Now that's a challenge, you know, just you up against the impersonal market. Those who know *how* to play the game best win most."

This banker proved himself a man by beating other men on the complex financial chessboard of the "impersonal market." He found the greatest meaning in that challenge not because of why the money was important nor because of the way the profits would be used, but merely because he performed his tasks with greater success than his opponents. He had the same fragmented, technique-oriented outlook that characterizes the old awareness on every front of the generation gap. The banker had forgotten to ask *why*. As he bragged about his stocks-and-bonds game, I wanted badly to ask him, "Who loses because you win?" Do those that win really need to win? I wondered, thinking of the bank president feeding his Arabian horses while the ghetto children turned to petty theft.

The young mind tends to be an ideological mind. When young people realize that businessmen treat money as having intrinsic rather than potential human value, that businessmen are the source of manipulative and insulting advertisements, or that businessmen comprised half the delegates to the stagnant Republican convention—they tend to turn away from business altogether. It is easy for young people today to forget that the most dynamic and capable members of earlier generations went into that field.

Once business, along with science, appeared to hold the solutions for social problems. But to the young today, those endeavors seem to have merely covered those problems with a layer of technology and industry. They covered the problems and then said they didn't exist. They covered the problems and then called for law and order. And whoever didn't conform to their conception of order was somehow not a man.

Well, this generation is turning the tables. What once was a challenge is now a cop-out. Anyone who is sensitive to young people's need to prove themselves in a meaningful way must realize that capable college graduates cannot nowadays go into business with the same purposes their elders had—increasing corporate profits and hastening personal promotion—when this is not at all the same world. As Bruno Bettelheim, a man whom *Time* magazine has called one of America's leading psychologists, wrote in an essay entitled "The Problem of Generations":

> What if existing manhood is viewed as empty, static, obsolescent? Then becoming a man is death, and manhood marks the end of adolescence, not its fulfillment. . . . One cannot realize one's values by climbing the ladder of the business community, nor prove one's manhood on the greens of the country club; neither can one settle into security in an insecure world.[7]

Preachers of Equality

Preachers of equality
Think they believe it . . .
One of these days I'm gonna stop my listening
Gonna raise my head up high.

—Janis Ian

Implicit in young people's lack of interest in business is their awareness of the misleading, almost hypocritical, ideas that American society
ingrains in the individual, concerning domestic equality and international
progress. Whenever young people feel that they are being misled or
"snowed," they react by condemning without leniency the interest behind
the front. The sometimes overdone criticism directed against the "organization man" personality is a manifestation of this attitude. It is clear that
business must occupy itself with the concerns of youth in order to combat
the decline of interest. So it is in civil rights: the only way to combat
youth's criticism of adult society's attitudes is to make theoretical equality correspond to actual equality.

Once again, affluence has had a role in changing this generation's attitudes. Many older people would scoff at the idea that young people are
today less prejudiced than adult society. Poverty is not immune to progress, but for some reason they think that prejudice is. This is because
their viewpoint is strictly material, not psychological. They recognize
only the tangible effects of change, and not the psychological.

The fact is that in the past economic competition and insecurity were major factors causing prejudice in the individual. If the necessity for tense competition decreases, and material security increases, these factors may be eliminated. The anti-Semitic and anti-Negro discrimination of the early decades of this century was a result of the influx of great numbers of immigrants and the economic difficulties and insecurity of the majority of Americans. For many of the postwar generation, however, the economic bases for these prejudices are no longer present. And the decrease in these traditional prejudices has been one factor in the civil rights activism of this generation.

Young people today are asking that a society which professes freedom and equality make these viable realities. That the young have been the most energetic and devoted participants in civil rights protests and marches is well known. Their support for federal programs that actually help the poor is equally acknowledged. In this area, the liberal element in adult society has looked favorably on this generation. The young are trying to right a glaring political injustice that has long been the greatest American hypocrisy. But to understand the attitudes of today's critical youth no further would be to miss the most forceful challenge to hypocritical adult society.

As might be guessed, it is once again a psychological challenge. If one reads the underground, hippie papers or frequents hippie communities, or if one is familiar with college areas, or if one is aware of the numerous interracial singing groups, one cannot help seeing a person-to-person racial equality that is not very evident in adult society. Interracial couples are frequently seen in youth-culture areas, but for such couples, rather than the pat-on-the-shoulder approval given for civil rights activities, many adults shows nothing but repugnance. Here is where youth feel the deepest hypocrisy.

Adults point to Negro baseball players or Congressmen or Army officers to show how liberal and free of prejudice they are. But that is as far as they think equality should go. *They are willing to grant equality to the Negro as a laborer, or as a soldier, or as a sportsman, or as a government official, but they stolidly refuse to consider him equal as a human being.* The young in general, but especially the most alienated, flaunt their independence from these hypocritical attitudes. This psychologically involved generation is just as angered by a prejudiced attitude as by a prejudiced law. Both limit the fullness of human relations and of life.

If one looks at the roots of the issue, it is the psychological orientation of this generation that separates it from adult society as far as civil rights are concerned. Adults' consciences seem to be involved only in so far as laws and jobs are concerned. "Look!" one Northern lawyer began lecturing me. "We got the bigoted laws off the books. We're seeing to it that there isn't any job discrimination. What happens from here on out reflects the Negro's own abilities. From now on he can pull himself up or get left behind, as far as I'm concerned." If blacks have equal political and economic opportunity, many adults want to write off all other racial problems.

From what I have already said about this college generation it should be clear that it cannot share this attitude. Since college students have had to analyze the psychological, not the political or economic, roadblocks which mass society placed in front of them, all they have to do is turn around and see the infinitely greater psychological obstacles in the way of young blacks,* and they may realize that adult society is leaving untouched a major area of racism.

Really to move ahead in American society, a man must have self-respect. Having a job and being able to vote, in themselves, do not guarantee this, for it is difficult for a man to respect himself unless he feels society as a whole accepts him as a worth-while human being. This acceptance has been denied the black man. Young whites today have realized that having only *white* teachers, that seeing only *white* movie heroes, that reading only about *white* children in the first-grade reader, that hearing only about *white* landlords and *white* store-owners, that watching *white* television talk shows, that being told only about the great *white* men in history—that all this can kill a *black* child's self-respect. Especially if a black child's parents have accepted the stereotype of inferiority that white society so willingly provided, he may find it almost impossible to become an adult who can hold his head high. All this that's going on inside a black child's head is a very quiet psychological process, not a noisy political event. The newspapers don't cover it. But it is much more real in the lives of black children than any legislation that makes the headlines.

I once worked as a recreation leader in a church located in a poor

---

* In youth culture the words "colored people" are not used, although in adult society they are still frequently heard. Young blacks have decided that there is no reason why they shouldn't call themselves "black" with the same pride that whites call themselves "white." Young blacks have also rejected the word "Negro," for it is a name created by white men for black men. Young whites have simply disagreed with their parents' language and agreed with the language of the black members of their generation. In this sense, at least, generational lines have cut through racial lines.

urban area. One of the smartest and kindest twelve-year-olds I worked with became my good friend. His name was Larry, and he was black. He wanted to exchange comic books with my little brother, so one day he came home with me after church. That day I realized why I like him so well. He looked as if he respected himself. His vitality showed in his dark cheeks. He stood up for his little sister when guys picked on her. His alert brown eyes were alive and absorbed every action, every emotion. He made a day become more alive and interesting for everyone.

As every middle-class white who does social work soon discovers, one's affluence remains an ineradicable difference between the people one is working with and oneself. Larry mentioned how nice my house was. "I've only been in one like it before," he confided in me. "It was Mr. Browning's. Did you know him?" I told him I didn't, and he went on. "Mr. Browning was the church organist before you came. He sure was nice."

I was surprised to hear him say that, since I didn't often find that the black kids really liked and respected a white adult. I asked him why such a nice man had left the church. "I don't know," he replied. "Mr. Browning moved down to a place in Missouri, I think, and he said I could visit sometime."

Perhaps prying, I asked, "Have you heard from him since?"

"Nope," Larry replied casually. "It'd probably be too hard to manage, me coming all the way. Besides," he added slowly, his face tightening, "they don't like niggers down there."

The rest of the day was depressing. Larry's eyes never regained their fire; they had been clouded by his renewed awareness of prejudice.

It was the first time I witnessed the effect of centuries of racism on one day in the life of one black boy. I thought of all the little white boys I knew. They too certainly had moments of disappointment and sadness. But none of them ever experienced anything like what Larry had in that moment when he thought of the mass of unseen people who condemn him and his heritage as inferior. White legislators could pass laws, the government could initiate programs, but no one, no one at all, could ever erase this experience and all the others like it from the memory of my friend Larry and from the memories of all the little boys like him.

And then when I found out the kind of teachers that often end up in ghetto schools, when I found out that in many cities less is spent per school child in poor neighborhoods than in rich ones, when I found out about the lethargy and prejudice of some school systems,[1] only then did I begin to realize the extent of discrimination that Larry and other black children must encounter. I did not wonder why some black children grew up to loot stores or to talk of black power. I wondered how they grew up at all.

The same message came through to me again when my girl friend, who was working for the summer in a slum-redevelopment project, told me about a conversation she had with a black man of twenty-one. "There's one thing," he told her, "that you can't understand, no matter how hard you try. I was nineteen before I became proud that I was black. Nineteen! My father is almost fifty, and he still isn't proud of being black. Tell me," he asked her, his words cutting sharply, *"how old were you and how old was your father when you both became proud that you were white?"*

Maybe this is why today's college generation has so much dedication to civil rights. The scales of racial pride are being equalized. For young blacks have finally realized that "black is beautiful": they have regained some of the pride that racism stole from them. And many young whites have realized what their race has done for centuries, intentionally or unintentionally, to blacks: they have lost some of the pride of being white.

One Push of the Button

Bob Dylan sings a song, "With God on Our Side," which
is his version of the cold war. He explains how he was
brought up to hate the Russians, and points out that
with "one push of the button" civilization will die—yet
apparently adults think hate and destruction are all
right because "God's on our side."

Today's young people first began criticizing adult society by attacking
its lethargy in domestic matters. This is quite natural. With Harlem
across the street from the dorm, or with one of the worst ghetto school
systems just a mile or two away from campus, domestic issues are what
hit a young man first. The great increase of students in the social sciences
has also had an effect. It is the purpose of these disciplines to make the
student aware of the flaws and historic inequities of the American social
system.

But also part of a modern liberal-arts program of study is the student's exposure to other forms of political and social systems. Information about other cultures of the world has increased, because of both
academic studies and increased political interaction. Of course, not only
has the information itself increased, but this generation's opportunity to
study it has grown dramatically. It is one thing to view another culture
from beneath an army helmet or through the sights of an artillery gun
during a time when one's own culture is being threatened. It is quite
another experience to study other cultures academically and personally,

in a time of prosperity when America's standard of living has doubled in the past three decades while the growing majority of the world lives in unchanging poverty.

This very difference is reflected within many families and reminds me of one situation in particular. A friend of mine who is a student in sociology was looking forward to spending his junior year in Japan in order to study how the culture was adapting to rapid industrial development. In many ways he was disappointed with what America had allowed industrialization to do to its cities and its values in general, and so he was curious to see how the Japanese were handling it. When he was accepted in the program to study in Tokyo, he couldn't understand why his father wasn't as elated as he was. In fact, he told me that his father got irritated whenever his upcoming trip was mentioned. His relationship with his father was pretty distant anyway, so he just figured his dad was bugged because he wouldn't have him there to yell at for a year. Only after wondering about this for a long time did my friend remember that his father's younger brother had died fighting the Japanese in World War II.

He realized how distant that war was for him and how real it was for his father. He approached Japan, in fact all countries, as just countries; as places where people were wrestling with the same problems of population, modernization, security, and so on. To his father, many countries were still enemies or friends. My friend's relationship with his dad improved after this, for they both began to realize the kinds of things that can come between father and son. In a sense, they began to bridge the gap.

Because of their historical unrelatedness, young Americans have been able to relinquish many old predispositions about the absoluteness of social and political values. Just as their education made them aware of hushed-up domestic ills, so did it make them aware of the relativity of cultures. They realize that social facts which they had considered absolute are, in fact, unique to the Western industrialized nations. For example, this realization is implicit in young people's new attitudes toward business and science, which question the assumption in adult society that whatever science, industry, and the GNP need, the individual should sacrifice. These assumptions are uniquely American. They are not, as young people were first made to suppose, inherent in human social life. Young men have begun to ask the kinds of questions their parents do not ask, because certain social attitudes have been seen to be variables rather than constants: How does the GNP rise? At whose expense? For whose benefit? With what accompanying psychological manipulation? And with how much occupational channeling?

Unlike society a generation ago, today's young people have taken social relativity as a means for understanding more fully human needs and human potential. The standard attitude in adult society is an outmoded one.

> The sophisticated modern temper has made of social relativity . . . a doctrine of despair. It has pointed out its incongruity with the orthodox dreams of permanence and ideality and with the individual's illusions of autonomy. It has argued that if human experience must give up these, the nutshell of existence is empty.[1]

As the author of these words, anthropologist Ruth Benedict, later says herself, this attitude is an anachronism. It is not part of youth culture, because the postwar generation knows it is in the "House of Mirrors."

Quite naïvely at first, young men realize that the problem is ethnocentricity—cultural narrow-mindedness. In the tenth grade, in our country, high-schoolers are taught that in Euclidean geometry "the whole is equal to the sum of its parts." But in America, as one grows up, one sees that this truth has not been applied to the world and its nations. It is possible to grow up in America thinking that our way of life is in itself the whole.

As I grew up, my biggest doubt and question grew up inside me. I feel that as much as I possessed eyes, I possessed the seed of this question inside me, and my experience only made it grow. How strange it is, I thought, that with myriad national systems and peoples and beliefs, I have been born in the best and most righteous nation, with the only true and rewarding religion, into the finest race, and brought up in the most free and just civilization that has ever existed. Mathematically, I thought, how the odds are against this happening to me! Perhaps I'm lucky, I thought. But then again, perhaps I'm just being fooled. This was simply the germinal stage in the growth of my doubts. Such questions grow slowly. But the interaction of cultural values today is creating dissent in old and young alike who might have otherwise allowed their questions to be lethally sprayed by governmental and mass-media rhetoric.

Many aspects of the educational system reinforce ethnocentricity. The public-school system manages quite successfully to offer a diet of, and to inspire an appetite for, products exclusively from this society, whether on the ideological or cultural menu. In retrospect, a young man notices that in pre-college education he never heard of cultural anthropology.

A comparison of modern cultures is limited to a highly indoctrinated discussion of pure capitalism and pure communism (two nonexistent economic forms). A study of "primitive" societies is even more completely absent. If he came across the names of Malinowski, Mead, or Benedict, it was purely chance. It is a telling comment on our society that ten-year-olds know about the physical theory of relativity but that, until recently, twenty-year-olds did not know about the social theory of relativity. Furthermore, psychology courses are given in strictly American terminology and approach. Biology deals inadequately with the question of race. History courses are usually about Western and American civilization. To today's college students, it seems as if their culture is afraid to tell its children about other cultures.

Young people feel that no longer is it enough for an individual to conform to the cultural system in which he was born. As acculturation accelerates, individual development must be such that one understands not only one's native culture but also foreign ones. Certainly, a purpose of education is to make good citizens, and children should be made knowledgeable about their own society. But can they be fully aware of their own, both its merits and its shortcomings, if they have no knowledge of the nature of other societies? The young cannot help wondering whether present intercultural conflicts might have been prevented had it not been for this composite isolationism. A nation's policies can hardly be more enlightened than the nation's education.

This generation fears that the ethnocentric handicap is one of the most stubborn elements causing America's unresponsiveness to the needs of the emerging nations. Americans continue to get richer without becoming at the same time more concerned for the world, which is getting poorer. American young people today feel like children in a family living in a mansion in the slums.

The work of Gunnar Myrdal, widely read on college campuses, has been a continuous analysis of the rich countries from an international viewpoint of great impartiality. With one major exception,* his work has been exclusively aimed at showing the rich countries what their responsibilities are to the underdeveloped countries. His conclusions challenge the beliefs that are uniquely American. Myrdal demonstrates that the standard of living is not improving in the underdeveloped countries; that America's role has not been that of benefactor or leader in achieving the goals of the poorer countries; and that aspects of American

---

* *An American Dilemma* by no mere coincidence criticizes the other aspect of society that young people are concerned about: racial inequality.

society do tend to make its citizens sluggish and apathetic in improving the economic position of the underdeveloped nations. In his book *Beyond the Welfare State*, Myrdal explains that

> a negative corollary to this increase of national solidarity within the Welfare State is . . . a tendency to a decrease in international solidarity, and, generally, to the weakening of the people's allegiance to international ideals. *The national state and all that goes on within its framework becomes the practical reality for everybody, while internationalist strivings are unpractical dreams.* [Italics mine.][2]

Myrdal's description of adult society's attitudes is valid, but he did not consider the generation gap and the differences it might cause in attitude.

Young people are also critical of this ethnocentricity. They feel with Walter Lippmann that "affluence is not greatness," and also that affluence in the growing poverty of the world is callousness. Their feeling is similar to one experienced frequently in athletic competition. Take a high-jumper who has been trying hard to break the city record. He has been working at it for years, steadily approaching the record mark. The last track meet of his senior year his team is set against the rival team with whom they are tied for the championship. With great effort, the high-jumper clears the bar and sets a new city record, but his team is unexpectedly clobbered by the opposing team. Can he be ecstatic with his victory when his teammates' hopes have been shattered? Can a young American complacently reap the benefits of material affluence when his fellows around the world remain in poverty with unachieved aspirations?

Alienated college students feel the guilt of affluence quite painfully. This is evident throughout the generation but it is seen with greatest immediacy in people who have served in the Peace Corps. They have been moved from affluence to poverty and back to affluence again. As if watching a movie that has been spliced too often, they are often unable to find a sense of continuity as they look back on their lives, and their identities blur.

One girl, who served in the Peace Corps in Latin America after graduating from an Ohio college, was a good example of this. She told me after she returned to America how disconnected her life appeared. "My junior year in college," she began, "I gained weight so rapidly that I went on a special exercise program at a health center. It cost two hundred dollars, and the only reason I needed it was that there was too much food and not enough physical work. Two years later I found myself living with people who were starving—people who worked the whole day the whole year round and earned less money than I had spent for reducing! *How can you live with yourself after something like that?"* No other group but the postwar generation has asked this question with such bewilderment.

In 1930, there were 4 Latin Americans to every 5 North Americans (108 million/134 million). In 1965, there were 30 million more of the former than of the latter. And, amazingly, the projected census figures of the United Nations for the year 2000 indicate 2 Latin Americans for every North American.[3] In another three decades the number of very poor, illiterate, and often exploited inhabitants of this hemisphere will outnumber the rich, 2 to 1.

This generation's parents, many of whom had to climb out of poverty themselves, can approach the situation of the poor in two ways. First, they can treat the poor with patience, reasoning that just as they were poor once and are now relatively affluent, so too will the poor in the ghettos and in the underdeveloped lands become better off. Or second, they may treat the poor with criticism, thinking: We had to work hard and had to sacrifice a lot to get where we are. If the poor today, especially in the slums, would work, if they really *wanted* to improve themselves, if they wouldn't bite the hand that feeds them, they could improve their standard of living just as we did.

The postwar generation clearly cannot share either of these possible adult attitudes. The young assumed affluence; they didn't work for it. Only in adolescence did this college generation realize that the comfort it had enjoyed since childhood had been denied to many people. An open and unlimited concern for the less privileged was a consequence of this realization.

The Bomb is also a factor that must be considered in this context. As I have mentioned, this generation has achieved "freedom from fear" because nuclear power made war obsolete. The postwar generation cannot hate other countries or ideologies, because all men live under the spectre of the mushroom cloud. What must be realized, in order to understand young people's ambivalence toward their own country, is that their freedom from fear of other men has been more than replaced by a fear of mechanical worldwide destruction through the inventions of modern technology. The postwar generation in America has been the only one to have grown up amidst discussion of fallout shelters and of the effects of radiation, practice air-raid drills every month in school, documentary movies about the consequences of nuclear war, and novels such as *Fail-Safe* and *On the Beach*. With the ambivalence inherent in technology, the possibility of annihilation has become more remote and at the same time omnipresent.

One result has been a difference between the generations concerning the underdeveloped countries. As Vietnam so tragically illustrates, adult society still fears Vietnamese Communist guerrillas and the "international Communist conspiracy." It still fears people and politics different from its own. Implicit in the postwar generation's anti-war activism is the fact that its members fear open conflict and the possibility of nuclear war much more than they fear Vietnamese peasants attempting to rid themselves of foreign armies. The young are painfully aware that what really threatens their lives is not Vietnamese or Chinese but Russian and American. The button which they have learned to fear is not in Hanoi or Peking but in Washington. This generation's fear cannot be directed at a convenient "bad guy" far away but must also focus on the missile, anti-missile, anti-anti-missile network of nuclear overkill that its own society perpetuates.

Another consequence of nuclear arms has to do with the postwar generation's emphasis on psychology. As young people look at the history of international politics, they realize that it is merely the history of international war. Past wars have resulted in the reconfiguration of political power, but future war will destroy the very elements of that configuration. This generation reflects the need for a change in approach, a move toward nonviolence and away from aggression. The young emphasize the importance of understanding the social and psychological origins of war and hate in order to prevent the need for disastrous political or military action. The emphasis on psychology is a search for the means for resolving the issues of violence in a nuclear age.

Violence has been a part of this generation's adolescence in a unique way. For, unlike past generations, today's young people see violence not only as something done by an evil enemy or by psychopathic criminals, but as something deep in their own society and in themselves. Especially for those involved in demonstrations, the issue of violence cannot be easily resolved. For earlier generations, violence seemed to be justified because it was inflicted on wrongdoers in the cause of "the right." But for those who have been clubbed by cops at Century City in Los Angeles or at the Penatgon or in Oakland and Berkeley, in New York or Chicago, for those who feel much closer to ghetto residents who have been shot or maced or clubbed than they feel to the policemen who have done those things, for those who are opposed to a war in which high-altitude American bombers rain tons of napalm on peasant villages—for them, violence is something else entirely.

In a sense, when what is right is not being questioned, there is no such thing as violence. There is only punishment. But when what is right is the basic issue, when that issue is so unclear that it divides the nation, violence becomes violence again (or rather it is seen for what it always was). Then it is something which seems to be used, not necessarily by the right against the wrong, but simply by the powerful against the powerless.

These are the circumstances which have defined the radicals of the 1960s. Their means are basically nonviolent, whether legal or illegal. And their goal is to gain power. And with power in the hands of the nonviolent, they conclude, we will be safe in a nuclear age.

When and if historians look back on these times, I hope they remember to look at them from the point of view of the young as well as the old. They will realize that the Vietnam war, the longest in the nation's history, coincided with the postwar generation's adolescence. They will realize that, in a very personal way, violence enveloped the adolescent years. This generation, hoping for the youthful revitalization of politics, lost a hero in John Kennedy; deeply committed to civil rights, it lost a great man in Martin Luther King; passionately against the Vietnam war, it lost its most powerful political hope in Robert Kennedy. The historians will realize that, for this psychological oriented generation, violence was inside, not outside. And so the young will follow only leaders who impress them as being very self-aware, very much in control of their own motivations and drives, very hip. The criteria for choosing one's leaders is different for a generation that has lived only "in a world where the mildest irritation, multiplied a billionfold by modern technology, might destroy all civilization."[4]

This generation has lived only in a world with these new issues of wealth amidst poverty, multilateral nuclear power, and violence. No wonder its members are impatient for action on the part of their country which acknowledges these new realities. At present, they see the United States' Vietnam policy as continuing evidence that the government is retaining the old priorities, now out of place. Change in the world has simply come too quickly for rigid policies and attitudes to keep abreast.

In response to rapid social change, French philosopher Gabriel Marcel writes that, if it is our aim to understand the generation gap, "we have to take note of the fact that life is being less and less felt as a gift to be handed on, and more and more felt as a kind of incomprehensible calamity, like a flood, against which we ought to be able to build dykes."[5] This is because most individuals in the older generation increasingly feel removed from the powers that determine policy; they feel that life is calamitous because they themselves seem to have no control and often no knowledge of the crucial questions.[6] And if an adult begins to feel more and more a spectator to the events of political and social change, he can detach himself from what goes on and become a permanent citizen in a world reality that yearly passes further into the past. One may continue to apply precepts that in their time were logical responses to developments, to problems of a later world in which they are irrelevant or at best secondary.

But adults must protect themselves and preserve their authority. In order to do this, there is only one recourse. They must affirm with absoluteness the view that "young people are always radical." They must cling to the idea: "Youth is a time of naïve, idealistic radicalism. 'Let's make the world over,' young people seem to think. But once they get out into the world, they'll come to their senses. They'll realize it's a tough world; they'll settle down, and they'll look back at their radical episode as one of the mistakes of growing up."

This logic applies pretty well to the youth of the 1930s. But what about the generation of the 1950s? An international survey of college students made by two distinguished psychologists in the early 1950s demonstrated statistically that no national group was less concerned about social problems than the American student sample. There was no trace of radicalism.[7]

This apathy was not simply because of the war, for a case can well be made that the same was true in the late 1950s. A book entitled *Revolt on the Campus*, describing campus political activities at that time, concluded that a new wave of conservatism was sweeping the nation's colleges and universities. Written by M. Staunton Evans, one of the most articulate conservatives today, this book quite elaborately discusses the growth and eventual predominance of conservative political organizations on campuses, and the virtual nonexistence of radical groups. Evans makes the case strongly that if young people were noticeably different from their elders, it was in that they were more conservative.

Quite clearly, then, if we look at the issue historically, the simplistic interpretation of youth and politics—that the young are always radical

—is just not true. We are forced to accept that, in a time of rapid social change, the old clichés don't work. And when adult society has realized this, when it finally learns to listen to what some of the sensitive, intelligent young radicals are saying, it will find, to its surprise, not naïve, youthful idealism but legistimate social concerns.

A Fading Dream

The English minstrel of love, Donovan, tells the older
generations that in Vietnam they are playing the game of
life "with your blackest queen." Donovan's dream for
peace is fading, for he refuses America's freedom
when it is packaged "in a lie."

Because the attitudes of the generations are so different, we begin
to find one generation regarding the other's views not only as untenable
but as incredible. The extraordinary exception to this is Dr. Spock.
Responsible for the relatively permissive child-rearing practiced by the
parents of the postwar generation, pediatrician Spock has aligned himself with the children he helped rear and not with the parents who bought
millions of his books. Spock has unequivocally supported draft-resisters.
He has decided that the young generation is right and the millions of
silent adults, who "patriotically" support the laws and institutions that
are permitting the destruction of Vietnamese society and the division
of our own, are wrong.

Were the differences between the generations limited to merely political
opinions, they could be resolved in political debate. But this is impossible, since the lack of credibility has taken root in deeper soil than
the political controversies of the day. Distrust has become embedded
in generational differences that extend beyond the political into the
psychological. Neither generation realizes the differences between their

respective childhoods, and so their "facts" are different. With the same set of facts, one can have an intellectual debate about the conclusions. But when the facts themselves differ, the debate becomes personal— and violent.

The difference between father and son generations seems so great that each considers incredible not only the other's rationality but also the other's humanity. In youth's phraseology, "God, my parents are unreal!" one sometimes fails to realize that the reaction to generational differences is similar to that which occurred when racial, religious, or ideological differences were encountered between adults. One group feels so radically different from another group that, in order to preserve their status as human beings, both groups must degrade each other to something less than fully human stature. Throughout history, whenever this has happened because of national, ideological, religious, or racial differences, war or prejudice had inevitably resulted.

Today's differences, however, are not between men divided by national boundaries or by the color of their skin. They are between men who are part of the same communities and families. Their differences are not dealt with by war or by traditional prejudice, but are avoided and allowed to grow by mutual tacit agreement of indifference and minimal communication. Quite literally today, "a house divided against itself cannot stand." The issue has been restated in relation to the present war by Arthur M. Schlesinger, Jr., in his critique of American foreign policy in *The Bitter Heritage*: "Whatever the outcome of the Vietnam debate or of later debates that may darken our future, the essential thing is to preserve mutual trust among ourselves as Americans."[1] As indictments of Dr. Spock and others on charges of conspiracy, and mass emigrations to Canada by young men, have tragically demonstrated, it is precisely this trust which we have begun to lose.

It would be inaccurate to mention only the distrust between generations. The rift in the nation has also divided the younger generation itself. The scene of the massive Pentagon march in October 1967 illustrates this. Young men in uniform, helmeted, with unsheathed blades pointing outward on their rifles, surrounded the massive front walls of the Pentagon. At the other end of their bladed guns stood tens of thousands of young men, variously dressed college and high-school students, professors, mothers, radicals, and curious onlookers. Two groups, both comprised mostly of members of the postwar generation, stood in their country's capital, facing each other across loaded weapons.

There are always some in such a gathering who have suffered so greatly from the mistrust which pervades our society that they must hate the opposing group in order to sustain their self-image. Some soldiers taunted demonstrators; some demonstrators taunted soldiers. But the vast majority of young men on both sides experienced not hatred but rather a painful awareness of the absurdity of hatred.

I personally could not help thinking that I might have grown up with one of those soldiers. The soldier who lacerated the head of the student by whom I was standing could have been a high-school buddy. What is it about American life, I and many others wondered, that takes a young generation and divides it so completely that it confronts itself like opposing armies?

It was the bitter memory of these thoughts that remained in my mind after the Washington experience. But the thoughts then were abstract wonderings. It was not until I went home at Christmas that I realized my thoughts were grounded in reality.

I was hitchhiking into town to buy some presents when a guy I know picked me up. We had both missed making our high-school basketball team a few years earlier and so had played together on an intramural basketball team that won the championship. We had been really good friends. As we discovered by the time we reached town, he had been on the other end of the rifles from me in front of the Pentagon.

We shook hands as I got out of the car, but we knew that the conversation had been awkward after our startling discovery. We both realized that, although each had attempted to trust the other group at the Washington confrontation, the bitterness and mistrust that were so pervasive had deeply affected us. Our handshake was a reminder that, because of our nation's foreign policy, an extended rifle was just as likely as an extended hand between two members of the postwar generation.

There are very few times when one can blame fairly only youth or only adult society for the loss in communication that has occurred. On virtually all issues the blame is shared because the ignorance of the changes is shared. But on the issue of the Vietnam war, young people come as close to being blameless as they can get.

College students have repeatedly requested a dialogue between State Department officials and anti-war speakers. Only the latter were willing. Young men have asked for explanations, for valid statistics, for credible reasons. But they have been met with silence or rhetoric. An extremely broad cross-section of student-body leaders from campuses across the country—200 in all, from 200 colleges in 36 states—sent a series of letters to President Johnson, trying to state with moderation and clarity the position of a growing number of college students against the war. The first letter, sent in December 1966, got little response from the administration, and so they drafted others. The last letter to date by that group, further questioning the logic and morality of continued escalation, carefully and sincerely expressed the doubts of these student leaders. Their aim was to offset the radical actions of the draft-card-burners and campus SDS groups which had received adverse publicity, but at the same time to succeed in informing the administration of the growing turbulence of dissent within their ranks.

But all these moderate campus spokesmen received was silence. Their last letter stated that "it seems inconceivable to us that the government would abstain from any honorable effort to regain the confidence of the generation which must bear the brunt of the war if it were aware of how deep the loss of confidence has been." The student leaders warn that "it would be a sad misconception about the nature and depth of the dissatisfaction to think that it can be eased by slogans, rebukes, or patriotic exhortations." Yet to their ears, after the replies have crossed the generation gap, shallow rhetoric is all they have been given.

These young men who are being brushed aside are not the fringe or the outcasts of the generation. They are the leaders. The students who organized a war protest at Princeton, for example, were not a radical student fringe. They were the captain of the football team and the presidents of the junior and senior classes. And the two hundred student representatives who drafted the series of letters were the elected student-body leaders, not social outcasts.

The young keep trying to communicate their opposition, but, since their voices have not been recognized, they have changed their message. One hundred present and former student-body presidents from such schools as the University of Michigan, MIT, Yale, Harvard, and Union Theological Seminary drafted a letter to President Johnson which read in part:

> Along with thousands of our fellow students, we campus leaders cannot participate in a war which we believe to be immoral and unjust. . . . We publicly . . . express our intention to refuse induction and to aid and support those who decide to refuse. We will not serve in the military as long as the war in Vietnam continues.

The leaders in adult society ignore the radical adult fringe, so it is not surprising that they have ignored what once was the radical youth fringe. *But today, the generation gap has widened to the point where the leaders of adult society are forced to ignore not the fringe but the leaders of youth.*

A medal-winning soldier in the Special Forces in Vietnam, James Sloan, has written a startling novel entitled *A Small War* about his experience. After a military career which took him into the thick of the jungle and of Army bureaucracy, Sloan has conveyed the stupidity of our involvement in Southeast Asia and the destruction it has caused, not through ivory-tower criticism but through his own Army experience. The protagonist of his novel, Tom Thane, returns home from the war a hero but is a dissenter in disguise.

> Thane lived at home the life of the returning hero. The duty of a hero is to answer cowards' questions.
> How he would have liked to tell them: "You want to find out how it was in Vietnam, get off your own fat ass and go.
> "You want a war fought over there? Go fight it for yourself."

Although supporters of the war continue to pretend that this generation's dissenters are nothing but an isolated campus fringe, the fact remains that young soldiers as well as young students are finding their own young awareness.

High government officials know of the generation gap. It is impossible for a government speaker at a college commencement to watch dozens of the graduating class walk out in the middle of his speech without being aware of it. But awareness is not understanding. Government leaders do consider the generation gap as something that must be eliminated—but, unfortunately, eliminated by crushing the attitudes of the postwar generation rather than listening to them. Government leaders cannot seem to recognize that the attitudes of the young are a valid response to a changing world reality that has moved too quickly for them to follow. Adults are still trying to reverse the clock by making youth's attitudes conform to their own.

Former Vice-President Humphrey is a good example. He is aware that the generation gap is a major factor in today's unprecedented dissent against the war. "This new young generation has never known a depression or a war, and it hasn't learned about these things from hard experience," Humphrey told a reporter. The immense dissatisfaction in the young generation, he felt, "isn't limited to anti-war feeling about Vietnam. It's a more general kind of self-indulgence."[2]

By impugning the sincere motivation of this generation, Mr. Humphrey dismissed the generation gap as the result of the absence of some sort of self-control that would have made this generation agree with his views. He automatically considers his view of history right and the attitudes of youth wrong, so it is not surprising that he concluded that youth somehow lack the moral fiber that his generation fortunately possesses.

Former Secretary of State Dean Rusk revealed the same rigidity. He also thinks that this generation is having difficulty understanding the meaning of history: "World War II is twenty years away now, and World War I twenty years before that. A lot of years, and a lot of answers get forgotten. And some people now aren't even old enough to remember them."[3] Since the answers to the dilemmas of the present and the future are to be found two or three decades in the past, Mr. Rusk found it quite understandable that the younger generation is less aware of the "answers" than are he and his cronies. And the "some people" he blithely referred to as not being old enough to remember are the twenty-five-and-under generation who comprise over half the population of the country he was helping to lead!

Rusk considered this historical unrelatedness to past fears and military tactics a real hindrance in dealing with the problems we face today in a nuclear age. "The young people who haven't experienced any other war," he explained, "feel that the war in Vietnam is something that is all fresh and different, that it has nothing to do with other crises. A lot of arguments I hear now against the war are the same ones people used during the thirties." He viewed a fresh or different approach to future crises as an alarming danger. We must continue to apply the precepts of the past, he seemed to be telling youth.

But this generation can see in the fiasco of Vietnam what the same stale approach has achieved in a changing world. "Fresh" and "different" are compliments today, not criticisms. The young realize that Rusk's approach can be used until hell freezes over, or, more likely, until life is consumed in a thermonuclear flash. Mistrust and fear, resulting in the fantasy of a worldwide Communist plot, can continue to shape our policy and our tragic future. And if the rigidity of men like Rusk and Humphrey smothers the fiery freshness and differentness of this generation, that apocalyptic future will be inevitable.

Youth and Psychology

Increasing numbers of young men have only a secondary interest in the functioning of their government. Their primary interest is in psychology, in the functioning of the human mind. Politics must still interest them because intergovernmental affairs hold the immediate fate of the world in their committees and their missile systems; and, more constantly, because the government impinges on the day-to-day reality in which young people live. But the academic division between psychology and politics, an expedient creation of Western education, is not a clear one in the psychologically oriented eyes of this generation.

Because of their preoccupation with the workings of the mind, some young people try to minimize the control that social pressures exert upon them. They try to break the dichotomy between their public and private selves by making their whole lives private. The student quits school, hops on a drug kick, manages to get a psychological draft deferment that exempts him from military service, works as a waiter in some little coffee shop on MacDougal Street in exchange for a room upstairs and meals, and enmeshes himself in a small underworld that can still manage to survive despite the omnipresent federal and metropolitan eyes. He becomes an Outsider and so frees himself from the entanglements in which an Insider inevitably involves himself. He removes himself from the mainstream of social life and from the values that always flow with it, and he chucks the responsibilities and hassles with which modern American life tries to burden him. He gains "freedom."

But by so doing, he precludes the possibility of doing anything to change directly the society in which he grew up and which he had to reject. He felt within himself no incentive to join the rat-race and social-climbing syndrome, and, on the other hand, he felt the many convincing reasons that made the Outsider life look better than the aspiring-collegian-from-good-family role which he had lived before. *Yet he is planning to leave society essentially the same as it was, without trying to change the elements in it that drove him away.*

Many young people feel the same criticisms of society that prompt the Outsider to reject it. But most of them have in the past felt that the unhealthy, irrational parts of society that are detrimental to individual fulfillment should be weeded out; that each individual is striving for the same fullness in life that they are; and that in this free and democratic country those individuals will support him in his attempts to change the disliked elements of society. These young people obviously would retain some interest in politics. They feel, unlike their social dropout counterpart, that many people nourish within themselves the same goals and beliefs for a better society as they themselves do. All that needs to be done is to make people aware and active in fermenting this social change. And the realm where this change should be brought about is in political action.

It is the thin line between feeling similar or dissimilar to other people that divides the politically active young from the politically apathetic. Keniston's *Young Radicals* documents this interplay of forces: each of the young Vietnam Summer workers he interviewed experienced an intense period of self-examination and self-doubt because of "differentness." Those who came to feel that what made them different was not a psychological malady but an intelligent awareness of political problems became activists. Those who failed to achieve such a realization remained silent. It is the extension of political alienation into psychological alienation that precludes meaningful political participation.

One cannot help seeing that the political process of a modern mass society is integrally related to the psychology of its members. For if social authorities convince young people that their political dissent is nothing but youthful rebelliousness (in other words, their own personal psychological problems), then they will bury their dissent within themselves in order to hide their alleged immaturity. But today these young people are acting on their beliefs; they are changing attitudes into behavior. However, if mass society can succeed in convincing young people that their dissent means not that they are politically concerned, but that something is psychologically "different" about them, then they will become dropouts, not activists.

One of the most outspoken scholars to realize the interrelatedness of the political and psychological aspects of modern life is political scientist Herbert Marcuse. "Psychological categories," he says without qualification, "have become political categories."

> The traditional borderlines between psychology on the one side and political and social philosophy on the other have been made obsolete by the condition of man in the present era: formerly autonomous and identifiable psychical processes are being absorbed by the function of the individual in the state—by his public existence. Psychological problems therefore turn into political problems: *private disorder reflects more directly than before the disorder of the whole, and the cure of the personal disorder depends more directly than before on the cure of the general disorder.* [Italics mine.][1]

No one feels this with more intimacy than today's young people. The difference between the social dropout and the politically active and dissident young man is this: *the former emphasizes the fact that his personal psychological dissatisfaction reflects the disorder of the whole, and so decides to remove himself from the whole; while the latter emphasizes that his own dissatisfaction with the prevalent way of life relates directly to the sickness of society itself, and so decides to establish himself in such a position that he may change the social whole.* The difference between the young man who leads the Outsider life, which is generally considered to be unproductive, and the one who tries to become an active catalyst for social change is the degree to which each feels estranged or alienated from society.

The division of social dropouts and activists may sound academic or abstract; an illustration of the difference might clarify the dichotomy. Take the issue of draft-resistance, for example. The activist would say: "America has gotten involved in a war that is really opposed to her ideals. She is suppressing nationalism and supporting colonialism. Elections will not provide the American people with a choice in foreign policy because the military-industrial complex has interests that will support only candidates with at least moderately hawkish attitudes. Because a power clique has developed in this country, the individual must act outside of the political system to make his dissenting voice heard. To stop the mass slaughter in Vietnam, individuals must act, regardless of the personal consequences. Through our actions we may stop this unjust war, and bring about a change in the political system which allows such policies to develop."

The psychological dropout would have quite a different explanation. "The problem is not primarily in the political system," he would reply, "but in the minds of men. Your mind has the same hassles the government and miltary have. You work with the same priorities they work with. You think in terms of power; you look at different factions with hate; you want to control and organize others. The way you have had to live has made your mind work like theirs, whatever your political differences. First, solve the problems of your own mind; then solve the problems of the world." (The Beatles state the psychologically alienated position succinctly when they sing: "If you want money for minds that hate, well, you'll just have to wait.")

The psychological insight of the latter young man is wasted, for he does not engage in a way of life that will in any way improve the aspects of society which he criticizes. His awareness is never translated into social action because his alienation was so overpowering that he feels any political action is doomed to failure.

We live in an era of abundance and, believe me, we have an abundance of alienation. Now the question seems to me to be: What is going to happen to this alienation? Is it going to manifest itself in the form of the "happy waiter" who waits on tables as he waits for society to change? Or is it going to provide the Western nations with a generation of young people highly enough motivated and free enough of tradition to overcome the social inertia which is leading the nation ever closer to the brink of nuclear destruction and the individual ever closer to absorption by mass society?

The process of alienation must be understood for what it is. Alienation is first a dissatisfaction with an approach to life. This is a rebellious, "negative" stage. Since human beings cannot exist without some relatedness, this stage is temporary. Depending on the individual, three outcomes of alienation present themselves.

1. Some alienated young men feel the isolation and lostness and so return to the unfulfilling social pattern of behavior with the rationale

that "it's better than nothing." The germ of their awareness of their unfulfillment does not leave them unaffected, however, for they participate in society in an egoistic and destructive manner. Society did not give them what they needed in life, and so their frustration is directed at others.

2. The second group calls the first reaction "selling out." It does the individual no good at all, this group feels: because the first group could find no outlet for alienation, it sold out to the *status quo* life that makes living appear to be an unfortunate calamity. An increasing number of young people are reacting against the "sellout." They know that because their alienation is so great, a return to the traditional, even externally, would be a sacrifice. They have no choice; they *must* look for alternatives. Since they feel on one side of that thin psychological line, they remain within society to change it. They are sure of their dissatisfactions, and so have the conviction and the strength to function as critical dissenters. This group can do so constructively—out of a concern for the future rather than out of frustration for having sacrificed themselves to "the system."

3. But when alienation becomes so overwhelming, when the feeling of differentness extends beyond the intellectual, when the young person feels so removed from society that he believes there is no common ground between his values and that society's, he often decides to extricate himself completely from the social whole. Ties are severed completely, and the individual turns to other cultures to find his values, if indeed he finds any at all.*

It is not hard to see which of these groups has been predominant in the past. During the 1950s, the first group's reaction to alienation was the prevalent one. In the early 1960s we began to witness the second. But the social forces breeding alienation grew so quickly that in the late 1960s groups reacting in the third way became visible. It was the failure of a stagnant adult society which did not incorporate the values of the activists that led to the political apathy of the psychological dropout.

The relationship between activism and psychology is illustrated by some interesting facts about student activism at Berkeley and Harvard, two of the most volatile campuses in the nation. Each of these college communities experienced periods of intense activism in which students temporarily felt they might finally have some effect, in one case concerning "free speech" and in the other concerning the Vietnam war.

---

* The section "Youth and Identity" discusses these groups of alienated behavior in the spectrum of youth culture more fully.

The psychiatric units at the health services of these two universities, normally quite busy, found that the number of students coming for psychiatric help declined dramatically during the period of concerted political action. The students, it must be concluded, found an external outlet for their intense concern and so temporarily were less caged in their own minds.

But mental frustration returns and grows after these all-too-short episodes of activism. The college psychiatrists stay in business.

Even if they end with chapters enumerating all their hopes, eminent sociologists, psychologists, and philosophers sound pessimistic when discussing the future of the individual in our society. They foresee doom unless the individual in mass society can gain a measure of autonomy and self-awareness. Many of these scholars conclude what the young have realized by other means: that although life in America has obvious advantages over life in other environments, it has psychological drawbacks that gain additional significance because the individual is unaware of them. Especially if one is part of college youth culture, it is impossible to avoid the recurrent themes in sociopsychological literature which indicate from many, many perspectives that the inner part of the individual is slowly being absorbed by the necessities of modern life.

Adults have made themselves aware—and indeed are constantly being made aware by the prestigious voices of the media—of the benefits and strengths of the American system, but most of them have not recognized the detrimental aspects of the way of life. "The diffuse and anonymous authority of the modern democracies is less favorable to autonomy than one might assume"[2] states Riesman cautiously. "The era tends to be totalitarian even where it has not produced totalitarian states,"[3] says political scientist Marcuse plainly. Both groups of young people, the Outsiders and the activists, can feel this without reading it. More and more of them are turning to psychology as a primary interest and method of understanding modern life.

The immediate personal consequences are what concern the young first, not political repercussions. A young man feels: Perhaps my public self cannot be changed, but I can and must control my private life. I must preserve my self-awareness within the confines of mass society.

A modern young man, whether a social dropout or a critic, is aware that he must free himself from the limiting aspects of mass society in order to live, as Camus says, "to the maximum." In this endeavor to free themselves psychologically from society, both the Insider and Outsider become united. And both believe that, like the Outsider of literature (as described by Colin Wilson),

> men are in prison: that is the Outsider's verdict. They are quite contented in prison—caged animals who have never known freedom; but it *is* prison all the same. And the Outsider? He is in prison too . . . *but he knows it.* His desire is to escape. But a prison-break is not an easy matter; *you must know all about your prison*, otherwise you might spend years in tunneling, like the Abbé in *The Count of Monte Cristo*, and only find yourself in the next cell.[4]

Substitute the young people's term "bag" for the prison cell, and you have the situation of modern youth. When a hippie says derisively, "What kind of a bag are you in?" he means in what kind of cell, in which set of socially patterned frustrations, are you living (or rather *not* living) your life.

Today's young people, unlike adult society, know they are in prison. They want to know their prison—their society—and they want to know their cell—their minds. The young today are forced to want to escape because their society has become one where the demands made upon the inner self are too great to withstand.

Today's young man reacts as did twenty-year-old Thomas Wolfe in *Look Homeward, Angel*: "Every move I have made . . . has been an effort to escape. I *shall* get me some beauty, I shall get me some order out of this jungle of my life. I shall find my way out of it yet," he tells his mother, Eliza, "although it take me twenty years more—alone."

"Alone?" asked his mother then, as adult society now asks its children. "Where are you going?"

"Ah," the twenty-year-old answers, "you weren't looking, were you? I've gone."

What Did They Put in Your Head?

Your father sits watches stocks,
Your mother has tea with society.
You started your lesson at half-past three. . . .
What did they put in your head today?
What kind of games do they make you play?

—The Seeds

To know oneself has long been a tenet of Oriental philosophies; it crept into the Western world through Socrates, but one does not hear much about it in adult society today. When one hears a person being praised in everyday life, one soon becomes aware of what personal characteristics are valued in our culture.

The corporation man is looked up to because he can really keep *cool* at an important board meeting. The office assistant is respected because she is so *efficient*. The union official is considered indispensable because he is *tough* and can hold his ground. The factory employee is valued because he is *compliant* and *diligent*. The student admired by his teachers is *conscientious* and *obedient*. A child does not live long before he realizes what personal characteristics are considered valuable by his society. His parents and his teachers cultivate precisely the traits they think he will need as an adult—that is, the traits that are most in demand in society.

This generation realizes that this is merely the process of socialization. But it cannot avoid the realization, also, that as society has been transformed, the process of socialization could not help also being transformed. Young people can feel the new demands of this process of "making social."

When the pace of technological innovation and social change was slower, authority in the family and child-rearing remained traditional. The father was austere and respected, his wife reinforced his authority, and the children were obedient. The parents were conscious of their role in socialization: in religion, politics, education, morals, the parents inculcated their values in their offspring. Parents knew what was right and were going to fulfill their duty as parents by teaching what was right to their children. Teachers and the public-school system heartily accepted this pattern. The teacher had unquestioned authority, and the child had to be obedient.

Clearly, with this pattern of family and school authority, people's behavior could not be made to change rapidly because of the virtually complete correspondence between the older and the younger generations' values.

In both the family and the school, this authoritarian method of socialization underwent a rapid social change which most strikingly changed the postwar generation. First, women gained equal rights and began to assert their equality within the family. Legally and emotionally they destroyed one level of the hierarchical family authority pattern and made the family more egalitarian. And, as any on-the-ball eight-year-old can tell you, that was an important change. It enabled the child to play one parent against the other—a tactical weapon in a child's strategy that had never before been so potent.

Next, accelerating social change along with the increased importance of higher education gave young people in the second half of the century a more nearly equal footing *vis-à-vis* their parents. Accompanying this change came the so-called "permissive school" of baby and child specialists, such as Dr. Spock, which advocated a less punitive, authoritative method of child-rearing. The door was opened for children to be not only seen but also heard.

All this was not pushed on parents: *they were looking for a way out.* "Most urbane, educated parents knew that they had been raised for a world very different from the one they lived in," says educator Christopher Jencks, "and they at least suspected that their children would grow old in a world they could barely imagine. In such a context it was hard to be sure about anything."[1] And if parents weren't sure what was right any more, much less what would be right when their children were adults, they weren't sure what to tell their children. And so many of them didn't tell them anything. They left the "telling" up to the public: the church, the school, the media, and the peer group.

In this situation, obedience was no longer such a simple thing. A father's system of rights and wrongs had usually been clear, and when it wasn't he would make it clear behind the woodshed. But when his authority became diffuse and anonymous, when it was parceled out to many institutions, which often gave conflicting instructions, a child was in a complex situation. The question was not of simple obedience, but of obedience to *what*. The question is not how well one looks in the mirror, but which mirror one should look in. This generation had to grow up without the time-honored gift from father to son: a firm set of beliefs and guidelines to accept or rebel against. The generation joined Bob Dylan in his lament: "I've got nothing, Ma, to live up to."

This change in the patterns of authority revved up the engines of social change. New tastes, new fads, new values, new buying habits—all could appear in one generation because guidance was coming primarily not from the parents but from the public apparatus of mass society.

The young generation discerns scholars who have also noticed this change. Sociologist Riesman's concept of "other-direction," psychologist Erikson's awareness of the "mechanization of man," psychologist Erich Fromm's idea of the "marketing-oriented" personality—these terms all denote an academic awareness of significant changes in various patterns of traditional authority. These scholars find large audiences in today's generation because they all realize that the interaction between culture and individual psychology is rapidly changing and must be examined closely in order to preserve individual autonomy.

By no means do the young today generally have the objectivity of these learned men, but young people's alienation does place them outside of society so that they may examine it at a distance. Today's psychologically oriented generation criticizes modern society because it has seen that, in spite of all the emphasis put on individuality and happiness, society has nevertheless made the individual feel that the purpose of his life is perseverance in his work, in his striving for social success, in his endeavor to keep pace with the socially ideal personality. Fromm writes: "Money, prestige, and power have become [man's] incentives and his ends. He acts under the illusion that his actions might benefit his self-interest, though he actually serves everything but the interest of his real self. . . . He is for everything except for himself."[2]

Well-known economist John Kenneth Galbraith provides the economics to support Fromm's psychological assertion. The natural tendency of men to work until they think they have enough, and then to stop, has been overcome by the needs of the industrial system for ever-increasing consumption. Now men are made to think that they always need more, so that they will work more. The advertising media reach out to create consumer wants and, at the same time of course, create the consumer's need to work. "In 1939," Galbraith says, "the real income of employed workers in the United States was very nearly the highest on record and it was then the highest of any country in the world. In the next quarter century it doubled." Yet, despite the hundred-per-cent increase in real income, there was actually an increase in the average hours worked per week! Galbraith adds with a touch of sarcasm, "This was a remarkable achievement."[3]

The change in the consumer was psychological, and so too were the tools that achieved that change. Advertising and salesmanship created the wants, the continually changing wants, of the consumer. Galbraith concludes that "the wants so created insure the services of the worker. Ideally, his wants are kept slightly in excess of his income. Compelling inducements are then provided for him to go into debt. The pressure of the resulting debt adds to his reliability as a worker."[4]

From an economic perspective, too, the young conclude that modern, affluent man is no longer working primarily for himself. The intellectual or religious justification for such an attitude toward work and life stems from what Max Weber called the Protestant ethic. In tracing the growth of capitalism, he concluded that identical with capitalism is not only the pursuit of profit, but the pursuit of *ever-renewed* profit. Weber said that the Protestant ethic actually tried to create a type of personality[5] —a personality that values above all "restless, continuous, systematic work in a worldly calling," so that "man is dominated by the making of money, by acquisition as the ultimate purpose of his life."[6]

A phrase that is peculiarly American is: "What is he worth?" It means "What is his income or what is the value of his total estate?" The question is asked usually about men of great wealth. It would be embarrassing indeed to ask the same question about a poor man. One would then have to answer, "He's not worth a red cent," a reply which is, among other things, very un-Christian, for the same would have to be said about Christ.

This is only language, of course, but it is the set of values which supports such language that this generation of alienated college youth finds unacceptable. Young people know too many adults (as is evidenced by their criticisms of business) who are "worth" thousands or millions but who are worth a great deal less as concerned parents or compassionate human beings.

The psychologically oriented young are concerned about the completeness of what they and others experience. Young people are looking more and more within themselves rather than into society for the answers to the problems of their dead-end adolescence. Society is changing so rapidly and authority is so fragmented that the young feel that as long as an individual looks for his own balancing-point in his external world —by identifying with the Company, or by blind loyalty to The State, or by chasing the Madison Avenue Joneses, or even by glorifying a remote God—he will never come fully to examine himself or his society.

Young people are merely reacting against a society in which men succeed if they use their own abilities as salable commodities. As Fromm puts it, the individual's true abilities then become "masked from him because what matters is not his self-realization in the process of using them but his success in the process of selling them."[7]

Adult society's acceptance of an external image, of the self-image reflected by the mirror of mass society, provides a paltry substitute for the security and permanence which its members lost by their self-alienation. The psychological orientation of youth is emphatically declaring that, for a person to be mature and self-aware, the external is not enough.

Adults, for their part, can barely contain their ridicule of a youth who is engaged in working to know and understand his self with psychological depth. If adult society is not aware of the loss of self, it is not surprising that it finds unreal the search for self.

This is the aspect of the generation gap I have often found most tragic. I have known so many young people who, distraught and depressed and running away from their own problems and their real selves, were nevertheless encouraged to stay in college by their parents because it's just the thing one should do. After all, "Dad" would have loved to go to college if he had only been able to.

Finally these students' problems became too overwhelming. They could no longer run away from them successfully by reading about life rather than living it. These young men left college (without much trouble before the Vietnam war was escalated, anyway) and traveled to communities where there were other young people of their breed—working, involving themselves with people, often taking drugs, sometimes reading books of social criticism, of psychology, or of Oriental philosophy. By concentrating on finding out who they were, by trying to know their prison and their cell, many of these dropouts gained freedom from their former imprisonment. Liberated from academic pressure and social control for the first time in their lives, these members of youth culture often came to terms with themselves, found out where "their heads were at," and made what they considered the psychological leap from youth to adulthood.

What was so tragic in most of these cases was that this process of gaining an identity went unrecognized and was criticized by these young people's parents. All they could see was that their Johnny was wasting his time. How did these supposed changes translate into real life? they asked him. "You're no better prepared for earning a living now then you were a few years ago," they went on. "And look at Fred and Irma's boy: he's already one year into med school."

Mom and Dad were troubled about their dropout son. What could they tell the neighbors that Johnny was doing? Could they say that Johnny was "finding himself"? No, they'd be laughed clear across the office or across the back-yard clothesline. The parents wanted to know what the change meant in terms of social recognition of it. How do these changes affect Johnny's standing in society?—that's what Mom and Dad are interested in. Johnny says the changes were beneficial, but he is looking inside himself. Mom and Dad say the changes are detrimental because they are looking at society.

When parents in this position say that their son is farming and fishing in Mexico, or working an ocean steamer, or waiting on tables in a Los Angeles coffee shop, or picking fruit with migrant laborers in Oregon, their fellow members in adult society try to feign a smile, but their disapproval shows through the transparency of politeness. *Why isn't he in college?* their eyes demand of Johnny's parents. *Couldn't he make it?*

Few of the parents have the courage to ask the real question: Why didn't Johnny *want* to make it? This question challenges their framework of goals and social priorities. When today's sons pass up the opportunities that parents wish they could have had, it challenges the older generation's goals, and parents know it. And so, quite often, adults cannot accept what Johnny's experience means to him but only realize what it means to them.

The hero in the movie *The Graduate*, fresh out of college and a star student and athlete, could have met the challenges of his parents' society.

He could have made it big—big house, big parties, big name. But he didn't want to. He saw beneath the affluence and propriety of high society an emotional emptiness that he refused to accept.

When the movie began to look as though it might be the biggest money-maker of all time, the movie pundits couldn't figure it out. What was so special about *The Graduate*? It was simply that it told the story of a young man growing up in a society he could not accept, the same story that millions of young moviegoers knew so well.

A decade ago an alienated young man like the one discussed in this chapter could have been bullied back into conformity. He had no support anywhere, it seemed to him. Today, however, there is a youth culture that stands behind him. Simon and Garfunkel, whose songs have very profoundly criticized life in mass society, provided the music for *The Graduate*. Dustin Hoffman, the leading actor in the movie, campaigned for Eugene McCarthy. Simon and Garfunkel donated earnings from several concerts to McCarthy's campaign.

Without looking too hard, alienated young people realize that a large corps of youth shares their opposition to most of what the old awareness stands for.

They All Look
Just the Same

And they all play on the golf course
And drink their martinis dry,
And they all have pretty children
And the children go to school,
And the children go to summer camp
And then to the university,
Where they are put in boxes
And they come out all the same.
—Malvina Reynolds
  (as sung by Pete Seeger)

Johnny's parents can find no positive reason for his behavior. Yet, in his own way of thinking, their son must somehow be reinforced in order to continue his quest for self-knowledge in the face of mass society's criticism. If society negatively sanctions his psychological undertaking, what reference points strengthen his conviction that he is doing the right thing? What is the way of thinking that sustains a psychological dropout?

With their psychological orientation, members of this generation view dropout behavior from a perspective different from their elders'. Their view of adult society as a collection of individuals who act on the basis not of what *they* need but of what *mass society* needs makes the vast majority of jobs appear to demand a considerable sacrifice in individuality. Young people do not criticize those who do have an occupation that is challenging and that demands the worker's full development of his capacities. But in the image that adult society gives them, those with fulfilling jobs appear to be in the small minority.

Adults seem to expect to develop themselves personally only in their leisure time, if then. Work is the time when one sacrifices oneself and discharges one's duties as automatically as possible. And one behaves in such a way that one may become able to sell one's time more profitably. In Erich Fromm's words, one becomes a man "who does not realize himself in his labor," whose "life has become an instrument of labor," and whose "work and its products have assumed a form and power independent of him as an individual."[1]

In the affluent society created by their parents, young people's rebellion against the nine-to-five system is perhaps the most widespread indication of dissatisfaction. They consider it a sacrifice of self because the nature of modern, industrial labor requires alienation, and requires daily activity where the *whole* man is not involved. "Work . . . does not exist in a nonliterate world," says McLuhan. "The primitive hunter or fisherman did no work, any more than does the poet, painter, or thinker of today. Where the *whole* man is involved there is no work."[2] The primitive man works for necessities; he works for himself. But modern man works for conspicuous luxury; he works for the industrial system and expanding production and a false sense of social prestige.*

This daily period of automaton activity, psychologically alienated young men feel, exacts its price from the happiness of modern adults. A young service-station attendant in Oregon, for example, explained his observations to me concerning adults: "If they come into the station in the morning," he began, "they can still be friendly and talk like they're human. But if the same people come in sometime after work, it seems like a completely different crowd. They just stare straight ahead through their windshields while I fill the tank." He stopped and then added, "That's why I like to work weekends."

His solution reflects the attitudes of today's young people. Sociologists have become aware that, with the possibility of a shortened work week, leisure has become a potentially important part of life again. Riesman argues that it would be in the best interest of the individual "to depersonalize work, to make it less strenuous emotionally, and to encourage people to decide *for themselves* whether and how much they want to personalize in what the culture inescapably requires in the way of work."[3] What he is advising is precisely what youth is doing.

This generation, striving for involving roles, not for detached jobs, is searching for two kinds of work. On one hand, its members are looking

* In conjunction with this psychological criticism of labor, of course, is the change in attitudes concerning science and business. Many occupations—police work, civil service, medicine, and others—seem much more stereotyped today than they did a generation ago. Occupations appear to be as impersonal as mass society itself.

for jobs requiring but a few hours a week and very little emotional attachment, which are taken merely in order to subsist minimally. Advancement, promotion, fringe benefits, social prestige—these young men search for these things not in work but in leisure, in their own self-development. Their measure of advancement is psychological, not material or social.

On the other hand, young men are looking for roles, occupations that demand the whole man. They are searching for occupations with progressive ideals and demanding challenges so that the value of their "work" will be such that they can devote themselves to their social role entirely. They want their work to be a cause or a creation, something that involves them completely. In both types of jobs, the "all-involving" and the "noninvolving," this generation avoids the self-division of labor man and leisure man, and of detachment in one's work.

These latter types of occupations are the hardest to find in adult society and, in terms of prestige, have been the least highly regarded by the mass of adults,[4] because mass society has seen to it that its members are judged primarily as labor men, not as leisure men. Mass society judges men not on how creatively they use their leisure but on how efficiently they use their labor. And why shouldn't this be the criterion of judgment? Creative leisure does nothing for the GNP!

Galbraith writes: "Men will value leisure over work only as they find the uses of leisure more interesting or rewarding than those of work, or as they win emancipation from the management of their wants."[5] On both counts, today's young people fit Galbraith's description. Because they are so involved psychologically, their songs filled with such phrases as "travel first class . . . travel with your mind" and "take a journey to the center of your mind," they know that it is in their leisure time that they will be able to develop their inner selves more fully. And because they are so alienated from mass society and its media, they are indeed coming to be "emancipated from the management of their wants." They are opposed to acquisitiveness, against the idea of false social prestige. They'd rather have another two weeks' vacation than spend that two weeks' earnings on a flashier car. They would rather spend the time that would earn them an expensive suit in pursuing their own personal goals.

When this generation's parents began working, it was a real challenge to gain an occupational niche in society—at least, a challenge to gain one with more prestige than one was accustomed to. A man was measured by how far he moved up the ladder of material success. But today too many parents have been able to tell their college sons, "You've got it made, boy!" And then they ask in the same breath, "What's the matter?"

No youth, who wants to become a man, wants to have it made. He wants to make it. And when by one set of public, prestige-oriented values he has it made, he begins to emphasize a set of private, individual-oriented values which still provide a challenge.

But many parents can't understand this, and their sons think they know why. Young men perceive that, although this society professes for the most part to believe in one of the various theistic religions, it really lives by a quite secular, materialistic, power- and prestige-oriented set of beliefs. Adult society does not live by its religious beliefs because they do not fit *in practice* in mass society. As far as the young can understand, adults do not know in fact by what standards they are really living, and the young criticize them for not living by their professed values. Young people need examples, not speeches, and it is the former, not the latter, of which they are critical. The striking lack of self-knowledge in adult society does not inspire them to attain this society's conception of manhood.

To return to the psychological dropout's conflict with his parents: clearly a rejection of adult society's criteria for assessing the value of an individual is not enough to provide the strength for continuing his quest for self-knowledge. Revolt through alienation is not enough; one must also find Camus' freedom and passion for life. The reinforcement for these young people comes from two sources: their notion of social relativity and the writing of psychologists and social critics.

The recognition of social relativity demands the ability to view an individual in reference not to others in his particular society or social class, but to what he as an individual could potentially become, and how his environment limits or enhances this growth. Young people establish a socially relative perspective on personality because they are sufficiently alienated from their native society, and also sufficiently aware of character ideals that have existed or do exist in other cultures. They are concerned not primarily with how they measure up to the standards of adult, industrial, detached, mass society, but rather with how they measure up to their own conception of human capabilities.

Implicit in this idea of social relativity is the realization that what is common and accepted as normal in one society may well be uncommon and considered abnormal in another. The psychological orientation of this generation leads its members to see that society has imposed self-limitations on the individual, but the commonness of the condition obscures it from the individual's own consciousness. To define normal behavior in terms of one particular culture, especially a culture as mechanized and specialized and removed from nature as our own, is relevant only in that culture and only during a specific span of time. If what is considered to be the socially ideal personality is determined by the needs of the society, then what is considered normal or acceptable behavior in modern mass society certainly differs from what would have been considered normal or acceptable in other cultures or in our own culture at another time.

Since young people today have an awareness of and involvement in other cultures unparalleled by that of their parents, and since they are separated from society by their alienation, they are the most vociferous in criticizing the predominant mode of acceptable and normal behavior. (Witness the American Breed's blunt statement: "You gotta be a little insane if you wanna get along in this world.") They have begun to define their own personalities less and less in terms of what their own mass culture expects them to be, and more and more in terms of their own youth culture or in terms of another society or time whose modes of living seem desirable. They feel that the time simply to adapt to "progress" unquestioningly is over: man can no longer simply follow technological change and mold himself to the machine called mass society. To mold oneself to the form of mass society is to lose oneself.

The tenets of modern psychology reinforce this generation's belief that stronger and more pervasive threats are being directed against the individual's sense of self than ever before. Since Freud opened the field of psychoanalytic psychology, there has been a steadily increasing emphasis placed on the importance of individual identity and the way it relates to society, and a lessening of emphasis on certain aspects of Freud's sexual theory and its effects. The fields of "culture and personality" study and inquiries into "national character" have developed since World War II; only the postwar generation has been exposed in great numbers to the information and theory which these fields have established. They are part of a more general movement in psychological research toward studying the individual primarily in terms of social influence rather than solely in terms of instinctual drives and family patterns. Kenneth Keniston, in *The Uncommitted*, states this trend concisely:

> In discussing mental illness as in explaining mental health, psychoanalysis increasingly points to what is missing and present in the patient's ego. . . . The basic trend in psychoanalysis is away from the study of the harmful effects of repression and toward a study of the ego.[6]

These psychoanalytic terms may make this change sound abstract, but in youth culture the change manifests itself everywhere in very real terms. For example, a book by Alan Watts entitled *On the Taboo against Knowing Who You Are* now graces campus bookstores. The long line of books about taboo subjects and taboos themselves has come to its logical end—man himself. Taboos against nature, against sex, against profanity, have culminated in the subject which a wise man might have predicted—the taboo against the identity of man. It is doubtful that a book like Watts's, criticizing modern society's "rusty-beer-can type of sanity" because it prevents a man from finding his own identity within himself, would have appeared before the change in psychological emphasis which Keniston describes. The new technological pressures of mass society, the field of culture and personality, and Watts's book, all appeared with the postwar generation.

Although the young are intimately involved with achieving a knowledge of self, their view of the psychological condition of society is limited. Gallup Polls can collect statistics on many things, but identity is not one of them. The main source of personal information for young people is their own contact with others in youth culture who are trying to avoid selling out to the psychological malady they feel prevails in society. Youth's own experience provides great motivation and interest in psychological questions of normality and self-awareness, but it provides little objectivity.

The importance of the academic literature that confirms and articulates young people's questioning cannot be overestimated here. Trained behavioral scientists who come in contact with many individuals and who gain intimate knowledge of their patterns of behavior can investigate and describe objectively what the young can only sense. This generation is the first to grow up in a culture—a youth culture—where the reading of academic criticism by social scientists is widespread. Freud's *Civilization and Its Discontents* stood alone as a psychological criticism of society for almost three decades, and it was read by a comparative handful of people. Today the book market is brimming over with much more digestible social criticism by men from many disciplines, and the college consumers provide the largest part of the market.

The generation gap is so all-inclusive that some young people feel removed from psychiatrists because they think they are attuned to the problems of adult society and can gain only a limited understanding of youth's problems. But, at the same time, young people can have respect for the perceptive analyst because he is singularly aware of the unhappiness and unfulfillment of many members of adult society and so is more capable of understanding youth's criticisms.

Often, alienated young people need the sound perspective of psychological writers in order to push on through their alienation. When they begin to feel their unwillingness to conform to the socially ideal personality, they first succumb to personal doubts. They wonder if their criticisms of society are but projections of shortcomings that are inherent in their own personalities. They feel they are alone, too, because in high schools (and at some colleges) the most desirable attributes are popularity, attractiveness, and involvement in the "in" activities. Obviously a young man's questioning of these attributes challenges the set of traditional attitudes that support them. So at first he remains silent.

But then comes college. His alienation from adult society grows, he is exposed to the social relativity of accepted behavior, he reads the psychological and social critiques of this mechanized society, and he increasingly views himself in relation to youth-culture standards rather than mass-society standards. In finding out where his head's at, he often also finds a number of other young people who share his attitudes. These factors support alienated young people and save them from being as completely isolated as they have been in the past.

The alienated need this support and reinforcement to continue their quest for self-knowledge, for they are in a society that urges people to find *security in sameness*. Members of adult society may feel apathetic toward life and frustrated and isolated in personal relationships, but at least they feel normal. All the individuals around them also feel this same detachment from life. Their dissatisfaction is culturally patterned, and it saves them from the feeling of differentness, unrelatedness, and insecurity that leads to actual clinical mental illness.

Conversely, what these psychological dropouts are trying to do most, clearly does not provide this security of sameness. In our culture, to question the socially patterned frustrations and the structures of society that reinforce them is most certainly not culturally patterned. So young people are searching for their security not externally in the reflection of themselves in society, but internally in their self-knowledge. They want *security of selfness*. And this security of knowing who you are can be gained only by understanding the relativity of what this society calls normal. "From the point of view of single culture," wrote Ruth Benedict,

> this procedure [of defining normality clinically and statistically] is very useful. It shows the clinical picture of the civilization and gives considerable information about its socially approved behaviour. To generalize this as an absolute normal, however, is a different matter . . . the range of normality in different cultures does not coincide.[7]

In other words, what Benedict is saying is that we all live today in a "House of Mirrors."

Members of this generation are increasingly aware that the types of individuals this society wants differ greatly from the type of person they want to become. They realize that the behavior society desires, and the type of experience and thought it has discouraged, have shaped their personalities throughout childhood. How to free themselves from this molding process, how to analyze themselves in order to judge what capacities were discouraged or limited by society, how to understand the way society confined and controlled their individuality—these become the immediate tasks of the young people whose goal is self-awareness. They become the new challenge for the young man who is not satisfied that he has been classified "normal" in an "abnormal" society, or that he looks okay in front of one mirror in the "House of Mirrors."

Continue to Pretend

Simon and Garfunkel state the dilemma of the young
student trying to find relevance in his artificial world.
If you can't decide what's really you, and if you
are separated from what you feel, they advise
sarcastically, just "continue to continue to pretend" you
are who you are supposed to be.

A young man who is analyzing his earlier childhood can discern
the beginnings of some of his adolescent problems. Of course, as a child
he could not realize the nature of the social forces bearing down upon
him, but as an alienated young man he is much more able to find the
crucial problems.

As I was walking in a department store, I wandered into the toy
department. The entire back half of the store was filled with towering
spires of children's games: "Life," one was modestly titled; and "Management," for the child who was being directed toward the heights of the
business community; and "Finance," "Campaign," and of course
"Monopoly" for the child of the acquisitive society. Young couples (it
was around Christmas time) would procure in the span of a few minutes
an armful of brightly colored boxes, each filled with the appropriate
board, pieces, money, accessories, and instruction booklets.

Grandparents too walked the aisles, but more slowly, looking at
the games with an uncertainty that revealed their misgivings about the
new form of entertainment for which their grandchildren were clamoring.

That the children's enthusiastic desire for certain toys had been mechanically induced by the commercials sandwiched between the Saturday-morning cartoons seemed to make little difference to the shoppers, except for some of the really old folks.

I could envision with bitter clarity, a few weeks hence, all the nation's living rooms at Christmas. Child after child would be opening the same bank accounts and play money and instruction booklets. And this is just the beginning. By their early teens, when young people are beginning to "think for themselves," their imaginations and individual characteristics have been fenced in by their legacy of identical Book-of-the-Month Club children's selections, of uniform stay-pressed this and slim-Western that, of mass-produced Ginn and Bobbs-Merrill texts with versions of the world approved by every Chamber of Commerce, and of the omnipresent voices in every home of television, radio, and the Columbia Record Club, not to mention the black-and-white voices of the same comics, newspapers, *Readers' Digest*, and *Time*.

And as the children meet at school, sons and daughters of Catholics and Jews, of laborers and executives, of immigrant and indigenous parents, the seeds of their homogeneous heritage have been sown within them. All these external influences have already begun to work on the child before he even leaves the home for school.

During the preschool years the child, by climbing up on the couch by the big picture window, could watch the "big" children going to and from school every morning and afternoon. When he gets "big," he finally leaves for school, after what seems like an interminable wait, with the awareness that indeed something "big" is happening. For the next sixteen years or more, his mind will come to revolve more and more around the matrix of people and pressure of the classroom environment and less and less around the family. His parents have been developing in him the qualities that would prove valuable in school communication and competition, and now the school in turn begins to get the child ready for the competitive college and adult worlds.

Most parents, thinking that school obviously prepares the child for a good job and patriotic citizenship and prudent marriage, feel no need to question the method of education much further. *Parents blame most of their child's difficulties in adjusting to educational experience on slow or inadequate development of the child.* This attitude draws the college student's first criticism. In terms, again, of a single culture, this is perhaps the correct parental attitude. The constrictions placed upon a child's individuality and spontaneity during the school years are merely preparing the child for similar limitations to be placed on him during adulthood. But in terms of the individual and of youth's awareness of social relativity, this process of grooming for adulthood has drawbacks. On one hand, it is a painful process of desensitizing the individual characteristics of the child that do not conform to the personality pattern adults have found to be the most valuable. And on the other hand, it is a process of cultivating the aspects of personality that, whether or not they are naturally part of the individual, have been found to be most valuable in adult society. The young see that they have been shaped by this two-edged sword; they feel they have been manipulated by the integrated effects of these processes of desensitization and cultivation.

In his book *Culture Against Man*, Jules Henry points a critical finger at some of the emotional effects of mass-society elementary education. He shows in a cross-cultural study of American education that attitudes developed in children in the classroom cause an emotional compromise of character that in other cultural systems would be unconditionally condemned. He illustrates this with one example quite familiar to today's college youth.

A common figure in American classrooms is the child who, because of emotional problems at home or deficiencies in his educational background, is noticeably slow in responding to the teacher's questions. As he sits at his desk, the teacher repeats her question more forcefully and the child droops further behind the math book, which is practically as wide as he is. We, the good students, are waiting impatiently for the first sign of defeat. As the teacher turns brusquely away from him saying, "All right class, can any of *you* answer the question?" we take our cue. A cluster of little hands shoot up in the air, waving for recognition. Whoever is picked answers the question with the pride befitting the situation.

And the daily blow to the little boy's self-esteem is completed. He can barely be seen behind the green and orange math book with the big blue letters: *Arithmetic Can Be Fun.* A young man sees in retrospect that the competitive attitude is begun not in the business world or in college admissions, but in the world of the elementary classroom. What hits the college student the hardest is that he realizes that, while the drama was taking place, he never once thought on his own, and never once was made to think by the teacher, of the feelings of the little boy behind the math book. It all seemed so natural, so normal. After all, as the gym coach says, everybody can't be a winner.

The Conspiracy against Childhood, a forceful book by a child psychologist, brings home the point that education overemphasizes IQ at the expense of personality, and technical skills at the expense of human relationships. The author describes how the increased competitiveness and mechanization of the adult world have invaded the schoolroom, and says:

> When much of the curriculum should be scrapped and teaching methods should be changed, where there should be small discussion groups and personnel equipped for conducting classes in human relations, we are instead providing teaching machines. We just go right on as if nothing at all had happened [in society as a whole], talking about how to teach children more facts faster.[1]

The elementary schoolroom is a fascinating setting in which to view the adjustment of young personalities to the pressures of adult social values. But my concern here is primarily with the late adolescent. I wish to stress simply that today's questioning young people not only examine the problems confronting them as they face manhood, but also place their childhoods under their personal psychological microscopes. Although Freud first wrote almost seventy-five years ago, it is only today that alienated young people are really reaching back into their childhoods to find the psychological roots of their dissatisfactions. This is another aspect of the concern this generation has for the younger ones, for the yet younger children who are facing the same detrimental social pressures, but more strongly.

As college students turn their critical eyes toward their immediate situation, they have to cope with something that affects the majority of them at one time or another: a feeling that what they are doing is irrelevant. And when they analyze the intellectual and psychological reasons for this feeling, they run into the conflict of the old and the young awareness once again.

Irrelevance pervades not only the college experience. An admissions officer at one college told me about a New York high-school student who had asked his principal if some students could form a Vietnam discussion club. The student himself had no set feelings about the war; all he knew was that he was confused about it. He thought it might be very instructive to invite pro- and anti-war speakers to discuss the subject. After all, he figured, there were a Visual Arts Club and a Science Club. "Isn't the war at least as relevant to my future?" he must have wondered.

The principal was enraged at the idea. He didn't want any trouble at the school. After a long argument with the student, he sent him away with the angry statement: "The public schools, young man, are not the place where controversial subjects are to be discussed!" If that is really his school's policy, it should not teach anything beyond science, shop, and ancient history. The faster social change occurs, the more there is that is controversial. Young people like the New York student are left with the hope that college will be a freer, more relevant, and so more meaningful, experience.

At too many colleges the searching student is disappointed. Professors giving lecture courses are often well past middle age and have been assigning the same course material for the past thirty years. If not much had happened during that time, this might not matter. But to young people's eyes, all spheres of social life have been radically changed in the last three decades.

At many smaller colleges students have won significant victories in getting new reading material assigned and new courses formed. It seems to me that the Sorbonne and Nanterre student rebellions in France are American colleges' warning, for one main criticism of French students was the outmoded course structure and degree requirements. For students everywhere, when courses are describing a world that no longer exists in the same form, education can seem quite irrelevant. Students' knowledge of new and interesting and relevant material goes ungraded; their knowledge of the old and seemingly distant material is thoroughly examined. They begin to question why they are studying at all.

The reason given a child throughout his education, to explain why he is doing things and studying subjects which he doesn't care about, is that he is being prepared for the next stage of schooling or for the job market. "You can't get a good job any more," he is told, "unless you finish high school and go to college. You can't get into Nearby U.," he is reminded, "unless you work now." Only very rarely does a parent or a teacher give a self-sustaining answer, an answer that explains why the learning is intrinsically valuable. Learning is thought of as a possession to be acquired, which is apart from the individual and with which one can attain the desired social objectives.

This indoctrinated "pay now, fly later" attitude is directed toward college, and the students' questions that have been answered with this deferred-benefits logic remain unsolved until the college experience is under way. The answers provided by adult society are then seen to be shallow. Those who go to college are forced to find valid answers as to why they should study.

Many students try to evade the shallowness by continuing with the deferred-benefits logic. I am preparing for my adult life, the logic begins. I am developing my skills so that I may earn more later and be more socially respected. My life will be just that much fuller, and my ability to advance that much greater. This is the age of the highly trained specialist, and without special training I will be of little value.

In its own framework this is consistent logic. It satisfies parents, anyway. But for many of today's college-age young people it has some fatal inadequacies.

No one sees or hears the expression "experiencing college," and only from deans of admissions does one hear the phrase "the college experience." The expression today always seems to be "to get a college education" or "get through college." Job applications say ". . . must have some college." *Even verbally, college education is considered apart from the individual, a thing to be possessed.* And no longer does one hear someone say "a well-educated man"; he always "has" or "got" a good education. One goes to the University for an education just as one goes downtown for a pair of shoes: make the trip and pay the money and wear the purchase in comfort for years to come.

This generation alone realizes that money is not the only price that is paid. There is a sacrifice of individuality, a sacrifice of emotional involvement, a sacrifice of open communication, and a great sacrifice because of the feelings of personal isolation and inadequacy due to all these losses. But although these words speak clearly to young men in college, parents cannot understand them. There is, once again, a generation gap.

The fantastic increase of students pursuing higher education—the number has doubled in the past decade—makes a comment on the family situation in many homes. Today many young people have parents who have never been in college. The parents see college as an experience they missed out on: their child is getting a fairer shake from life than they did. For the most part, they cannot fathom what their child's college experience is all about. The only tangible connections they have with it are grade cards they receive and money they pay; and so they assume that grades are most important and that the experience is essentially one to be purchased.

Even parents who did attend college did so in an institutional environment radically different from that of today's universities. From the point of view of size, whether one looks at a "small" college such as Southern Illinois or a large one such as UCLA, one cannot help concluding that what once was an individual-oriented intellectual community has now become an increasingly massive, bureaucratized organization—what *Newsweek* has called a "megauniversity" to go along with megalopolises and megatons. As usual, however, numbers tell only a small part of the change, for in our society the most important changes are not quantitative.

Today more and more students attend resident colleges often located away from their home towns and even from their home states. For most, college is the first experience of living outside their families. Also often for the first time, they meet others not from their own community or background. They find themselves in an environment psychologically so different that to understand it we must contrast it with that of the average man.

The average adult man does not feel a direct or absolute dichotomy between himself and his personal world. He sees himself, his identity, in his wife, whom he has chosen, and in his children, whose existence is a product-creation of his own actions. His family is also part of his identity in that it is dependent on him for its livelihood and for his affection and approval. The dichotomy is also absent between the adult man and his object world. His home, if not built to his own specifications, was chosen partly on the basis of his tastes, and the objects and their arrangement within reflect his own desires. He works in the same office each day, in the business he chose, and each day sees new projects or deals that he made possible. He works for the dual purpose of accomplishing something for his self-esteem and of providing for himself and his family. At least (and this is the crucial thing) it seems that way to him.

The college student has none of these things. Often far from home, he has no woman who is his and who depends on him. He has no children, and no longer any brothers and sisters around wanting his approval. The place where he lives was chosen not by himself but by a computer in all likelihood, and it looks like a hundred other rooms in the high-rise dormitory. The objects he has can all be placed in a couple of suitcases; the desks, chairs, furniture, and beds are identical to those in tens of hundreds of other rooms. The work he does is rarely of interest to him, since courses and majors are set up not according to his interests but according to long-standing university traditions. Certainly no one is dependent on his productivity: papers on Charlemagne or *Wuthering Heights* can't support anyone. He receives no paycheck, but has only a grade card, which he disdains, to show for his efforts. Finally, he is still being partially if not totally supported by his father, who gives him money, often with strings attached.

These appear as two distinctly different worlds—the first with external relatedness, the latter without. Parents, without moving from their world, want to understand the other. Worse yet, they feel they already do. They were already working at their son's age. All he has to do is go to classes and do his work, and when he's finished he'll be able to earn more money than perhaps they can.

Some students, of course, react to their emotional isolation and increased inability to communicate with their parents in a quite logical pattern. Many try to simulate the home environment: they quickly try to find a girl whom they persuade to become attached to them; they find an instructor or administrator who becomes their substitute parental guide; they begin as rapidly as possible the acquisition of material things —from books to calendars, from personalized stationery to distinctive clothes—and they try to redevelop a corps of similar students with whom they can be alone together. This is the reaction that would tend to support adult values, for the young man is preparing to become a member of the "lonely crowd" of adult society.

It is a reaction one sees less and less on college campuses, because, as alienation grew, the attempt to simulate the previous semblance of adolescent "security of sameness" appeared increasingly shallow. The absence of many external reference points, and students' unrelatedness to their immediate environment, accentuated their detachment from society's values. These young people are forced to redefine their individuality without the factors by which they previously defined themselves. Not just historical circumstances, now, but also the personal circumstances of these young men augment their feeling of unrelatedness. The modern college student and the Outsider fringes that have seceded from society feel the alienation of the age with greater impact than does any other segment of the population.*

Those who try to reconstruct the elaborate social attachments of their precollege lives also tend to continue with the deferred-benefits logic that was discussed earlier. Much as they did in high school, but now

---

* With one exception: the postwar generation of black young people. If for white, middle-class students the courses seem irrelevant and the material biased, how must it appear to black students! Trying to establish a black identity while attending a white university accentuates the problem of growing up today, and is one reason why black activism has increased so dramatically.

oriented toward a more advanced goal, they concern themselves with acting in a manner and engaging in activities that will ensure their acceptance by a graduate school or that will make them appear the most outstanding candidates for the occupation market they are considering. They try to establish the acquaintances and to gain the knowledge that will most facilitate the attainment of these goals. They attempt to develop their personalities and their mannerisms so that they will be most acceptable in adult life. They continue to prepare and pretend.

Many college students, however, have begun to realize that this plan of deferred living—of continually putting off being oneself—is really more than a guide for student study habits. *It has become a way of life.*

Those who live by deferred-benefits logic think that they are preparing for their years of specialization or breaking into business, which will be preparation for anticipated promotions and the next higher echelon and wage bracket, et cetera. Today's critical members of the young generation cannot accept this. They have become what some have called the Now Generation only because adult society and the education it necessitates have continually told them: "Later! Later!" Freedom *Now*! Stop the War *Now*! This generation knows that an industrial, specialized society needs recruits with extended education, but it is also making clear that it wants to live *now*, not later. From their psychological perspective young people realize that, once a person has accepted the programed pattern of preparation, and decided to defer being himself and being involved in life, it becomes habit. He becomes unable to live fully because he has lived for so long artificially. He gets his $15,000-a-year job and split-level home with two-car garage, but he has lost in the process the capacity to be passionately involved in life.

What the preparing ideology demands is an artificial existence. No action may have any inherent value. Its value is what it can get, what future possibilities it may open up. Like the evasive socially ideal personality which the media encourage, this attitude toward life develops a concept of deferred contentment that never comes. It is the substitute for heaven in a secular culture.

This approach to the college experience encourages a kind of egocentrism in which one sees oneself in isolation. One does not feel related to the community, or to humanity, or even to one's fellow students.[2] Unlike the job world, where teamwork and group effort and cooperation have become universal, college demands that the student work alone. Only in the world of sports does he ever work with others for a common goal.

The violent conflict between the Majority Coalition and the Students for a Democratic Society at Columbia University is a good example of the effects of this issue. Alienation, a feeling of isolation from others, is prevalent on this diffuse, urban campus. The only feeling of real group membership at Columbia is found in three activities: SDS and fraternities and sports. (A high percentage of athletes are found in the frats.) In these activities alone, students work closely with others for common goals. And it was precisely these groups which fought each other during the campus riots: SDS against frats and jocks. The rest of the student body, those who belonged to no coherent groups, were the so-called silent middle. The surest way for on-the-ball administrators to maintain an orderly campus is to make sure that each student feels utterly alone and unrelated to any larger body.

So a college student is supposed to prove his manhood, not by going out into the world but by withdrawing from it. In trying to prepare oneself in this detached way, one loses the capacity for compassion, concern, and sympathetic involvement which each person originally has in abundance.

In contrast to the college experience, the young see the Peace Corps experience. The Peace Corps has found acceptance in youth culture because it is so out of place. It was not designed originally as preparation or training for anything. The experience had value in and of itself. "You can't help becoming involved!" has been the consensus of Peace Corps Volunteers, because the service is done for itself. It is both means and ends. *It is not an artificial experience because the value and challenge are within the experience itself.*

The experience of the Peace Corps is wonderful because it credits the participant with being an adult. He is asked for those qualities of maturity—compassion, concern, resourcefulness, and sympathetic involvement—which are the natural human responses to relationships in life. But they are the very qualities his education experience fails to emphasize, and even ignores. Young men in America feel they are not challenged to manhood in this society. The educational process tests such qualities as malleability, perseverance, and subservience, but it certainly does not provide a meaningful challenge for capable young people. It does not ask for the development of the qualities of maturity which the Peace Corps requires.

College offers a shallow challenge in comparison to that of the Peace Corps. Students know that different levels of performance in college are largely due to the amount of time one spends specifically for tests, or, more colloquially, how long a guy "grinds it out." To excel means to spend time meaninglessly. All good students want to learn; but all good students also have their own *personal* ideas of what they want to learn. All good students want to learn all that seems worth while to them as individuals. But the one who excels learns both the personally worth-while and the personally worthless. He works, as Fromm words it, for something other than for himself. His work does not have value in and of itself. What values it has rest in the future, in a future that often is disappointing.

The issue of grades demonstrates the gap in values between adult society and youth culture. When most adults ask a college student, "How was the year at school?" the student feels he is expected to divulge a grade-point average. Grades are taken by adults as indicators of the relative success or failure of a year in college, much as net corporate profits would be considered in the adult world. Adults consider grades the most important criteria for assessing a student's own satisfaction with the college experience. This is because adults assume that the student's aim is the attainment of the traditional goals of adult society, for which good grades would indeed be the most important preparation. Despite the fact that this college generation often has goals and values in opposition to those of adult society, parents and even educators continue to nourish their misconception.

As evidenced by student activism directed against the grading system, an increasing number of young men refuse to share adults' concepts of excellence. For when the conversation is between these young men themselves, and the question "How was school?" is asked, grades are often not mentioned. What is important is not whether one is a 2.97 or a 3.03, but if something has finally been found to which one can become related and committed; if one has been able to meet and know genuine and warm people; if one knows where one's head is at, a little better than a year ago; and if one has managed to survive the depression and purposelessness that often seem unavoidable at college. The idea that scholastic achievement is identical to personal development sounds ridiculous to this psychological generation; as Dr. Harold Taylor, past president of Sarah Lawrence College, said: "To identify growth with grades is to deny the meaning of life."

Know Who You Are

The Beatles tell everyone who listens to them, "Baby, You're a Rich Man," not if you have money but if you know who you are. If you know where your head's at, then you can answer the question, "What do you want to be?"

This generation is turning away from adult society's idea of the self, and so is rejecting the way one is supposed to come to know the self. Psychologists call this development of self-awareness "identity-formation." The young are rebelling against the accepted pattern of identity-formation because they feel that the identity is formed more and more by the society and less and less by the individual. To be sure, the gaining of an identity is brought about by the interaction of culture and personality, but there are many different kinds of interaction. Individual personality and cultural reality, to use Camus' illustration, may interact in the same way as "a man armed with a sword attacking a group of machine guns." A young man's individuality may be mowed down before the sword of his self-awareness has ever left its scabbard. Or, as this generation is trying to do, a young man may gain a measure of self-knowledge and a strength of identity, a form of armor, with which to confront the barrage of social pressures on a more nearly equal basis.

Alienated young people realize that in adult society one's identity is supposed to be gained by seeing one's reflection in the mirror of mass society's needs and standards. Perhaps a bird's-eye, diagramatic view would be the best presentation:

(infant dependence and childhood control) =

EXCELLENCE + OCCUPATIONAL ➤ SOCIAL ➤ SELF- ➤ IDENTITY
                  CHOICE   DEMAND   ESTEEM

(personality   (job)   (labor   (income)   (social
& training)   value)   prestige)

Traditional identity-formation in adult society is seen as a response to the standards, needs, and values of mass society. Either by criteria of social prestige or because of one's cultivated abilities, a young man is supposed to pick out a certain occupation. The period of preparation then follows, during which the youth demonstrates the degree to which he can perfect the necessary skills and develop the necessary personality characteristics. The degree to which one masters these, and the nature of the occupation one has chosen, determine the social need for the individual's services.* Because of the demands for one's personal and technical skills, one becomes aware of being needed and so gains self-esteem commensurate to that need. The nature and magnitude of the social need determine the nature and magnitude of one's self-esteem. Finally, this in turn determines what the individual feels is his just occupational goal and social position, which are equated with identity.

In an other-directed society, for which parents are trying to prepare their children, this developmental process of identity-formation certainly seems to be suited to the demands. Young men who follow this pre-scribed pattern can retain the inner malleability that can respond to changing social needs for personality types and technical skills. They are made to defer defining themselves and becoming aware of their own selves.

Innate abilities cannot be changed, so parents help their children to engage in the pursuit of the other factors for gaining the highest social prestige, the "best" identity. First, children are given the best training possible in order to procure both the knowledge and the cultured person-ality necessary for social success. Second, they are placed in the college environment most likely to provide the best connections in business and society, which could provide opportunities for advancement after col-

* Surpluses and shortages of various types of trained personnel, as well as changes in the manpower needs of the industrial system, would of course cause the labor-value standards to fluctuate.

lege. And third, they are coached to enter the proper fields of endeavor, which will enable them to achieve social prestige in mass society.

Only in a very few people is this pattern as pure as it is here described, but *it is this whole attitude toward identity that today's generation is rejecting with conviction*. With adult society's attitude toward identity-formation, the young argue, the individual must treat his *self* as a commodity to be produced in the most acceptable form. One must be so conscious of defining oneself by limiting one's identity to those qualities that are found to be useful or salable that one fails to gain the self-knowledge and individual autonomy that are characteristics of healthy, mature personalities. One's identity and even sanity rest upon the foundation of external factors such as job attitudes, prevalent opinions, degree of material wealth, and the amount of social prestige one possesses because of them. In any life these elements come to have some importance, but what young people stress is that *individual identity should find its strength primarily within the context of the individual, not in the context of mass society and its standards*. A sense of self should not depend completely on the logic of society. Perhaps a diagram of youth's idea of identity like the following most strikingly points up the differences between it and the traditional concept of adult society.

(infant dependence and social control) =

SOCIAL AWARENESS	➤	ALIENATION	+	SOCIAL CRITICISM	➤	INDIVIDUAL AWARENESS	➤	IDENTITY
(social definition of self)		(meaninglessness of social definition of self)				(individual definition of self)		

The social definition of self is easily gained. A young person's physical appearance, his social class, the way his parents treat him, his grades and athletic ability, and so on—all these things define him in terms of society. By his early teens, he has been given a social awareness of who he is. But the nature of mass society and the consequent psychological orientation of this generation disrupt this streamlined socialization. Most often during the college years, the shallowness of this definition becomes painfully clear. If a young man utilizes his alienation and isolation, he forges his own awareness. He analyzes how society formed him, and he analyzes how social pressure made him react and defend himself. He overcomes the meaninglessness of the social definition of who he is and finds a sustaining self-knowledge. And *after* the social definition has been discarded and he has gained a measure of self-awareness, *then* he engages in achieving excellence in the occupation he, not social necessity, has chosen. Or, to paraphrase the Beatles, now that, *first*, you know who you are as an individual, *then*, what do you choose to be as a social being?

If this is not just a lot of hogwash, if this is indeed the new progression of identity-formation in this generation, then some very definite and visible changes should be occurring in our society.

Following are the four most closely related social effects of this change in identity, with special stress on the final point.

1. Because identity now is determined within the framework of the young person himself and his youth culture rather than in reference to the social demand for his training and personality, then we should be beginning to witness a shortage of some types of skills that society needs and a surplus of people unwilling to fit into traditional social niches.

2. Because now it is self-knowledge that permits a feeling of identity rather than attainment of occupational excellence, the real challenge and goal in the eyes of the young should be learning of and coming to terms with the self, rather than the educational or training process itself. This should be evidenced by lessened importance placed by these young people on grades, and a greater willingness to forgo the experiences associated with a formal education for other experiences that would tend to increase one's self-knowledge or sureness of identity.

3. Because identity now must precede the achievement of excellence or the acquisition of training, jobs should less and less be chosen by this college generation primarily on the basis of anticipated financial reimbursement and social prestige.

4. Because of the self-probing that is going on during the college years, there should be increasing mental preoccupations and difficulties during that period.

I believe that in the course of this book I demonstrate that all four of these expected manifestations of youth's identity-formation are becoming evident. They are becoming social reality.

First, we are witnessing a shortage of people anxious to go into business and of those satisfied with fragmentary, alienated jobs that characterize a technological, industrial society, accompanied by a simultaneous increase in psychological dropouts who populate hippie communities such as Haight-Ashbury and communes throughout the country. *Second*, we are witnessing student campaigns at scores of colleges for less emphasis on grades and rankings, and an increased desire to live outside of the traditional campus structures, combined with a desire for Peace Corps or junior-year-abroad experience, and a sudden increase in those students involved with psychedelia and the "expanded consciousness" that is supposed to accompany it. *Third*, we are witnessing in this age of affluence an increasing demand to be engaged in a meaningful occupation and a corresponding lack of concern about income brackets and material goods. *Fourth*, as the psychological orientation of this generation makes clear,* we certainly are witnessing a tremendous preoccupation with the mind which is precipitating "mental illness" or "maladjustment" on college campuses reaching such proportions that it cannot be ignored.

For every 10,000 college students, 1000 have to seek professional psychiatric help to cope with their problems; 300 to 400 will have periods of extreme depression that will be great enough to impair their ability to work; and about 200 will be apathetic and disoriented or will be seriously affected by family problems; and others will need to seek treatment in mental hospitals. Finally, the national rate for suicides and threatened suicides is 50 per cent higher among college students than among Americans as a whole.[1]

The suicide statistics offer a simple sociological proof of my earlier assertion that college students experience the least social attachment of any social subgroup. Emile Durkheim's famous conclusion in his book *Suicide* was that the less an individual felt integrated in society the more likely he was to commit suicide. It is this lack of integration, this Outsider position in relation to mass society, that enables some young people to analyze society and liberate themselves from its socially patterned frustrations. But for other young men, overwhelmed by rootlessness and alienation, this position leads to suicide.

Each time I hear of a student suicide—and on almost every campus hardly a year goes by without such a death—the same heavy thoughts weigh on my mind. Would he have killed himself, I ask myself, if he had known the pleasure of sex and love and the joy of having children, *experiences which his non-college counterpart has probably had*? Would he have killed himself if he knew the bonded feeling of working and earning and supporting others who depended on him? Would he have killed himself if he had seen crops that he had planted in the fields around his home grow and feed his family? Or seen the house he built shelter them? Would he have killed himself if he had ever been given

* One literary critic has even called youth "the Freudian proletariat."

the opportunity to be responsible and related to something beyond himself and his own preparation?

My questions go unanswered: most college suicides have never done any of these things. They have rather been encouraged to withdraw, to absorb, to remain uninvolved—and this at a time when fidelity and commitment are the most important elements for gaining adulthood!

From a social rather than an individual perspective, other questions trouble me deeply. Would he have killed himself if he had been shown some concern by other students? Would he have killed himself if those who saw him withdraw and heard his mutterings had felt some responsibility, some relatedness, to the young man now dead, and had done something? The catch phrase in youth culture—"Just let him do his thing!"—is the young individual's response to the broad spectrum of different behaviors that emerge because there is no acceptable image of adulthood. But involved in the apparent tolerance of letting someone else do his thing is also an unwillingness to take responsibility or show compassionate interest in the problems and dilemmas of other students. How many suicides might have been prevented if a guy down the hall, or a roommate, had felt responsible for someone else's well-being?

One can cheat on tests today and "friends" won't say a word—to the cheater or to anybody. But that same silence can extend to relationships in general and can permit someone to be cheated out of life —out of a hold on life which today is very tenuous.

In addition to young people who are seriously troubled, there are many more who experience similar inner conflicts but bear them inwardly. For them, life loses its vividness and they lose the passion for living that at birth is present in everyone. Bearing these conflicts inwardly is like driving with a faulty clutch or with poor wheel alignment: the machine can still be driven, but after a few years many parts of the system will be in much worse condition because of it.

Adult society and its media do not demonstrate much insight into these problems. The potentially valuable magazine article that provided the mental-health statistics I have used offers no approach to the widespread mental difficulties and suicides. All it manages to do is advocate that more extensive mental clinics be established at colleges. To psychologically alienated young people, this proposal alone sounds analogous to an absurd suggestion that the federal government should invest in oxygen masks to combat air pollution. Instead of solidly and critically investigating the nature of the society and educational institutions in which necessary changes must be made, members of adult society in leadership positions plan to avoid making the changes altogether. The same mentality that attacks the problems of ghettos by forming commissions to study them attacks the problem of youth's mental problems by setting up psychiatric clinics.

Today's generation of college students views itself as a microcosm of society with the external social crutches taken away. Their alienation, disorientation, and unrelatedness only reveal the illness that is part of society itself. They can see the absence of self-sustaining identity in adult society, and therefore change their approach to the concept of identity itself. Those young people who reject the traditional pattern of identity-formation often appear "maladjusted" to adult society. But these young men who appear different do not pity themselves. They pity those who did not reject the system, for they will be manipulated callously by the social pressures and patterned frustrations of mass society.

"We have young people who find themselves failures at age twenty. When the grades go sour, they feel it's all gone" (Assistant Dean Lorrin G. Kennamer at the University of Texas). "Students are frightened. If they don't do well, they'll get punished and pushed into the draft. Even the very brightest kids feel threatened by this" (Dr. Phydras at Emory University). "Most kids . . . resort to defensive procedures. Grade-getting is one of them, and the kid retreats into the grinding rat-race" (Dr. Coplin at Amherst).

I need not go on. A young man does not have to wait today for educators to tell him about social pressures. Nor does he need to turn on the radio and hear the singer wailing, "You're pushing too hard! You're pushing too hard on me!" All he has to do is look within himself and see the empty detachment from life by which he has preserved himself.

Today's critical young people are reacting against this syndrome. They set up their own values, their own path to identity, their own concept of mental health. Unlike the magazine article on college breakdowns, young men themselves do not think that "the tragedy is that too few college kids get help." This generation is convinced that *the real tragedy is that they are made to need help at all*. The tragedy is that there are students like the case history in the magazine article who, after an attempted suicide, is coached back into the rat-race, convinced that "I'm okay, really, I'm okay." The tragedy is that, in the first place, the day of the razor blade and thirty sleeping pills ever had to happen. But this tragedy would be unpleasant to think of for the adult magazine-readers with children in college, so it is not mentioned. Adults are sent happily on their way to the next article in the magazine, after being assured that more psychiatric clinics are being set up in college communities. It is much more comfortable for adult society to pretend to fix up the effects of alienation than to look at its causes.

The tragedy is not simply the absence of social integration, for it is through the freedom of that Outsiderness that the young gain insight into the mechanisms of society which attempt to control and define who they are. *What is tragic is that too few utilize their alienation from society.* They fail to gain an understanding of the social games, of the socially patterned frustrations, which cause the breakdowns in youth culture. A little slowly, perhaps, too many young men resume their positions in the rat-race after their mental crises without having liberated themselves from the social pressures that caused their crises in the first place.

Since young men themselves experience the same pressures which cause these crises, they cannot complacently read the article, as do settled adult readers. This generation faces the article with psychoanalyst Erikson's words in mind: "If we only learn to let live, the plan for growth is all there."[2]

But in so many ways this generation sees the plan for growth being limited, cut short, destroyed, being sacrificed for pursuits absurdly removed from the necessities of human happiness. What this generation considers mental health seems to be far from the major concerns of adults, who have accepted a limited, one-dimensional view of man and society. To sell oneself most profitably on the market of social personalities, to chase most blindly the socially ideal personality, to accept most complacently the socially patterned frustrations: this is the framework in which a young man is supposed to find an identity. These goals are youth's heritage. This, today, is a young man's shallow challenge.

Young people know that to meet this challenge would be a Pyrrhic victory—Pyrrhic because their goals are sensitivity, passionate involvement, self-knowledge, and these are the very qualities that are ignored in college. And they are the qualities that are most often sacrificed in order to achieve success in adult society. The victory is not just getting through college. If a loss of self-awareness is the key to the victory of getting through, or of being "in," then it will indeed be a sadly Pyrrhic victory.

Youth and Manhood

In all the public spheres of life there is for young people an absence of credible challenges. Because of the generation gap in social values, members of this generation can find no meaningful recognition by adult society of their manhood. Because the public means of proving themselves men seem to be closed, the private spheres of life gain greatly in importance. Today it is through private challenges that a young man must become a grown man. This is reflected in young people's preoccupation with the inner workings of the mind, which I examine once again in following chapters, in relation to psychedelic drugs. I turn my attention now toward the other sphere of life which has traditionally been considered the most private: sex.

With so many channels for relatedness, for involvement and emotional expression, cut off, sexual expression becomes of crucial importance. Establishing a complete sexual and emotional relationship during the college years is the overriding concern of the great majority of this generation. Social unrelatedness has magnified the importance of personal relatedness.

The age-old conflict between generations, the older trying to convince the impatient younger to wait for sex and marriage, has now taken on a new dimension. Progress has provided this generation with the Pill. The older generation has lost the standby reason for discouraging the younger generation from sexual involvement. No longer will premarital sexual pleasure result in pregnancy for a girl. Today dependable contraceptives are available, and the upcoming generations will use them more readily than does even this first postwar generation. Robbed of this reason for discouraging premarital sex, adult society has turned to the dangers of venereal disease. But scientific progress is not on the parents' side any more than it is on the side of the young generation. New drugs have made the dangers of venereal disease minimal in comparison to what they once were.

Because of these changes, the generational controversy over sex has become an intense battle. Hardly a suburban church in the country has been without its forum on sex and chastity. High-school health classes continue to expound adult society's warnings. Failing all else, the newspaper "tell me your troubles" columns daily discourage young people from engaging in premarital sex. Adult society, through its institutions, makes it quite clear that sex without marriage is socially taboo.

Once again, society has failed to hear the reasons for this generation's dissent. Adults still approach the question in terms of whether or not to engage in premarital sexual activity. Although marriage itself is simply a legal formality, they make it the crux of their argument. The real question in the eyes of the young is not whether sexual intimacy is combined with marriage, but whether it is combined with a deep and serious emotional commitment. *By emphasizing marriage and sex, parents have weakened their argument. If they emphasized emotional commitment and sex, they would have a very good case.* Parents have to weaken their case because, if they looked at the latter question, of whether or not sexual intimacy was a deep expression of emotional commitment, they would have to examine the basic structure of the dating pattern their children have been forced into.

As parents are well aware, all across America during school vacations and on weekends, along the small dark streets of urban and suburban areas, a multitude of conspicuously half-hidden cars with fogged windows are nestled against the curbs. In these simulated wombs, high-school students writhe in the wonderful liberty and warmth of sexual exploration. After a few years of having to be satisfied with basement parties and movie-house corners, they have found comparative freedom in the private parlor of modern society, the automobile. Car widths are the only hindrances parents can rely on, but even cars are getting wider. Mom and Dad can question Mary or Johnny about plans for the evening, but the fact is that, once the car keys have been given, their control is gone. No longer can mother and father allow their daughter only to kiss her sweetheart in the parlor after Sunday dinner under their critical surveillance. Today, in the post-Ford era, the daughter who is out on a date can be anywhere within a twenty-mile radius of their watchful eyes. Affluence has given the modern parent new problems.

But while the parents can avoid the problems that social change has caused, the children cannot. They must grow up among the new changes. They face problems of a psychological nature which they cannot conveniently ignore.

Before the Pill, despite the sexual liberties permitted by the automobile, intercourse was off limits. From around the age of fourteen or fifteen all the way through college, "Don't get involved" meant first of all not to get someone—or not to become—pregnant. All pleasure had to be derived from sexual foreplay. Hours of sex play were begun with the knowledge that intercourse was out of the question. But, especially for "steady" couples, everything else that is pleasurable was permissible.

Already an unprecedented and unnatural sexual burden had been placed on a young person. For probably the first time in history, prolonged and intensive sexual foreplay was socially patterned for males and females of mating age, but at the same time, sexual intercourse was socially taboo. From lower middle class to upper upper class, the young are told on one hand to be popular and on the other hand not to get pregnant (or get anyone pregnant).

Translated into the realities of high-school life, this meant: use sex for social popularity but don't get carried away! So the American adolescent tried to achieve the first, to be socially popular, which to a large extent in the modern high school went hand in hand with engaging readily in sexual foreplay. But the adolescent tried to achieve that, all the while making sure that nobody got pregnant.

The poor kids couldn't win. They wanted to be turned on and to turn their partners on—which means losing control. Yet they knew they were not permitted to lose control. And neither the boy nor the girl could withdraw from the situation because each would pay a high price in social popularity. Parents can withdraw from their problems: "Let

Johnny (or Mary) do what the Joneses let their kids do." But how can the kids escape from their dilemma?

Like any human being facing a social strain they do not think they can change, Johnny and Mary made a psychological adaptation. When they engaged in sexual foreplay they made a minimum emotional commitment. They made no permanent sexual commitment, since the purpose of their relationship was social acceptability. They detached themselves emotionally from what they were doing physically, and the detachment became more marked as the years of this kind of sex mounted up. It was the James Bond phenomenon again: the individuals were detached in their sex. Their detachment is the unconscious price they paid because of the distorted nature of their *prolonged and limited* sexual intimacy. In winning the public, social game, they lost the private, psychological one.

By separating their emotional selves from their sexual selves they made their personalities amenable to the socially patterned dating system. In high school and in some colleges, as in adult society, there is conspicuous consumption. But there is also conspicuous sex. Boys and girls pair off for car dates at night, and the next morning at school the boys cluster away from the girls and share their exploits among themselves. New sexual conquests are worn as proudly as new clothes. If by chance one boy is serious in his emotional commitment to a girl and wants to keep his relationship private, he encounters problems. He must either pretend that he really doesn't care and succumb to his friends' pressures for information, or he can sacrifice peer-group acceptance for emotional fidelity. To sacrifice emotional involvement is what is socially patterned.

This dating pattern has caused a significant change in emphasis on sexual desirability, a change which is present already in the media of mass society. There is a physically objective desirability in a sexual partner. The more she looks like a bulging *Playboy* fold-out, the more physically desirable she is supposed to be. But in bed, not on billboards, this desirability is not important. It is the capacity to desire that makes a woman desirable. The beauty of love is how the need for love of one augments the other's awareness of his capacity to love. Desire, and the desire to be desired, complement each other and make love a unique and beautiful experience.

The overemphasis on physical attractiveness in traditional culture is, of course, well suited to the needs of the industrial system. *Adolescents cannot prove their desirability by the sharing of genuine emotion, so they must prove it by sheer physical attractiveness alone.* As the chapter on

"Youth and Mass Society" demonstrates, mass society and its media are quite willing to use this socially patterned frustration. Mass society perpetuates the image of the socially ideal personality that is constantly moving ahead. The economic competitiveness of adult society becomes part of the emotional lives of young people who fail to reject mass society's values.

Teen magazines inform their readers (mostly girls) of the changing trends with which they must keep pace. "I don't like to read *Seventeen* especially," a high-school girl told me, "but I've got to. Otherwise I get so far behind." These magazines even feature dilettante Kinsey reports that inform their readers of polls concerning sexual behavior. They factually explain at what age what percentage of their teen-age readers started doing what on dates. They say, in effect, that what matters is not how much you care, but what others are doing.

Adolescents are thus kept consciously aware of the proper pattern of controlled involvement. They are informed about what they should do, what they should wear, how they should put on their make-up, even how they should budget their time. Throughout the advice, of course, what one should buy is the topic of paramount importance. Because it is to the advantage of established society, the socially ideal image constantly changes, and the young people who accept that image as their goal invariably feel inadequate—"so far behind."

College students of this generation have grown up in the pre-Pill period. They have been raised in a social milieu where the private is made public and where the public is controlled by mass society. In retrospect, they can see that they sacrificed emotional involvement for the necessities of social acceptability. They look back and realize that the acceptance of adult society's values caused psychological chaos within themselves. They look back in anger.

What this generation finally comes to realize in college is that *our culture exalts primarily what the individual's personality has been made to feel it is lacking.* The culture exalts God in its official documents, rhetoric, and coinage, but in no nation is a deep religious conviction less likely than in modern, scientific, materialistic America. The culture exalts slim waists and broad shoulders, but nowhere are these less likely than in America, where work and travel have been mechanized and the way of life has become spectator participation. The culture exalts being up-to-date in everything from foods to fashions to gadgets, yet in no culture is this more impossible than in America, where advertisers' goal is to make sure that the consumer knows there is always something newer. In every sphere of life one may find this same pattern: a high cultural valuation of specific characteristics which the nature of the social system virtually precludes.

To young people it appears that the same is true in sex. *The public exaltation of sexual attractiveness and sexual prowess correlates with private doubts about exactly those qualities.* One is made to doubt one's adequacy by the prolonged exposure to sexual foreplay and the impossibility of its consummation. But one is also made to doubt one's adequacy by the media. Whether it is a girl who is looking at the flawless face, complexion, hair, and figure of the woman in the Breck advertisement which she has seen on the back cover of her Junior and Senior *Scholastic* magazine since she was ten, or whether it is a boy who is looking at the handsome, well-built man on a television hair-lotion commercial, the results are the same. The young, impressionable person is made to feel that he or she must be something other than what he is in order to be the *right kind* of man or woman. Also, whether it is a new skirt length or a new eyeliner for girls, or whether it is a new pants width or new hair length for boys, the results are again the same. The young person feels he is falling behind the ever-changing socially ideal personality. He feels he must read the teen magazine or that he must go to the expensive walnut-paneled men's shop if he is to keep pace— not with the Joneses down the block but with the mythical Joneses of Madison Avenue.

The result of all this is the addition of another reason to the initial one of not getting involved. A young man fears his inadequacy. He fears he is not man enough. He fears he does not measure up to the standards of mass society which define what being a lover and being in love should be. So traditional adolescents decide not to be open but to divide their inner feelings from their external behavior. Some call the behavior "cool." But it is nothing more than the disguise of inadequacy.

If young people do not reject the traditional standards of adult society, they must complete the noninvolvement process that was begun because of the socially patterned avoidance of intercourse by accepting the socially patterned fear of inadequacy. When little boys between the ages of ten and thirteen begin carefully avoiding girls and expressing their distaste for the opposite sex to their friends, parents assume that it is a natural and inevitable stage in development. Most parents do not view their child's behavior from the perspective of anthropology, which would make them realize that there are many cultures where such a stage never happens. The same lack of perspective colors adult society's view of adolescence. When sixteen- to eighteen-year-olds begin showing signs of "cool" behavior, of emotional disengagement and outer toughness, parents assume it is a natural and inevitable stage in development. In fact, "It's just a phase he's going through" has become adult society's cliché.

When the cool, cynical toughness begins, these adults reason: It's certainly expecting too much from such young people to establish an emotional involvement with another person. Surely as they grow older and—magically—more mature, their ability to involve themselves emotionally with others and to care intimately about others will grow too.

Unfortunately this is not the case, and only those completely ignorant of human psychology can maintain that it is. The separation of inner emotion and outer sexual behavior is a splitting of the self, and it is not easy to revert to the natural state of unity and wholeness when social legalities finally make it acceptable. Critical young people— whether they are dubbed "hippies," "free lovers," or just "immoral youth"—are psychologically oriented. They do not view these social frameworks, which cause extensive sexual foreplay and yet forbid intercourse, and which cultivate a feeling of inadequacy, as if they were temporary moral restraints that exert only minor influence after a marriage license has been purchased. Although the machine age is trying, men as yet cannot be turned on and off. A marriage license cannot tear down the walls within the self which it took years of patterned behavior to construct. If one accepts the dating system and its emotional isolation, marriage will not be the key that unlocks all doors.

These problems are, in two respects, less severe for the half of the generation that does not continue education past high school. Members of this group may get married, and many do get married, soon after high school. Young men who do not go on to college can get jobs, support wives, have children, and essentially lead an adult life. Sexually they can be "adult" before they are twenty.

But for the vast majority of middle- and upper-class young people who go on to college, adult sexual opportunities are still far off. Most colleges, and virtually all the big state schools, do not allow women in men's dormitories. Some schools allow women in for a few hours a week, but often the doors of rooms must be kept ajar for surveillance. Even at the more liberal schools, of which there are very few, the rules regulating a woman's presence in the dorm severely restrict natural relationships.

The student is made to ask why he must remain a child while his less educated counterpart is able to have the responsibilities of adulthood. It cannot be said that young men who do not go on to college are more emotionally mature than those who do. Nevertheless, till the age of twenty-two or more, the college student is forced to live in a situation that continues to define and confine his relationships long after his non-college counterpart has become independent.

In addition to living in different circumstances, the college half of the generation—the half which is still treated as being sexually immature—reads the kind of books that have become well known only in the postwar era. In this psychologically oriented generation, it is no surprise that the most widely read book on love and sex is written by a psychoanalyst. Erich Fromm's *The Art of Loving* might well be the most common book on college bookselves. Unlike earlier manuals of love, Fromm's book probes deeply the psychological basis of love. He does not give fifty positions for intercourse, nor does he explain that intercourse is good only when it is used for the exaltation of God. Rather, he devotes an entire chapter to "Love and Its Disintegration in Western Culture" —an analysis of the reasons why modern, mass-society life has made genuine, mature love a rare emotion. Fromm's change of emphasis is of crucial importance. Dr. Spock influenced this generation's childhood, and Dr. Fromm influences this generation's adolescence. He does not discuss love as a compartment of religion or as a precondition for sex. He discusses it as the goal of human existence. And when he indicts modern society for having commercialized sex and streamlined love, the young generation that reads him joins in his criticism.

The young's rebellion against the sexual values of adult society is perhaps the most widespread rejection of tradition by this college generation. The generation is characterized by psychological orientation, need for an involving role, and awareness that the essence of life is human relations. In contrast to this, the acceptance of social values leads to emotional isolation. It is little wonder that many young people reject the socially patterned sexual frustrations with such vehemence. Even marriage, which society offers as the answer to their problems, comes under criticism. This generation realizes that marriage, on sale as the solution to unrelatedness, sexual frustration, and inadequacy, has also become something other than what is advertised.

Now a Man

I'm now a man
But why did it take me oh so long
I'm now a man

—The Seeds

Adolescent initiation rites are among the most nearly universal social institutions found in cultural anthropological studies. Called *rites de passage*, or "ceremonies of passage," these rites mark the official change of status of the youth in early societies from child to adult. The change is accepted simultaneously by the youth himself and by his adult society. These initiation rites often require feats of endurance, or of bearing pain, or of resourcefulness or courage. The young man is removed from the world of his youth, and adult control is decreased as the youth is given adult responsibilities. Often, seclusion with the men of the tribe is involved in the initiation rites, during which time the young men learn the tribal lore of manhood. They feel challenged to manhood.

When the young man returns from the period of isolation and when the rites are successfully completed, his status has changed in the minds of the women of the group. He is now a man. He can have a man's sexual life and he can look for a wife. He decides upon and courts a woman, not as a child or adolescent, but as an accepted adult male.

In western societies there are clearly no longer any *rites de passage*.

The very existence of terms such as "teen-ager" or *Halbwuchsiger* (half-grown) shows that the absence of this social institution results in an "in-between" stage. All too often adult society avoids this whole question by regarding those in their teens in terms of the high-school health book definition. Adolescence, it says, is the period when "the person is no longer a child but not yet an adult." This is defining the concept of adolescence by avoiding it altogether.

The generation gap has become so marked that late adolescence for many young people in America is the period when they feel they have left childhood and gained manhood—but they are judging by youth culture's values. The difference in criteria for judging maturity between generations is so great that by adult society's standards they remain adolescents. Adolescence today is a time of feeling individual maturity without social recognition of the fact.

Despite the fact that there is no recognized, culturally accepted initiation rite, there remains the necessity in any culture for a similar function. By default, so to speak, other established or just developing institutions take the empty place of these rites. Adult commentators on growing up in America first point to such things as sports or fraternities to demonstrate that our culture does have various kinds of initiation rites. These commentators have a very incomplete idea, evidently, of what rites of manhood are meant to signify. Sports, first of all, can hardly serve as the means for gaining manhood. That sports are games and have little relationship to the dilemmas and contradictions of real life is painfully clear to the young man who looks at competitive athletics critically. Moreover, how can sports be an initiation rite if only a small minority of males in American high schools and colleges are able to participate in athletic combat? Fraternities, too, are a painfully inadequate means for gaining manhood. Except for token "community service" projects once a year, most fraternities have no relatedness to real society, either youth or adult. The fraternity is a self-serving organization which nourishes its own members. Fraternities also tend to find homogeneous membership, dividing divergent types of students, who might have provided each other with challenges, into different frats. One frat gets athletes, another gets the brains; one frat gets the radicals, another gets the "big men on campus" of the traditional variety; another gets the undesirables or ethnic minorities. Finally, how can fraternities provide a socially recognized initiation rite when they involve only members of the younger generation? They do not go off into seclusion with the adults of the "tribe" but go off into seclusion with themselves.

Clearly, the institution that assumes the real burdens of the absent intiation rites must be other than sports and fraternities. But before this institution can be properly understood, some understanding of why initation rites in their traditional forms are absent must be gained.

Societies in which there is a functioning institution marking the transition from childhood to manhood are generally referred to as "backward" societies—now politely called "underdeveloped." This means that the bulk of their populations have no personal idea of social progress or change. The fact is that where a society's members are conscious of progress, initiation rites cannot exist in their original form. In a society that does not change, the older men command the most respect, writes anthropologist Elizabeth Marshall (Thomas), and for good reason. "In a society that is not developing, the case of a stable primitive society, particularly one that is not undergoing complex industrial changes, the older a person becomes, the more he knows about life."[1]

And "life" has one virtually unchanging meaning. The older a man is, in these stable societies, the more completely he has seen the vagaries of life, and the more able he is to judge the best course of action in the face of sudden changes in condition that challenge the group. Even after these old men have passed their prime in terms of hunting prowess and strength, they retain their positions of authority. The young men, although admired for their individual qualities, are always in positions of lesser status. Mere survival to the age of the older men is a great tribute to their stamina and sagacity.

All this changes rapidly with the acceleration of culture change. In our society, as social reality changed in the span of a single generation, and then began to change in terms of years, and as more and more people began surviving to greater age, older generations came to have less and less knowledge of the new developments and pressures that affected their children. Younger men who had grown up in the times of the social changes with which they were forced to deal were often found to be the most capable in dealing with new situations. Young men of twenty-three could solve problems of technology that older men in industry had never thought of. They could cope with problems of communications, of racial disharmony, of molecular biology, and so on, because the issues had come up in their minds when they were fifteen, not fifty-five.

Our contemporary world is characterized by a vanishing present. By the time the factors determining the present era are understood, they are a decade in the past. Realms of technological and social change have appeared on the scene in a single decade, and often only those who grew up during that change are aware of its existence. The young have no roots to pull up, no traditional ideas to discard, no firmly established beliefs to relinquish.

The difference in values between generations is the product of this ever-accelerating social change. The existence of youth culture and the absence of an accepted point at which a young man becomes an adult are both by-products of it. As was mentioned, because of the absence of *rites de passage*, other social institutions have tried to serve as substitutes. Adult writers have examined everything from fraternities to street gangs, from athletics to car cultists, from "cool" behavior to sexual promiscuity, to determine what social activity has become the initiation rite. They have looked at these peripheral activities, it seems, in order to avoid looking at the traditional institution that has been most affected by the missing rites of passage—the institution of marriage.

To avoid looking at marriage, I fear, adults would still like to consider almost any other institution as our culture's initiation rite. Boot camp, however, because of the present status of the military in youth culture, is not the meaningful challenge that it may once have been; besides, college students often avoid military service altogether. Nor does setting out on one's own have the romantic flavor it once had, for the young man leaves home today with a college diploma, a job paying as well as his father's, and insurance. Nor can mere employment denote manhood: a fresh-out-of-high-school construction worker would be a man at eighteen, while a postgraduate student would not be a man until his late twenties.

Furthermore, as the reader might surmise from the section on "Youth and Psychology," high school and college lack basic elements necessary for demonstrating the change from adolescence to adulthood. In our era of specialization, high-school diplomas cannot prove the attainment of manhood, either to youth or to middle-class adult society. College work requires some mental ability and a good deal of subservience and egoism, but certainly does not require the qualities of manliness and maturity. A college diploma could be considered to make one "a man" in the labor market, but does not give one the status to enter the adult social world. The road to a college diploma is so smooth, and so oriented toward what it *will* be worth in adult society, that at no point can it be considered to initiate the student to manhood.

The experience of a friend of mine illustrates this clearly, and returns us to the institution of marriage. Julie won a scholarship to spend her junior year in Europe, and she returned home at the age of twenty-one after a marvelous year of living in complete freedom from parental authority. Julie's home town was also the town where her college was located, but she had decided that, rather than live at home as she had before, she would get her own apartment near campus. To her, this seemed perfectly natural after a year of freedom abroad. But her parents tried to veto the idea, saying that she was still their child, she was dependent on them, and she should live at home. Julie was baffled. They were still treating her like a child although she had had a year in Europe and was twenty-one.

She hit upon an idea. "Mom and Dad, I think Steve and I are going to get married," she said one day, although she had no intention at all of getting married yet. The next week she had her own apartment. Her parents realized that she would show she was *really* grown up unless they let her have her own way. Nothing she might accomplish could make them think she was grown up; only getting married could do the trick.

The new initiation rite, the real entrance to the adult world, is marriage. Not only do a young person's own parents treat him with a new measure of equality, but adult society as a whole treats a young person who marries as if now, indeed, he is grown up.

Today's critical young people sense this new function of the institution. Marriage for a young man does not mean only taking a wife. It is difficult to have a wife without having a job and permanent commitments; and it is difficult to retain these unless one had already served in the armed forces or is a member of the reserves; and then one often acquired a house and car and insurance and bills to pay. Marriage is not just holy matrimony but the acceptance of social commitments that irrevocably lead to occupational, financial, and social ties that are difficult to sever. Marriage is, in short, becoming adult.

Marriage is held out to pre-adults as *the* answer to their problems of sexual and social insecurity. To be wed entitles the couple to adult sexual privileges that are difficult to attain in any other way. Quite stringent social limitations are purposefully placed on any who try to achieve these elements of marriage without also accepting the social involvement that is traditionally part and parcel of the deal. Marriage is offered as the liberation from the frustration of unrecognized manhood.

Unlike more stable societies, this country sees marriage and initiation rites as one and the same thing. An adolescent does not become an adult in the eyes of society, and then later, upon his own choosing, get married. Rather, the wedding night—or more realistically, the period of courtship—is the time when a young man is proving himself both socially an adult and emotionally and sexually a husband. The psychosexual burden that is placed upon a wife because of this "double duty" of marriage is great. It limits and detracts from sexual relations and further destroys the possibility for open sexual expression. But the double duty of marriage involves difficulty not only with sex but with personal development.

The young man in earlier societies became an adult as he was initiated and so searched for a woman as an adult. The primary importance of initiation rites was that by virtue of them he could court as a man and identify himself (as well as be identified by his society) as an adult man. *The woman did not need to make him feel like a man; socially, he already knew that he was.* During the period between initiation and marriage, he of course changed greatly and began to develop a position as a man within adult society. It was a time of individual development and maturation, of viewing the world as a man, all culminating in the choice of a wife who had proved to be compatible.

In our society today this whole interim period of personal maturation must follow marriage rather than precede it. The young man does not live as an adult, and is not identified as an adult, until after he has become a husband with the expected responsibilities. It is inevitable that each individual will change after this kind of marriage because seeing the world from an adult vantage point and being treated as an adult significantly alter many adolescent notions about sex, married life, work, social responsibilities—in other words, about adulthood. Sex is not like in the movies, marriage is not like on television, and financial responsibilities are not as simple as kids think they are. Finally, *after* the marriage, man and wife begin to see themselves and each other in an adult context.[2]

Some young men still, even in my generation, accept this definition of marriage and involve themselves as the society dictates. This group consists of the ever-scarcer breed of college students who do not feel removed from the values of and critical of the patterns of behavior in adult society. For those who do not reject the system of dating, marriage, and social involvement,* the consequences can be seen on any

* Studies on college students have come up with a revealing conclusion. In contrasting students who want a date to be attractive and from a good school, to enhance their own prestige in the male peer group, with students who approach dating as a form of courtship and who make close emotional involvement their goal, Rebecca S. Vreeland found that students from the first group were "conservative in their political opinions and

graph of the rise of the divorce rate. What are the statistics today? The odds are getting to be around 50–50 that marriage will last until "death us do part."

What the statistics do not measure, of course, is the number of those who are unwilling to pay the social price of divorce even after they realize that they are incompatible with their mates as adults in the adult world. The practice in adult society has been to stick together, so the saying goes, "for the sake of the kids." But the home is conflicted; the children are divided emotionally; anger is constant. As Janis Ian says pointedly, "They think they're martyrs but they're kidding their kid."

In the past few years divorce has become more widespread, and so more acceptable. More and more parents, rather than living in bitter loneliness with someone they have grown away from, have simply left. Divorce as a common social practice has characterized only postwar society. The postwar generation has concluded that if the divorce rate is not to continue to rise, deep premarital relationships will have to become acceptable.

College students who face the world of adulthood feel that in a round-about way they are being pushed into marriage. "No, you can't live with your girl friend," adult society tells them. "No, you can't make love with her. No, we do not consider you a man. Solve your problems, son, and get married." But members of this generation refuse to marry this way because they have seen how it ends, and they know why.

This generation's solution has been, thanks to the Pill, for two people to try to know each other deeply and intimately, to establish a long-standing loyalty to each other by living and making love together, and then, when they know each other as adults, to get married. This is neither immoral nor harmful nor loose. It is simply an attempt to avoid divorce and to assure their children of a loving, two-parent home—the kind of home which an unprecedented number in this generation have gone without.

For those who accept what marriage has come to be, however, quite often divorce or marital unhappiness lies ahead. Not yet adults, they take on the responsibilities and face the statistics in order to gain the sexual intimacy and social security that were absent in disintegrating

---

traditionally religious. They subscribe to traditional middle-class ideas of the future. For them the most important characteristics of their prospective career are its income, prestige, and security."[3] These students are traditional in public spheres of life, and, in their dating life, are also traditional.

family relationships and the socially patterned dating system. However, when they finally are adults, faced with the realities that are often hidden to those not yet enmeshed in the adult world, the responsibilities and commitments of double-duty marriage take on new meaning, the hoped-for security and intimacy take on less, and young couples who did not reject the system often find themselves entangled on the other side of the statistical fence.*

Increasing numbers of critical young people in this generation are coming to understand their position in regard to marriage as analogous to that of a fish with a lure. Marriage is held out to them, and, once it is grabbed, a young man is supposed to embrace not only the woman he thinks he loves but also a social structure and values which he knows he cannot accept. And so young people try to find their own values.

What so many of the signs of "looseness," "immorality," and "free love" are trying to get across to adult society is that a young man today wants to know a woman and to be a man *before* they marry. As seems to be quite often the case, adult society is condemning the very behavior that its rules cause. It condemns a young man for knowing a woman *sexually* before marriage, yet, because marriage itself has become the *rite de passage*, it has become impossible to know a woman *socially* before marriage. It is the lack of social recognition of manhood that places the burden on sexual recognition in youth culture.

Young men are refusing to place the burden, at the same time, on marriage. They refuse to marry in order to be considered "grown up," for they quite rightly do not view the purchase of a marriage license as a valid index of emotional and psychological maturity. Whether in hippie or college communities, they try to achieve deep relationships outside of marriage in its traditional form. And now there is the Pill.

Young men turn to each other and lose yet more contact with adult society. They form a youth culture and find their own ways to prove their manhood. With this understanding of the dating and marriage system, which for critical young men is a closed door to manhood, we can turn to other, newer institutions and endeavors which, though they were at first associated only with hippies, have become new foundations of youth culture itself.

* For a perceptive analysis of these aspects of dating and marriage by a professor and a student, read Robert F. Winch's "The Function of Dating in Middle-Class America" and Sheila Tillotson's "Golden Girl: Examining a Certain Kind of Coed" in Winch, et al., *Selected Studies in Marriage and the Family* (New York: Holt, Rinehart, and Winston, 1962).

Go Ask Alice

One pill makes you larger
And one pill makes you small
And the ones that Mother gives you
Don't do anything at all
                    —Jefferson Airplane

Drugs are today a sufficiently new phenomenon on a popular scale and are sufficiently criticized in our Western culture that it is safe to say that very few of the present young drug-users started out being in favor of them. On the contrary, almost all users approached drugs at a younger age with the typical hostile outlook ingrained by the press and adult society's opinion. Too many adults are so ready to condemn drug-users that they fail to ask the most important and illuminating question: What is the evolution of thought that takes a young man from a stance against the use of psychedelic drugs to the acceptance of, and participation in, psychedelia? And this question also must be asked: What relatively new cultural situations have impelled far larger numbers of young people than ever before to use drugs?

Those who give drugs little thought, who accept adult society's attitudes outright, and who have no personal contact with the world of drugs, simply say that it is too dangerous to try pot or LSD; they know the reports in the media of the crazy things people do under the influence of drugs. But today alienation is so widespread that few young people accept adult society's attitudes outright, and too many singers are singing about drugs, too many writers are writing about drugs, and too many young men are using drugs, for any but the most isolated members of this generation to refrain from examining the question more deeply.

Those who move beyond the culturally patterned emotional outrage against drugs and who begin to approach the issue rationally are often against drugs as not being natural. They question the necessity of using psychedelics in order to experience happiness and pleasure. They remember quiet, warm nights when they were lost in pleasure with the girl they were sure they loved. In love, they think, was something natural, something intensely good, achieved independently of drugs.

This is the beautiful idealism of youth, which often is the first casualty of dating, college life, and the closed door to manhood. While the idealism remains, though, it is easy to stereotype those who do turn to drugs, because adult society conveniently provides the stereotype: drug-users turn to drugs in desperation, out of shortcomings or perversions which are part of their personalities. They must, like the heroin addicts depicted in high-school health-class movies, become drug-users because they have failed to adjust and develop normally and are in some way inadequate.

I remember in my first year at college, after a friend had stayed in our dorm for a few days, that a young girl came late one evening looking for him. She asked if the friend was still there, or if he had left something for her. She was extremely nervous, her whole manner one of sadness, despair, and lostness. He was gone, of course, and had left nothing for her. She inquired futilely for his address or for the whereabouts of another source. When she realized there was none to be found, the ray of hope that had reflected in the pool of desperation in her eyes disappeared and they became cold and dark. She mumbled meaningless regrets and left.

This was proof in my own experience that drugs were for messed-up dropouts. Like many other young people I was to see later, she was not looking for lysergic acid diethylamide. She was looking for the self she couldn't find. She was looking for courage, for excitement, perhaps for love. She was looking for the answer to her sad and lonely detachment from life and for the source of deep involvement in life. She was searching for a fantastic miracle that would change what was inside her and make her something other than she was.

I took this incident and others like it as proof that the only right decision was to avoid drugs. I then wrote on a wave of idealistic fervor:

> Is it really drugs that are able to expand the mind and increase self-awareness? No. I dcn't believe that man is the low level of life that can purchase self-realization for five bucks at the corner. I believe that the only way one can increase one's knowledge of oneself is without hallucinogenic aid. Something as important as self-knowledge cannot be bought with money. Only serious and concerned self-searching and sharing one's knowledge with others through love can bring self-awareness. The body and the mind are man's only shrines. Can we ourselves not believe in them and improve them without escaping into a world of make-believe? Is not this our challenge?

It is this type of thinking which the alienation of youth culture often destroys.

If one remains open to new thought, college is usually the stage when one sees that the issue of drugs is not so simple.* Often almost simultaneously, one realizes that the high-school simplicity of communism versus capitalism, "revealed" religion versus empiricism, sanity versus insanity, and psychedelics versus rational learning are not such convenient dichotomies as one was led to believe. So many convenient ways of thinking, so many easy ways of defining who he is, are proving to be shallow that the college student asks himself: Why couldn't I be wrong about this issue too? I mistrust so much of adult society and what it says, why shouldn't I also mistrust its attitudes towards drugs?

During the time when a young person is caught between his childhood acceptance of adult society's attitudes and the attitudes of youth culture, the question of whether to use drugs remains a tortuous analysis of pros and cons. But increasing isolation from adult society, combined with the circumstances of college life, provides a basis for changing his childhood beliefs. Powerful as his individual isolation is, it would in itself not be enough to make him overcome the fear of drugs ingrained in him throughout precollege life.

The first crucial break with past beliefs comes when one realizes that one's best friend smokes pot; or that the guy down the hall who plays

---

* Not only colleges, but the armed forces have been experiencing an influx of psychedelics. Most of it has been in California, but because of the mobility of servicemen, drugs have spread. One might expect drugs, for instance, at Vandenberg Air Force Base near Los Angeles and at Travis Air Force Base near San Francisco, and not in Nebraska. But they're there. Annapolis too has had an influx of drugs, as evidenced by recent expulsions of midshipmen for possession and use of marijuana. And, according to news reports from Vietnam, upward of 80 per cent of American servicemen have smoked pot. Vietnamese marijuana is easily accessible and, I have been told, far superior to the pot from Mexico and Panama for which college drug-users have to settle.

first-chair oboe in the orchestra has taken LSD; or that the respected friend on the Dean's List and the fastest glove at third base you ever saw is "up" most of the time. Pictures of sordid underworld figures disappear. Images of sick and desperate people in smoky, dingy rooms fade away. Another culturally ingrained idea has to be revised.

One comes face to face with the issue again, but now with a less limited viewpoint. One must acknowledge at least two possible effects of drugs—"freakouts," on one hand, and beneficial or minimal effects, on the other. And one's theory of causation—what makes someone turn to drugs?—is shot to pieces. These people, who are leading productive lives and who are one's friends, have not been destroyed by taking drugs, and they weren't desperate before they took them. One realizes that when friends are "high" on marijuana they are not different except that they smile more and have bigger eyes. One accepts, after seeing smiling faces and dancing bodies, that drugs are at least not the universal horror they are made out to be. When one hears a movie describe taking marijuana as a "trip to hell," and when one reads the United States Commissioner of Narcotics' report on marijuana, which explains its psychosis-producing effects, one is forced to realize again that mass society tells only part of the truth, if even that.

For young people who reach this point in the evolution of thought, individual personality and geographic position will determine how long it is before they smoke pot. Their growing alienation from adult society makes the use of drugs more probable. And concerning geography, on the East Coast and in California, and in college communities in the Southwest and Florida, and in the metropolitan areas of Denver, Chicago, and Detroit—in fact, wherever great numbers of highly mobile young people can be found—there is access to drugs. Some places—for instance Columbia, Missouri, or Lafayette, Indiana, or Orlando, Florida—are still pretty clean. But any young person who has seen through adult society's phobia about psychedelia can get drugs if he wants them.

For the growing number of people who get drugs and use them, the controversy about the subject illumines some interesting aspects of the generation gap. What hits hardest is the symbolic nature of the drug issue—symbolic of the ever-widening gap between youth and society. It illustrates the sharp division in logic between popular opinion and youth culture. The drug issue points up, whatever one's ideas about the value and danger of drugs may be, the slowness with which the majority of adults react to new developments within their society. The same lethargy which adult society manifested in coming to grips with the effects of the media, or with surging nationalist feeling in the under-developed countries, it also manifests in coming to grips with drugs.

Unaware of the nature of youth culture, most adults consider the popularity of marijuana as ephemeral as that of a new dance. "Oh, those kids!" an old lady exclaimed to me. "It's a new dance or a new singing group every few months. And now drugs too. The fads pass, but some of them are dangerous." This lady felt that drugs were something that just caught kids' fancies. Complacent adults sit back and wait for pot to go out like the hula hoop.

They see the psychedelic "fringe" in a rigid stereotype. The drug-user is to them a guy who couldn't make the grade, who because of his own shortcomings is rebelling against the established order, with sloppy clothes, long hair, degenerate morals, and generally unconventional behavior.* Drug use, then, can be called not only a fad, but a fad of kids who are abnormal.

What is frightening is how poorly these adults read the signs of their own culture. Rather than being a passing breeze (or smoke fume), marijuana is an element of youth culture that has taken root in the soil of this generation's psychological alienation. The plant will not be uprooted unless the deep roots of discontent are recognized. Drug usage will not diminish as long as the alienation in youth culture grows.

Furthermore, as for the idea that drug-users are clearly messed-up kids who couldn't make the grade, the Ivy League colleges quickly show this to be invalid. To the dismay of college administrations trying to get money from alumni, the number of students who use drugs is not small. A survey at Yale in 1967 showed 40 per cent to have used pot. And a survey at Harvard in 1968 showed well over 50 per cent to have smoked grass. The colleges considered academically outstanding in the country by and large have the highest number of pot-users. And this trend is rapidly gaining momentum. In the Harvard study, 5 per cent of senior-class members who were polled had smoked pot *before coming to college*; the figure for the juniors was 6 per cent; for the sophomores, 11 per cent; and for the freshmen, 23 per cent.† Pot use is becoming

---

* More precisely, society views the psychedelic "fringe" as anomic personalities, *unable* to conform to normal behavior. Within youth culture itself these young men are considered individuals who are able but *unwilling* to conform to behavior they cannot accept.
† In other words, twice as many in the freshman class entering in 1966 smoked pot as in the class of 1965, and twice as many in the freshman class of 1967 smoked as in the 1966 class. From all available information it seems that, prior to these years of rapid increase in marijuana use, the percentage of users remained very small and very stable.

prevalent not only in college communities themselves, but also in prep schools and high schools.

Clearly, the schools mentioned above are not for kids who couldn't make the grade. Rather, their student populations are made up of young men who, at their respective secondary schools, were often the most successful, intelligent, and dynamic individuals in their classes. *Time* magazine reports that in an affluent suburb of Los Angeles, police have estimated that 50 per cent of the high-schoolers have used drugs. Their counselors estimate 70 per cent.[1] To look at another example: a senior who was the main supplier of marijuana at his prestigious New England prep school told me that at least 40 per cent and perhaps 60 per cent of the student body had smoked grass. Even small towns are realizing that their high schools have become involved with drugs. In two years the town of Brattleboro, Vermont, for example, became a center of drug use merely because the high-school students were able to procure marijuana from a nearby college. All across the country, proper suburbanites have realized that they had better acquaint themselves with the "new" phenomenon. As one Manhattan mother complained, "None of us knows anything about it. It's so new."

She was referring to grass. She should have been talking about the attitudes of this generation. For it is the postwar generation that is new, not marijuana.

Marijuana was not invented in 1965. It is ancient. Even in America it has been used for decades in urban subcultures and in rural areas where it grows wild. The only thing that is new is the extent of alienation in white, middle-class, educated young people and their consequent openness to the values of pot-smoking. Much of the recent severe criticism of marijuana is the result not of new and more accurate research but of the spread of its use into "respectable" society. For the alienation from middle-class society which once characterized only the poor, the blacks, the artists, and the inveterate dropouts now characterizes a growing number of the sons of that middle-class society.

There is no doubt that youth culture is moving toward drugs. That young men begin adolescence by avoiding drugs and finish adolescence accepting drugs is a social fact. The sociological and psychological reasons why this has become a social fact are complex, but, when analyzed, provide an airtight proof that drugs are a force in modern culture to be reckoned with.

I Know It's Mine

The Beatles ask: When you're high and the room is dark,
what do you see? The answer comes: I don't know,
"but I know it's mine."

The first breeding ground for large-scale use of psychedelics was in
the social-dropout and artistic fringe areas, usually centered in a specific
and densely populated section of a large urban area—Venice in Los
Angeles and Greenwich Village in New York City being the prime
examples. It was in such areas in this country that drugs which had
been known in other societies for centuries, or (in the case of lysergic-
acid derivatives) had been isolated in laboratories decades ago, were
first socially discovered. The cores of these areas were populated by
confirmed social dropouts, by various deviant subgroups, and, more
recently, by a large number of alienated young people. While the alienated group was small, drugs remained in these areas and found no
means for entering the established, functioning circles of society.

The situation has changed radically in the past few years, and the
reasons for the growth of drug use are hard to pinpoint. Aside from
the increase in cultural disaffection, the most important sociological
reason is the hyperactive draft. Social dropouts of college age, if they
were men, could not remain out of school without being inducted into

the armed forces. They had to reconsider going to college. Numerically more significant, however, were those students who had once decided to work or travel or study independently in order to "find themselves" before going to college. Because of their interests or the extent of their alienation, these young men would once have gone through their "drug stage" away from the college campus. When they felt ready to return to established education, they would have left their drugs behind. No break in the education process has been possible for young men during the mid-1960s unless they want to end up in khaki, and so drugs have found their way to campus. Both alienation and drugs have left the enclaves of dropouts and entered the mainstream of young people which flows through our nation's network of colleges and universities.

The presence of the often bright and privately motivated young men who used drugs on campus changed an essential problem. The appearance of these individuals in college communities accounts for the increased availability of drugs. This original fringe group provided the college population with drugs and with the example of drug-users, both of which are necessary. A young man cannot choose to smoke pot if there is no pot. And it is less likely that he will want to smoke pot if he has never seen anyone who does.

Needless to say, the original pot-smoking fringe could not have affected the large mass of students unless striking social changes had come about. It is hard to dissect anything as nebulous and yet as real as the climate of alienation that has allowed the diffusion of drugs in youth culture. For purposes of examination, the social change that has caused the increase in drugs among the student population may be divided into the categories of chronological, philosophical, academic, economic, and political.

Chronological. Today's students do not find themselves a completely isolated, rebellious group having no resonance with established circles, to the degree that they were a few years ago. In the schools mentioned in the previous chapter, and in even more schools on the West Coast, there is already a crop of graduates from the early 1960s who have made their way into the lower echelons of the educational hierarchy. Established and upcoming people are beginning to write the same thoughts young people are having, and are making the once isolated voices from student populations more vociferous and numerous. The knowledge that the botany professor grows marijuana (actually the case at a prestigious East Coast college), or that the government instructor is a confirmed hippie, is a real factor in reducing students' feelings that perhaps drugs are only for lost adolescents.

*Philosophical.** The philosophic background of this generation lends itself quite readily to a drug-using ideology. Having acknowledged the so-called "death of God," and the absence of ultimate and absolute values in American culture, a young man asks: Where do I go from here? Drugs are an element of his answer, an answer that provides a very here-and-now, sensual-perceptual experience. The user knows that he cannot determine scientifically what happens on a "trip"; nor can he refute the scientific assessment of the distorting effects of drugs in a professional manner. That the average pot-smoker or acidhead cannot justify drugs in this way is quite understandable. That he does not mind this apparent inability is the key to understanding the philosophical basis for using psychedelic drugs today. Critical analysis and scientific discourse are what the student is forced to use during his entire student career. He is asked to read textbooks with laws and theorems that have no immediate relevance to his personal life. Ever since *Sputnik I* began circling the world, scientists have dominated the classroom. Today's young people have witnessed the exaltation of science as has no other generation, and they are reacting against the requirements that science imposes on the individual. The student has no desire to investigate rationally during his trip. He wants only to know that it was *his* experience, that he was living through his own senses and not out of a textbook. He wants to feel he was himself for a few moments, rather than just acting the detached part of the student reading a textbook thousands of other kids have read before him.

Academic. The burgeoning number of college students in the social sciences is in itself an interesting phenomenon. A good part of the social sciences is devoted to the study of individual psychology—to the study of human motivation and how it is translated into social action. As I explain in the following chapter, drugs are tools that aid in understanding oneself. If this is so, one would expect their use to be more prevalent in those fields of academic inquiry that are intimately involved with understanding human psychology. Such, we find, is actually the case. A poll taken at Harvard showed that the highest percentage of pot-smokers was found in the Department of Social Relations, a catch-all department for sociology, psychology, and cultural anthropology.

---

* The logic of the present drug philosophy itself is discussed more specifically in the following chapter. I describe here only the historical background.

In contrast to these social sciences, which analyze the bases of human behavior, the natural sciences and mathematics had a much lower percentage of drug-users.* Because what can be gained from a drug experience is similar to what can be gained through psychological research and study, it is not surprising that there is a strong correlation between the choice of that discipline and the use of drugs. Moreover, as the psychological fields come to play an ever greater part in academic life, it can be expected that the use of drugs will become yet more widespread.

Economic. Although the poor certainly exist in our culture, the majority of people are richer than they ever have been. They can get the basic things they want, and they can see movies, drive powerful cars, go to parks, buy special foods, and so on. Activities or objects that provided thrills or kicks and once made young people feel that they were really living are household items today. They no longer possess the special magic that they once had for an earlier, less affluent generation. The incorporation of drugs into the quest for pleasurable experience seems to be the subsequent step.

Political. The political climate which has caused alienation to become psychological does not encourage drug usage in a positive way. Rather, for youth, it seems that a negative force has been lessened. The ideological minds of young men tend to classify: once an identified force in society has been shown to be "bad" in one respect, its whole function in society is to be resisted. The government, for its less than charismatic personalities, its "credibility gap," and its Vietnam war stance, has been identified as monolithically bad by many drug-users. This rebellion against the source of law-enforcement has decreased this generation's hesitancy to "break the law."

All these factors combine to increase the fertility of the national soil for the cultivation of grass. The expansion of psychedelia into academia and suburbia has begun. From the University of Miami to Reed College in Portland, from Brown University to the University of Santa Barbara, drugs are an omnipresent campus phenomenon. On the West Coast, the society—more mobile and with less stable community tradition—has provided less social pressure against taking pot. Although Harvard and Yale might well be the highest in drug use on the East Coast, they would drop to well below sixth or seventh place in

---

* The statistics showed that 36 per cent of science and mathematics majors had smoked pot, which was the lowest percentage for any academic group. The highest percentage—78 per cent—was found in social relations.

relation to the West Coast schools. This is a "failure," I am sure, that the Ivy League schools' administrations would not regret. An additional factor is that, along the coast from San Francisco to Los Angeles, access to marijuana, mescalin, and LSD is easier, prices are lower, and fellow psychedelians are easier to find.

The sociological reasons for the sudden wide acceptance of drugs are certainly crucial, but they are still not enough. Drug use could not have gained such a pivotal position in youth culture without having been an expression of the psychological needs of individual young men. The same psychological circumstances that caused the formation of youth culture in the first place, that closed the door to manhood for this generation, continue to exert their pressure. Experience such as the kind drugs offer is necessary for individual development along the only path to manhood that remains open.

To Be a Man

Now she's the one who gives us all those magical things,
Reads us stories out of the *I Ching,*
Then she passes out a whole new basket of rings
That when you put on your hand . . .
It gives you the powers to be a man.

—Country Joe and the Fish

Today's psychologically oriented generation witnesses a whole spectrum of behavior developing at the supposed demarcation line of adulthood. At around the age of twenty, at the extremes of the generation are small minorities who accept all or who accept nothing that adult society can give them. With an unacceptable adulthood as the ostensible goal, this generation is forced to realize the cultural arbitrariness and bias involved in deciding which segment of it is normal and which is abnormal. No longer can young people conveniently say that only the desperate and inadequate turn to pot or other drugs. This generation has become aware that most drug-users, in fact, are searching for psychedelic experience as a reaction to, and as an effort to extricate oneself from, the quiet desperation and inner inadequacy that are socially patterned in our society.

The wide divergence of behavior and the wide use of drugs in this postwar generation are integrally related to the absence of definite cultural initiation rites. It is true that in some societies with initiation rites drugs are used. What I maintain is that their function in our society is quite different.

Drugs now provide simulated *rites de passage*.* Few young men approach pot or LSD ultimately in a quest for pleasure or for escape, although these are sometimes initial reasons. *Most college students go to these drugs with the desire to be tested, not coddled, by the experience.* The risk involved is part of the challenge. These young men want and need something credible and challenging to measure up to.

In this age of psychology, young drug-users want to flirt with psychosis. If at first the experience is "merely" pleasurable, by getting higher and higher, going up more and more and more often, and taking bigger and bigger doses, they are trying to lose their old socially identified selves. They are trying to destroy their ingrained patterns of reasoning and perception, to jettison in Cartesian fashion all vestiges of childhood indoctrination, and to test their minds as previous societies tested endurance or resourcefulness as a sign of manhood. They want to "blow their minds." Much as past generations told about their war experiences as initiations to manhood, so experienced drug-users talk about their near freakouts. Their goal is to push themselves as close as they can to the brink of sanity, without losing control.

The shortcomings of this type of initiation are as clear as are the shortcomings of marriage. Neither can bear the burden of being substitute *rites de passage*. The drug rite is an intensely personal experience, having no relation to accepted social institutions in this society. Only within the youthful circle of drug-users does this experience have any social significance, no matter how illuminating or forceful it may be. The value of the experience is not recognized either by young people's parents or by adult society as a whole, largely because the experience challenges the values of traditional adulthood completely.

This lack of recognition further isolates drug-users from the mores of the society in which they were raised. The dilemma is again posed: a young man feels he has transcended childhood and become a man, but this change is of course not recognized by his society. And so follows the result: the original isolation and alienation from society because of a gap in values is magnified because of the total failure in communication.

* Some initiation rites in primitive societies bore a striking resemblance to the modern drug trip. See Arnold van Gennep, *The Rites of Passage* (Chicago: University of Chicago Press, 1960), especially pages 65–81. For example: "In some tribes [the rite] consists of a physical and mental weakening which is undoubtedly intended to make him lose all recollection of his childhood existence."

The issue of drugs is the one issue of the generation gap about which there seem to be no common grounds for discussion. Drug-users couldn't care less what the United States Commissioner of Narcotics or what university psychiatrists have to say; and, unfortunately, the commissioner and the psychiatrists couldn't care less what drug-users have to say. I know young men who limit their friends to people who have "dropped" acid because they can't get along with people who haven't taken an acid trip. And I know psychiatrists and narcotics-squad officers who never use the term "drug use," but only "drug abuse"! Where are the common grounds for gaining mutual understanding in this controversy?

Alienated young people, unlike adults, are unable to make quick value judgments about drugs because this generation alone feels the absence of meaningful character ideals in mass society. But to reach this final conclusion, it is necessary first to examine the pro-drug and anti-drug positions. I feel drugs have attributes that adult society will not acknowledge, and dangers that drug-users will not admit. I disagree with both extremes in the drug controversy, for I think drugs are neither "a trip to hell" nor "a blessed sacrament."

Narcotics officials and psychiatrists and adults in general always cite the element of risk involved in taking drugs as sufficient reason to avoid drugs, and as sufficient reason to challenge the mental stability of those who don't avoid them. But this generation cannot agree that the question is that simple. Psychiatrists have placed the number of individuals using drugs who need personal or institutional mental therapy at 2 per cent or 5 per cent or 10 per cent. They of course cannot know the exact percentage because they can only very inaccurately estimate the number of people who actually use drugs. Because they underestimate the total number, their percentages of drug-induced psychoses are too high. Nevertheless, that even a small percentage of users have mental problems is enough to deter "straight" people from taking drugs. That there is any risk, in our age of insurance, makes taking drugs foolish and dangerous, to them.

This generation's argument would be that in the opinion of psychiatrists at least 5 per cent of the American population is in need of personal or psychiatric help and that, especially during adolescence, the statistics are even higher. The percentage of clinically ill cases in regular society is roughly equivalent to the percentage of clinically ill cases among drug-users. The statistical argument against drugs is quite meaningless, the drug ideology may conclude. Drugs only permit already present neurotic aspects of personality to manifest themselves in the open. That sixteen psychotic mental patients who have at some time used psychedelic drugs are sitting in a Los Angeles hospital makes sensational news stories. However, the drug-user would add that it is virtually meaningless in relation to the fact that tens of thousands of young people in California alone use drugs and will never need to be in a mental hospital.

The only negative psychic effect of drugs seems to be that latent psychotics manifest the symptoms of their mental problems. But United States Commissioner of Narcotics Henry L. Giordano, in his publication on the dangers of marijuana, implies that marijuana use is *generally* psychosis-producing. He goes so far as to quote a study which states that the low incidence of psychotic effects may reflect nothing more than a poor quality of marijuana. Quoting from a book called *Nightmare Drugs*, Commissioner Giordano goes on to connect marijuana use with criminality, violence, and insanity. And, in a final *tour de force*, he tries to convince the reader of his pamphlet that marijuana use leads to narcotics addiction. If his audience does not read his pamphlet with an extremely critical eye, it is most certainly convinced that marijuana must be outlawed because it is so dangerous for most individuals.

I want to look at some of his arguments critically, that is, from the point of view of a young man who is intimately acquainted with college drug use. First we can look at the commissioner's statistical reasoning that marijuana use leads to hard drug addiction. He says: "Of course, not all persons who use marijuana go on to use heroin, *but* actual experience leaves little doubt that a large majority of narcotics addicts begin their drug-taking with marijuana."* He constructs his sentence in such a way as to imply that the second clause contradicts the first.

If we change the topic, look how strange that sentence is: "Of course, not all women who have kissed go on to get pregnant, but actual experience leaves little doubt that a large majority of pregnant women began their love-making with kissing." It is clear that the commissioner uses such an absurd sentence structure in order to imply a direct causal relationship between marijuana use and subsequent heroin addiction. He is saying, in a sense, that kissing causes pregnancy.

The commissioner's subsequent statistical argument reveals the shallowness of his logic. When he speaks of "actual experience," he is not

---

* All quotations from Commissioner Giordano are taken from his *The Dangers of Marijuana. . . Facts You Should Know*, published by the government and distributed widely to college and other health clinics.

referring to his own drug use or to his own intimate familiarity with drug-using subcultures. What he is referring to when he says "actual experience" is the information gathered from 2,213 hard-core narcotics addicts at a hospital in Lexington, Kentucky. Of the addicts, 70.4 per cent had used marijuana prior to their narcotics addiction. He feels confident, then, in concluding that marijuana leads "many people" to use other more powerful and more addictive drugs.

A young reader cannot help being appalled at the logic of such a statistical discussion. Of course most addicts have used marijuana first. But, rather than ask how many heroin addicts *have used* marijuana, why not ask how many marijuana-users *go on to* narcotics addiction? Well, there are two reasons. First, people like the commissioner cannot get statistics on this so easily. It's easy to find the sickest addicts. They are sitting in the hospitals. But to find a comparable number of marijuana-users the doctors would have to go out into the world of healthy people —into colleges, universities, artistic communities, and poor areas. Second, people like the commissioner cannot ask how many marijuana-users go on to heroin, rather than how many addicts have used marijuana, because it would disprove their idea. I can safely say that of the thousands of students in America's most outstanding colleges and universities who have used pot, less than one-quarter of 1 per cent will ever use narcotics. There is no direct causal relationship between marijuana and narcotics. All that can possibly have been proved by the commissioner's statistics is that addicts have generally first used marijuana. *Nothing has been proved about people who are not already narcotics addicts.* So his arguments are not relevant in understanding the college marijuana-smoker.

Commissioner Giordano illustrates a general weakness in the reasoning of adult commentators, whether narcotics officials, college psychiatrists, or medical doctors. What these adults must realize is that everything they know which has been derived from those who have had psychotic reactions to drugs cannot be applied to all drug-users. For all a college psychiatrist knows, 100 per cent of marijuana-users might have psychotic reactions; all the marijuana-users he knows, *by virtue of the fact that they are known*, are "sick." Only the student with over a hundred drug-using friends, who sees one of them go to a psychiatrist, develops a balanced perspective. That student can see that it was the single individual's personality, not the qualities of marijuana, which was the original cause of his mental problems. Until adults who talk about drugs begin to study the 98 per cent of college drug-users whom they will never see in their hospitals or on their couches, the adults will never understand drug use as a whole. They will, unfortunately, have to continue to generalize about drug-users from a very small and very unrepresentative group, the clinically ill.

On this flimsy basis, established society categorically condemns drugs and says that all drugs are the work of the devil. So the hippie categorically defends drugs and says that all drugs are the food of the gods. In the case of marijuana or peyote, the scientific evidence against them is extremely poor—poorer than the evidence against alcohol. The weakness of the argument against drugs is painfully obvious.

The reasoning of drug-users should now be clearer. Despite their reflexive defense of all drugs, they acknowledge that for some types of people there is a definite danger in taking mind-affecting drugs. But, as a Boston dealer in grass and acid, who traffics annually in thousands of dollars' worth of illegal drugs, told me, "Sure, if you're psychotic, your trip'll show you how messed up you are. But if you know where you're at, if you're a groovy person, then you'll usually have a beautiful trip. It's a test, man, for your head." A trip shows you who you are. *You find out about yourself.* You cannot hide your socially patterned frustrations from yourself. You become able to deal with yourself and "travel with your mind."

Drug-users often see those in the social rat-race as the mentally ill, and see that "normal" condition as the one to be avoided at all costs. Drug-users feel that the vast majority of people who accept the socially patterned frustrations have a limited and distorted idea of what it means to live fully, of what it means to be an individual. Drug-users have decided they cannot afford the risk of *not* taking drugs because without drugs it is not easy to pull oneself out of the psychological quagmire of modern society. Without using drugs, they fear, they will fail and succumb to the prevalent social illness of detached and empty noninvolvement; they will not root out society's ingrained patterns in their minds; they will sell out their ideal concept of a compassionate and involved life to the distorted, mechanical concept of American society. They view drugs as a measure of assurance that they will not sell out, because psychedelics are not just negative rebellion, they feel, but a positive route to another way of life.

It Is So Quick

I believe in magic
Why?—because it is so quick
I don't need power
When I'm hypnotized.

　　　　　　　　　—Love

Sharing a given period of time in history does not necessarily mean sharing common experience. It is valid to question my ability, or anyone's ability for that matter, to describe the experience of an entire generation of college students. A Negro from an East Coast urban slum or a rancher's son from Nevada could rightfully ask me how I could presume to speak for his life and ideas. Or a student at a religious college in the South and a student at a brand-new junior college in the California coastal mountains could rightfully ask how a student at a New England college could generalize about them.

As I stated at the outset, I am trying to describe only the college generation, and only those of college age who seem to be the young people who would normally have become leaders in adult society. But beyond this, I am describing a generation that is growing up in an impersonal, mass society. All people are subjected to the same advertisements, movies, and television shows. All people live in a world with atomic bombs, wars they cannot understand, and political groups they disagree with. All people live in a time when good jobs will not be achieved without a college education. All people use the same school-books and read the same set of mass-circulation magazines. *What mass society means is that more information and more experience than ever before is being shared by more people than ever before.* Because this body of information and experience contains internal contradictions, and because it conflicts with culturally patterned life experience, those who are subject to it share the common cultural pressures. Of course, different individuals react in different ways to these common circum-stances. But without directly considering individual psychological dif-ferences, one may generalize about experience insofar as it is defined by common cultural background. And in mass society, the background of its members becomes more and more uniform. It is because of their shared experience in this standardized, mechanized society that many reactions to drug experience are shared by so many users.

I hasten to add that this is not a Huxleyan account of psychedelic excursions, nor is it a mystical, Learyesque interpretation. I simply wish to explain the manner in which social roles and attitudes are altered in an individual who engages in drug activity.

The almost universal reaction to popular psychedelic drugs in Western culture is that the individual feels he was not aware of his life to the maximum before he used drugs. Afterward, he feels that straight people have yet to gain this level of awareness and involvement. When he is high, objects or scenes that formerly provided no particular interest or beauty become overwhelmingly beautiful and involving. The trip itself is often not the high point. Rather, the cumulative effect of numerous highs is that one feels more aware of (i.e., more open and prone to perceive) the beauty that is part of life. The frequent reaction is that the drug-user realizes that, despite the luxury, the ease, and the conveniences of modern culture, its traditional members are missing much of the beauty and pleasure they could experience. This all, of course, reinforces the drug-user's dislike for the mode of life in our society.

Involved with this perceptual difference is a psychological one. After the high is "over," the same old reality seems more exciting, and one is more involved in it—not more involved in the social, artificial worlds but in the natural, inner world. Because varieties in taste are much more acute, because the differentiation of colors and their primary components is visually accentuated, because music and the interplay of rhythms and tonal qualities become involving and beautiful, and because not only the senses but all the bodily processes can be more fully experienced and enjoyed, the external world is appreciated in a way similar (the user thinks) to that of pre-modern man, whose body had not become so removed from nature and dulled and desensitized in its sensation. The natural world, users would maintain, is more real because the individual has gained more knowledge of it.

In terms of hippies' external appearance as well as their inner psychology, this greater sensitivity to the natural world causes many differences which are hard for straight people to understand. I once witnessed a rather heated encounter between a conservatively dressed businessman and a hippie. The adult said that he thought hippies made themselves look needlessly strange by the way they dressed.

"So you think we look strange?" the youth retorted angrily. "Some things are much stranger, I assure you. Haven't you ever wondered why man, born into a world of beautiful color, voluntarily puts himself in a gray suit and into the midst of other people dressed in gray? Maybe hippies are strange colorfully; but straight people are strange dully. Or haven't you ever thought about how strange it is that people hardly ever wear flowers, even though they were born in a land where every plain and mountain is clothed in its own beautiful pattern? Instead straight people wear flowers to formal dances, flowers that look starched and utterly lifeless. Even stranger, you people wait till someone dies, till it's too late, and then flowers become the thing."

The youth waited until his words had sunk in. "People who build gray cities, and wear gray suits, and lead gray lives," he said softly, "tell their children that what isn't gray is strange. Ever since I learned I liked color better, ever since I learned that I'd never get beyond messenger boy if I didn't wear gray, I decided to become 'strange.' I'd rather live strangely than die slowly in different shades of gray."

According to drug ideology, the inner, psychic world is made more sensitive, much like the senses. It is clear to the drug-user that mental associations are liberated from the constraints imposed upon them by cultural patterns. Memories usually repressed are freed to the "high" mind. The individual, if he has been involved in understanding his basic motivations, can gain insight into areas normally beyond his grasp. This college generation uses drugs as tools for furthering self-analysis designed to root out the self-defeating patterns of behavior that have been ingrained by mass society. The greater a young man considers the molding forces of mass society and its media to be, the more necessary he considers the use of drugs to be. Most often these psychological insights are not immediate, but are rationally explainable only after continued self-examination. But sometimes the gain of knowledge is immediately clear. Let me give examples of both.

An example of a simple insight gained through drug experience might concern an increase in understanding of a facet of academic psychology. Students, when first exposed to Freud's developmental theory of the oral, anal, and genital stages, often cannot accept it completely. Freud describes the change in focus on the three erogenous zones during personality development, which culminates in adulthood in the nature or genital or psychosexual stage. Young people exposed to this theory can easily accept the sexual, pleasure-producing nature of the genitals, and even of the mouth, but find it hard to accept the sexual, pleasurable nature of the anal period. They criticize this aspect of Freudian theory until they experience their first bowel movement while they are "high." Only then does it become clear that the master psychoanalyst may have been right after all.

An example of a more complex insight gained through drug experience might best be illustrated by the frequent effect of drugs on the socially patterned feeling of inadequacy that has been a recurrent theme in youth culture. Time after time I have met students who, after a good drug trip, have realized that a basic component of their personalities was a deep-seated feeling of inadequacy. These young men were, for the most part, extremely bright and extremely socially successful in terms of their academic achievements, athletic abilities, and family backgrounds. And yet, because of the associations which their "highs" freed to their conscious minds, they realized that what had driven them to succeed—in sports, in schoolwork, in dating, and even in the one-upmanship of casual conversation—was a feeling of inadequately measuring up to what they thought they were supposed to be (what society wanted them to be).

Although these young men, by external appearance, had been achieving social success, they had all the while been moving toward psychological failure. For what they had been achieving was not a reflection of their own goals; they did not themselves choose the endeavors in which they excelled, and they never really enjoyed achieving excellence. They were living, to use Fromm's expression, for everything but themselves.

After their "high" self-probing, they were able to discern more clearly what their own aims were, and in what endeavors excellence for them was worth achieving. There is no single response to newly found insight. In fact, the responses are often opposite in different people. For some, self-awareness means quitting playing a musical instrument which their parents had pushed them into practicing. But for others it may mean resuming study of a musical instrument which they had discontinued because high-school friends had laughed at it. For some it means picking up a sport which they failed to begin because they feared they wouldn't do well. But for others it may mean leaving a sport in which they had engaged compulsively in order to gain social popularity. For some, insight into themselves might prompt them to study more because they realized that they had purposefully not done as well as they could in order to get back at their parents. And yet, for others, similar insight might cause them to study less because they recognized they would rather concentrate on their own reading or on working with people.

Whatever the specific case, the young person is just that much less a product of adult industrial society, and just that much more an individual who feels he is aware of his unique needs and abilities. This is one kind of achievement in the form of psychological self-understanding for which many members of this generation are striving. It receives no social recognition, and the psychedelic means which aided it are still categorically criticized.

What happens with marijuana is that a person's underlying psychological problems, which are normally ignored because of peripheral yet seemingly more pressing considerations, are finally dealt with. As can be seen from Commissioner Giordano's interpretation, however, adults do not agree that drug experience can be beneficial.

Giordano writes that marijuana is psychosis-producing. In other words, he thinks that marijuana raises a person's personal problems to such a level of power that the individual is incapable of dealing with them. The commissioner mentions only one other possible effect of drugs. He writes: "At best, drugs provide only mechanisms to escape from problems." In other words, he also acknowledges the possible effect of drugs in suppressing one's problems so that one does not have to deal with them consciously.

From my experience in youth culture I would say that the commissioner has mentioned only the two most extreme possible reactions to drugs. If one were to represent reactions to drug use by a bell-shaped curve in a graph, the two reactions to drugs which Giordano recognizes would be the two statistically small groups at each end of the curve. I would say that there is a great majority of reactions to drugs which Giordano does not even mention. The reactions to drugs which make up the big middle bulge of the bell-shaped curve are not considered at all. Probably Mr. Giordano does not think they exist, because he does not find them in hospitals or clinics. But whether or not he has seen them, they do exist.

Now what kind of reactions constitute the large percentage which the commissioner never sees? If one extreme is the violent expression of aspects of personality and the other extreme is the complete suppression of those aspects, the other reactions to marijuana would fall between those extremes. For a great number of marijuana-users, *their normally suppressed personal problems are raised to the conscious mind*. Their normal mental framework, in which their problems were ignored and allowed to reappear in disguised form, was indeed "distorted" by drug use, as critics always say. But if we accept the dictionary's definition of distort as to "change the usual shape or appearance of," we must admit that this distortion might just as well be beneficial as detrimental to the individual's self-awareness.

The point I am making is that it is the vast majority of drug-users, whom Mr. Giordano does not see, who reap whatever benefits there are from drugs and who perpetuate what I referred to as the "drug ideology."

What is most tragic is not that Mr. Giordano will never see this, but that his and adult society's blindness about marijuana is causing many young people in turn to act blindly. Some young people discovered that they were right about marijuana and society was wrong. So they foolishly concluded that drugs could be used freely—as if they had found that a sunlamp did not cause skin cancer and so decide to sleep under it all night.

These young men smoke marijuana as if it were tobacco (which, according to statistics, *is* cancer-producing) and think that anything which makes them feel momentarily good is expanding their consciousness. They ingest anything that induces a high. They inhale fumes from any substance that affects their senses. They make a long-term diet out of artificial chemical compounds which give them a lift, no matter how costly that lift is.

I find it necessary to be critical about drug use on a number of grounds. First of all, too many drug-users forget that drugs are physically injurious to the body. This is not denying that drugs offer a potential short-term psychic benefit. But that benefit is gained at a price. Drugs cost in physical well-being and self-reliance what psychotherapy costs in money. Anything that must support men in their search for themselves costs in one way or another. It is a question whether the benefits outweigh the sacrifices.

Evidently many people think that urban living and its opportunities outweigh the deleterious physical effect of polluted urban air. So do many drug-users feel that what is gained from drug use outweighs the toll it takes physically. But too many forget that drugs do require a sacrifice. My opinion about long-term drug use, even long-term marijuana use, is that individuals are no longer weighing benefits against losses. They are using drugs as a permanent support, like the man who never leaves his psychotherapist. Whether it is destroyed lungs and constricted blood vessels from marijuana, or brain and possibly chromosome irregularities from LSD, or general physical inactivity from any drugs at all, drugs take their toll. And drugs do not give prolonged and continued psychic benefits which counterbalance this sacrifice.

The individual who uses drugs for a long period of time, and extensively, has lost. He is no longer looking for whatever possible psychic benefits of drug use there might be for him. He is forgetting that at best drugs are *means* for change, for he is making them an end in life. Drugs then are indeed what adult society calls them—a crutch. For young people, especially non-artists, I cannot accept as psychically or physically healthy the extensive, prolonged use of any drugs.

Too many drug-users in this generation, after finding psychic involvement and physical pleasure through drugs, fail to realize that drugs are not the only or the best way to achieve that involvement or pleasure. Rather drugs are a reminder of what a citizen of mass society can too easily be cut off from; they are a reminder that the real ways to those goals have been obscured. Running through rain in the forest, plunging into a fresh stream after work in the fields, enjoying love-making without guilt or anxiety, concentrating on a creative endeavor from beginning to end, listening or dancing with total participation to music—there are many paths to psychic involvement and physical pleasure. Drugs are but one way, and a poor one at that. *Despite the potential value of the drug experience, after a certain point it detracts from one's over-all strength and creativity rather than rejuvenating them.* Drugs are a good reminder of the kind of experience that mass society tends to overlook, but they are a poor substitute for it.

Furthermore, I must disagree with those who blindly conclude that, because marijuana is misunderstood by adults, LSD is also. Generally speaking, as the psychic effect of a drug increases, so do its deleterious physical effects. LSD more than any other drug is suspect: (1) it was made in a laboratory; (2) it has had no long history in a traditional culture; and (3) it causes experience which is not in any way naturally attainable.* Even if it enables an individual to attain some higher state, it destroys the individual's ability to know *how* he attained it. The LSD experience is analogous to a psychotherapist's telling his patient at his first visit exactly what is wrong with him and what he should do about it. The patient, like the acidhead, wouldn't know what to do with his knowledge. It would probably create further confusion rather than greater clarity, because the "answers" were given right off the bat. Neither the patient nor the acidhead knows *how* to get to the conclusions he has been given.

For the acidhead, continuity is lost. A young man who has completed the process of alienation is supremely conscious of the changes he has undergone. He knows *how* he got to where he is, and it is the "how" which is all-important. But it is, in my opinion, impossible for acid to cause equivalent character development, because the acid experience involves thoughts and perceptions that obscure the "how." *How could anyone think that ingested chemicals, much more unnatural than the interpersonal situation of psychotherapy, could bring about the same quality of personal change that is attainable by either psychotherapy or personal effort?* What is valuable is not experience in itself, but the ever-increasing capacity to gain insight from experience. To settle for experience alone is to sacrifice the human capacity to gain insight from it.

Adolescent alienation is similar to adolescent infatuation. Both are valuable because they are signs of psychological growth, of becoming aware of new possibilities for living. Alienation can culminate in greater self-awareness, just as infatuation can culminate in love. But everyone has seen the couple, immature and psychologically unprepared for deeply

---

* These three characteristics of LSD constitute an indictment of it that is hard for drug-users to overlook. Conversely, they constitute a defense for marijuana. (1) Made in a laboratory, LSD, unlike marijuana, is not a natural product. Marijuana is unique among the hallucinogens in that it is the only natural product without nitrogen that affects the central nervous system. Known chemically as tetrahydrocannabinol, pot contains only oxygen, hydrogen, and carbon. The logic that concludes that marijuana is unique among the hallucinogens is grounded in chemistry as well as in psychology. (2) LSD and other laboratory compounds have had no long-term use in earlier cultures. Marijuana, hashish, peyote, and other traditional hallucinogens have been used for centuries in various Asian and American Indian cultures. No injurious effects on users have been demonstrated. No such reassuring history stands behind LSD, Methedrine, Dexedrine, Benzedrine, DMT, etc. (3) Many of the effects of pot can be achieved (and in a more harmonious way) by various disciplines of eating, exercising, and/or meditating. The effects of LSD cannot be. In this sense, LSD could be called *absolutely* distorting.

committeed love, who attempt to convince themselves of their non-existent maturity by compulsively becoming sexually intimate. Their inability to achieve love causes them to settle for sex. And although sex is also part of mature love, without love it becomes an empty and mechanical ritual.

After deep introspection and constant observation, I personally have come to the conclusion that the prolonged use of drugs is analogous to this kind of sex. *Just as mechanical sex is the result of infatuation that failed to become love, so is the prolonged need for chemical experience the result of alienation that failed to become deeper self-awareness.* Smoking marijuana experimentally for a short period of time, or even using other nonlaboratory psychedelics, can be a valid part of the process of completing alienation. But the extended use of drugs can mean quitting rather than completing that process. Most clearly of all, the acidhead is quitting if he turns to a product of the very technology which caused his alienation, in order to make that alienation palatable. And when, through drugs, one becomes satistfied with alienation, it is no longer alienation but despair.

Give a Damn

If you'd take the train with me
Uptown through the misery
Of ghetto streets in morning light
They're always night
Take a window seat
Put down your *Times*
You can read between the lines
Just meet the faces
That you meet beyond the window's pane
And it might begin to teach you
How to Give a Damn
About your fellow man.

—Spanky and Our Gang

Clearly I disagree with those who say that no criticisms can be made of drug use. But the criticisms I make, the ones that I think are valid, are not those that adult society makes. I think this is because *my criticisms are rooted in a psychological concern for the drug-user himself, whereas adults' concerns seem to be more for the preservation of social order and conformity.**

The psychedelic experience is decidedly un-Western: the West is modern, psychedelics are ancient; the industrialized West is characterized by detached, fragmented lives, a high is intensely involving and unifying; Western society is geared in terms of productivity and external accomplishment, drugs make one more reflective and concerned about sensation and feeling.

---

* In police and narcotics squads this is most clearly evidenced. The law-enforcement agencies are often more concerned with enhancing their own prestige than with aiding drug-users to find a better way of life. This can be seen from numerous cases of unwarranted police actions.[1]

Many drug-users maintain that not only is the drug experience negative to the West, but it is in many ways positive to the East. The experience is Oriental in that it is "synthetic, totalizing, integrative, . . . nondiscursive, subjective, spiritually individualistic,"[2]—all terms generally used to describe the type of experience valued in Oriental philosophies.* A drug trip, they say, not only completely destroys one's native cultural patterns of thought but actually simulates the meditative cosmic consciousness that is the goal of Oriental modes of thought.

The most accurate statement, however, which can objectively be made is that the drug experience is nonmodern or uncultural. It is not specifically Oriental. What can undeniably be concluded is that the drug experience is truly out of place in modern mass society, for it weakens the aspects of personality which are socially patterned and reinforces those which are basically human. It takes the user out of his modern culture, for it makes him leave behind his culturally patterned priorities. That a young man is a Methodist, not a Baptist; American, not Mexican; rich, not poor; part of a technological culture, not a traditional one; a resident of the twentieth century, not the nineteenth: these cultural characteristics seem to have much less relevance to what a person is feeling when he is high. The drug-user feels not like a product of a particular society and historical period, but rather like an individual being who by chance finds himself at a particular point in space and time. (I heard one student say that being high was the antithesis of watching television; he knew that, looking at *Bonanza* or Johnny Carson, his experience was identical to that of millions of other viewers across the nation. No matter who they were, they were all feeling the same thing, but when he was high, it was his experience and his alone.)

Drug-users view the psychedelic experience as the ammunition for their revolution against the "cool," detached, deferred-benefits personality and the mass society that cultivates it. They find what they feel is another way of life, alien to modern Western culture and comparable to feelings in simpler cultures. They experience a style of living that is unified, not divided; involved, not detached; deeply emotional, not logically analytical. Their actions for once feel spontaneous, not contrived.

I would stress again the point I made in the previous chapter: when this psychic wholeness, this depth and unity of feeling, is experienced, it does *not* mean that drugs themselves are the answer. It means only that drugs have opened one's eyes to the essential question of cultural

---

* Cf. D. T. Suzuki's lectures in *Zen Buddhism and Psychoanalysis* for a lucid description of the East-West contrast.

influence—of how mass society limits one's self-awareness and detracts from the wholeness and spontaneity of one's life.

Drug-users experience an individual wholeness, the idea of which they had thought to be inconceivably utopian. As members of the psychologically oriented generation, they have often read extensively in psychological literature. They do not fail to notice that many writers consider wholeness and spontaniety the goals of psychoanalysis and the mark of a healthy personality.[3] It is this state of being which they feel they attain while using drugs. By merely making drug-users aware that they have been experiencing life incompletely, drug experience orients them toward a further investigation of their own minds and awakens in them a concern for psychological development—a concern that is certainly not encouraged in any other way in mass society. They are led away from the type of behavior and personality which modern technological society values and are consequently impelled toward character ideals foreign to mass society.

Drugs have fed the generation gap, and anything that widens the gap is feared by adult society. Not only are drugs such as pot, hashish, and LSD made illegal, but the mass media have continuously put out a barrage of one-sided sensational articles and movies on the drug question. The young men who comprehend the disparity between media analysis and the experience of their own youth culture are further alienated from their parents' society and find themselves, for yet another reason, turning away from the society that was theirs by birth. Not only is the manhood of adult society unacceptable to them, but the type of manhood they are looking for is condemned.

Adult society, of course, is only trying to protect and perpetuate itself. For, as I have said, adults seem to care about social conformity, not individual psychology. Older people think they fear the *psychological* consequences of drugs, for they fear that anything which might possibly lead to behavior which is not socially patterned is dangerous and should be forbidden. But young people know adult society's fear is really *cultural*. Adults tend to see behavior that is not socially patterned as automatically wrong or psychologically ill. They condemn it by calling it "antisocial." But young people, as they look at history, cannot fail to see that entire societies have themselves been antisocial. Perhaps in other times the socially patterned behavior was authoritarian and militaristic, while today it is detached and mechanized. Both are "normal" within their own respective societies, but neither are in the best interest of human beings.

Young people see adult society's fear of drugs as a primarily cultural fear because *it is a culture's attempt to exclude experiences which it has not patterned*. But adults still think their criticisms are psychological because they do not accept that behavior which does not conform to the culture might be more in the individual's interest than what he was patterned to do.

A friend of mine never danced. He figured out all sorts of elaborate reasons as to why dancing was repulsive—that other kids did it just to try to be sexy but really they looked stupid, that dancing was an expression of frustration, and so on. Otherwise this friend was a very physical person, athletically, sexually, and in his general movements. One would have guessed that he more than anyone would have liked to dance. So this guy smoked pot. He found himself moving, and enjoying moving. He found it fascinating to do with his body just what the music was doing. He said he was so tuned in to the music that he felt like a transistor in the stereo amplifier. The first time he danced, he danced for four hours. And thereafter, although he didn't always smoke pot before he went to dances, he found himself being thrilled by dancing. Dancing in itself made him high.

For this young man the experience was a breakthrough. It will not increase his income, nor will it raise his social prestige. It will only make his life fuller, more expressive, more enjoyable. His negative attitude toward dancing was so deeply ingrained in him that its loss caused intensive self-questioning. He realized that he had sacrificed many potentially exhilarating experiences because he had placed too much importance on things that did not really matter to him.

This is merely one example of how drugs provided a nonmodern experience for a young man who had been so hammered by the pressures of mass society that he had forgotten many of the simplest pleasures of being human.

It is necessary to be future-oriented in modern society, but the drug experience makes one much more present-oriented. This is not *culturally* valuable, I suppose. But for many young people geared completely to the future by their parents and their education, this new experience can be *psychologically* very valuable. The effects of drugs are once again "antisocial," but they are often at the same time "pro-individual."

It seems to me that adult society's fear of drugs represents the essence of the generation gap. Cultural isolation—political, intellectual, and psychological—is breaking down. Drug use among college students accelerates this process. It decreases the power of one's native culture's personality pattern. It makes the modern youth even more a floater than he already is, amid opposing character ideals. *Drugs do exactly what youth wants and exactly what adults do not want*: they liberate the user from some of the pressure for cultural conformity and they cause the absoluteness of cultural values and character ideals to appear even more inadequate than it did before.

Because most adults have not recognized many of these generational differences in the drug controversy, they still think they have said the final word when they call drug experience "an escape from reality." But alienated young people know that what is being referred to is *cultural* reality, and cultures are being transformed. For the college student in modern countries, cultural reality no longer forms the borders of his life but constitutes a starting point from which to go and find his own reality.

Every time I hear the phrase "an escape from reality" I am reminded of an experience a friend of mine named Stu had with an acidhead and a banker. Stu was sitting by the swimming pool of the hotel in which he was staying in upper Manhattan when a man wearing a sweatshirt with a New York college name on it sat down near him. He asked Stu, the only sympathetic soul he could find, if he could tell that he was tripping. My friend didn't use drugs, and he told the acidhead that he couldn't tell the difference. The guy who was tripping said he just wanted to talk for a minute, so they both went to his room.

Stu said that this guy pulled back the curtains of his tenth-floor window and just stared out for a moment. From the plush hotel room they could see into the windows of an eight-story tenement across the street. The building was no different from the hundreds that lined the streets in this area of Manhattan. The luxurious hotels were like oases of wealth, from which trickled little streams of money into bars and restaurants amid a desert of old, decrepit buildings.

"I sat here for two hours, looking out the window," the tripper told Stu. "I got so depressed that I had to go up to the pool on the roof and look at the sky. I had been looking at that tenement. The fire escapes seemed to be hanging like black vines around the building, holding it together like string holds together a cardboard box. People hung out of their windows, trying to escape from the glaring light bulbs which hung in the middle of their bare rooms. Kids were playing with a ragged tennis ball, bouncing it across the street through the heavy traffic."

He finally turned away from the window and looked at my friend while he spoke. "And then I thought of where I grew up. It was right next to a park. My yard was about the size of that whole building—that building which cages a few hundred human being just like me. If I had stayed in this room with beige furniture, thick green rugs, and gold-framed paintings for one more second, I would have gone crazy."

Stu told me that he was stunned by the intensity of this man's feelings. The acidhead was feeling so deeply the guilt of affluence and the pain of poverty that my friend was still thinking of him a few hours later when he went to the hotel restaurant for dinner. He was waiting, next to a very respectable man in a gray suit, for the waiter to show him to a table. Not wanting to have to wait any longer than necessary, he suggested to the middle-aged man that they eat together.

After they started talking, Stu found out that the man thought he had been given a bad deal by the room clerk. "After paying twenty-five dollars for a room, you'd think this place'd give me something decent. But no!" he complained to Stu. "They stuck me in a room facing that obscene building across the street, with the traffic blaring right under my window. I had to go back down and tell the fellow at the desk that I'd change the bank's hotel affiliations unless he got me a room farther up, facing the terrace."

It turned out that my friend's dinner companion was a banker who, because of extra work, couldn't return to his affluent Connecticut suburb that day and so had to stay in the city. Glad to have a young man right there in front of him to whom he could lecture (his own son was at prep school, and even when he was back from school, he wasn't around much), he began to talk about how the younger generation irked him. As they were leaving the restaurant, Stu told me, he finally hit on the subject of drugs.

"Drugs are escapes," he told Stu. "They are for cowards who couldn't face up to the cold, hard realities of life. Drug-users escape into a world of funny colors because they just couldn't take reality. I'm proud to say," he concluded with an air of finality, "that I've never taken any of that stuff and never want to. Escapes are just for people who can't make it."

And with "Good luck, son!" he was off, back up to his own beige and green room with gold-framed paintings. There he was: the man who stays in the finest hotels whenever he travels; the man who takes the walnut-paneled elevator but never sees the dingy gray stairway that the janitors and maids use; the man who could look at a green terrace, but not at a gray tenement. There he was in all his glory: the man who faces the realities of life.

Stu said that he walked out of the hotel and, for the first time, took a long, hard look himself at the tenement across the street. He wasn't tripping. He never planned to. *But what he saw was what the guy on acid saw.* The kids were chasing their tennis ball under a beer truck parked outside a dimly lit bar. The bare light bulbs in the rooms glared. The people still hung out of the windows, their old undershirts contrasting with the sooty walls of the tenement.

Stu didn't have to explain why he told me about this experience. His point was clear. Exactly who couldn't face reality? he had wondered. Was reality the lives of thousands of people in bare tenement rooms? Or was it the lives of people like the banker? *Wasn't the truest reality the acidhead's profound awareness of all those lives and the social paradox which they defined?*

I realized that this is what alienation is all about. The banker Stu was supposed to respect, he pitied. And the acidhead he was supposed to pity, he respected. His attitude toward all adults like the banker was the same: it was they who could not face reality.

Adults like the banker have the old, fragmented awareness. They earned their money, by God! No stupid room clerk is going to make them see life the way other people—especially poor black people— see it. As part of their success, they sacrificed their ability to see anything beyond their own narrow circumstances. These adults have so completely identified themselves with comfortable homes, pleasant lawns, and orderly, businesslike people, that when anything—a riot, a demonstration, a tenement, a hippie—pushes its way into their mechanical reality, *they have to push it quickly out of their minds.*

The society of these adults could not be this generation's future, for a generation with the young awareness does not adopt the way of life of the old awareness. The young have accepted no defintion of themselves, no fixed identity. They may feel more involved with elements of society antithetical to their own background than with those elements which typify it.

The young awareness, formed by modern technology, is all-inclusive, not fragmented. Young people cannot return to their Connecticut suburbs and go to church and hear "Blessed are the poor . . ." when they have not even looked at the poor. They cannot respect a rich man with all the status symbols, when he has sacrificed his ability to feel how other people feel.

What has happened is that the generation with the young awareness has realized that its awareness does not fit. Its members have realized that they do not want to become their society's kind of man. And so they have begun to look elsewhere.

The Neon Gods

People aren't listening to the voices of their own lives,
say Simon and Garfunkel, but to the blaring voice of
mass society. American society worships not the God
that made the world but "the neon gods"
of its own creation.

The music of youth culture is also an indication that the postwar generation is trying to find alternatives to mass-society values. Popular rock music in the 1960s has been transformed by psychedelic, soul, and Indian music. These three sources of new music have much in common. They have all aroused in this generation what McLuhan would call "all-inclusive participation." They have in common their opposition to some aspect, either technical or emotional, of the old moon-spoon-June lyrics and the maudlin melodies of the Frankie Avalon, Paul Anka, Fabian days.

But similarities between the sources of new music are superficial. I want to look at each of their origins closely because I think the real common bond between psychedelic, soul, and Indian music reveals something important about young people today.

Some young people might ask why I am not emphasizing protest music, for it is indeed true that there was an immense change in the mood of America's youth between the generation that listened to Elvis Presley's inane lyrics in college and the one that tuned into the intensely critical lyrics of the protest singers. But the straight protest song has had its day. It angrily called a verdict of "Guilty!" for the old awareness, but in itself it was only a premonition of the kind of music that the young awareness would create.

Psychedelic. Today's radios blare forth in both content and form the message from psychedelia. This powerful clarion of the alienated and hippie philosophies affects not only youth culture but mass society itself. Young and old alike must listen, for it is part of the language of radio.

Acid rock makes people move, as they did in the last time of peaceful prosperity, the 1920s. Involvement with psychedelic music is not detached or physically limited, but a submersion in unstructured physical activity. It is not a passively social endeavor but a very active physical commitment—not to another person, perhaps, but to oneself. Music has evolved, become more electronic, and gained an elemental, pounding beat. It has grown in primitiveness, for it demands the whole person.

This chance to be deeply involved appeals to the young; it is a chance to escape from detached lives. They want something like psychedelic music and psychedelic drugs, in which they can involve themselves completely. When psychedelia finally invaded the record market, its popularity grew at an amazing rate.

After becoming submerged in academic work for a semester, I was shown that I was already beginning to lose touch with what was happening. I was walking in the record department of a big Boston store during the spring of 1967 when I heard a girl of about twelve ask a very elderly saleslady where the psychedelic-record section was. I expected the gray-haired figure to turn around and reply. "Why, dear, we only have classical and popular." Not quite. The saleswoman pointed to the next counter, and as I followed the young girl to the section marked PSYCHEDELIC, I realized that I had better write fast. I wasn't as young as I thought any more. For today, of course, no member of the young teen set would be so naïve as to suppose that there wasn't a section specifically marked PSYCHEDELIC.

Even more clearly than the music itself, the lyrics of psychedelic songs demonstrate the young's alienation. The lyrics most critical of adult society seem the most popular; the messages that stress the major themes of alienation fill the songs that are on the hit charts. The Beatles' *Sergeant Pepper* album, for example, is a three-pronged attack on adult society, attacking its emotional isolation, criticizing the futility of the social rat-race, and offering a constant psychedelic "turn on" massage. Here on one record are the major themes of youth's rebellion, explained loudly by the world's top rock group. *Sergeant Pepper*, carrying the messages of alienation, has made its way into over a million homes. What made *Sergeant Pepper* such a success? It was the intensely critical message, which hit a sympathetic chord in the dissonant lives of this generation. Even though radio stations in many rural areas and some Midwestern cities exclude the most critical songs, the message gets through to virtually everyone.

Psychedelic music has the same underlying message that the drug experience does: "There is another, fuller kind of feeling, a deeper kind of awareness, that your parents and your schoolteachers don't tell you about." It is, once again, trying to offer other ideals of manhood.

Soul. Just as young people's criticism of the Western way of life is illustrated by their cult of the Orient, their disaffection from the affluent way of life is illustrated by their cult of poverty. The reflection of the former is in the psychedelic-Indian music, the reflection of the latter in soul music.

Why do alienated affluent kids from Portland suburbs or the New York or Chicago suburbs go down to the hippie spots in their respective cities with old clothes and bare feet? Why has so much of the music booming from campus stereos originated in the ghetto or in the impoverished rural areas? Why have blacks—Otis Redding, James Brown, Aretha Franklin, Jimi Hendrix—so completely been accepted by the predominantly white college generation? Why do young white singers so often search for that same kind of "soul"?

It is because many in this college generation feel that there *is* no soul in affluent America. They feel a spontaneity, a depth of feeling, a vibrancy in soul that was completely absent in the whitewashed music that the record companies fed young people during the 1950s. Call soul passionate, call it primitive, call it what you will. But whatever the vital element in it is, it is certainly something that could not originate in white, businesslike, middle-class society. Both psychedelic and soul music had to come from somewhere else. Soul especially had to come from somewhere that had not been penetrated by the mechanized, detached, "cool" way of life. It had to come from the part of society where the character ideals had not been molded by mass society. Soul, too, is challenging the accepted ideals of manhood.

Indian. The origins of psychedelic and soul music are next door compared with the origin of Indian music. When the album sales of Indian sitar-players soared, when psychedelic groups began playing raga-like pieces, and when even radio stations began featuring full-length ragas, the music pundits were at a loss. Why all of a sudden did a traditionally very ethnocentric group—American teen-agers—tune in to music from halfway around the world?

It was because the college generation, facing a manhood it could not accept, was looking elsewhere for character ideals. In the same way, the popularity of lower-class, black "soul" was witness to the young's disenchantment with the kind of affluence they saw around them; the popularity of psychedelia signified their rejection of adult society's character ideals. Indian music, which moved their minds as well as their bodies, was only an indicator of the general receptivity of alienated young people to Oriental philosophies and religions. Eastern thought itself has come to play a leading role in youth culture because it offers the most coherent, complete alternative character ideals to mass society's.

For the alienated young people who turned away from Western ideals because they seemed unfulfilling and misdirected, the most logical step is to turn to the apparent cultural antithesis. Coming from the technological, they wanted the traditional; coming from the West, they wanted the East. The ancient Oriental philosophies are one of the most noticeable ways that American youth culture has been attracted to other cultural ideals. The needs of the young that went unanswered in their own society—unity of self, relatedness to the world, historical continuity—are all found to be basic motifs of Oriental thought. The confusing contradictions in this generation's mass society—between what the culture values and what it makes the individual feel he lacks, between religious dogma and social practice, between external appearance and inner reality—are resolved by attaining a unifying, natural, potentially harmonious way of life in the context of Oriental philosophy.

It was long ago pointed out by Jung that

> while we are turning upside down the material world of the East with our *technical proficiency*, the East with its *psychic proficiency* is throwing our spiritual world into confusion. We have never hit upon the thought that while we are overpowering the Orient from without, it may be fastening its hold on us from within. [Italics mine.][1]

This is not a devious or subversive infiltration by the East, as Jung's wording might make us think, but a very natural occurrence.

A vacuum-packed jar sucks in air when the lid is removed. In our shrunken world, the lids have been removed from all cultures—East and West, traditional and modern. If something is strikingly missing in one culture, it will attract that element from another culture which has it. The young have been given plenty of "technical proficiency"; they are looking for "psychic proficiency." As the group the Association sings in their song "Enter the Young," young people want to "learn not only to think but to care."

The two intellectual avenues by which the alienated young discovered Oriental thought were psychology and religion. This is not surprising, because they are the only two fields that appear to be involved directly with character ideals.* They alone are trying meaningfully to answer the questions: What should men strive to be? On what set of character ideals should men base their society?

What members of the postwar generation found missing in their culture's ideals of manhood, they searched for elsewhere. Their psychological orientation made a turn to the Orient probable. Young people who pursue psychoanalytic thought with personal involvement invariably find that the Oriental tradition has been much more cognizant of man's unconscious and the nature of his behavior than have the Western religions (which essentially had no inkling of these ideas until Freud, and are still denying those ideas).

Although the means are of course different, the aim of both psychoanalysis and Zen Buddhism (the most frequently "adopted" Oriental mode of thought) is the same. It is to be conscious of the unconscious, to become aware of the motivations that have been repressed and influence the individual unknowingly. Reinforcing the young person engaged in the quest to know his *self* rather than the misleading social reflection of it, psychoanalysis and Oriental philosophy show that awareness of the self, of one's relationship to the world, leads to actions serving the interest of the whole self rather than merely feeding the frustrations of self-alienation.

To understand further the appeal of the Orient, we must also look at religion—at the young's reasons for rejecting the modern version of the Judaeo-Christian concept of the nature of man. Young people feel that the idea of the basic evilness of man, as propounded by the religions in which they grew up, is an inhibition to mature human development. The concept of man's basic evilness has served as a rationale for repression

* This is true, of course, only insofar as young men are concerned. Psychology, as far as many academicians are concerned, should be made a science without any involvement in ethics, values, and social issues. It is not this mechanistic concept of psychology but rather the humanistic concept with which this generation is involved so deeply. Nor does philosophy (with the exception of existentialism)[2] appear to be primarily involved with character ideals, for, as it is presented academically, it seems too removed from social change to be relevant to the search for manhood.

because it has conjured up a morality that kills self-awareness by convincing the individual that he must indeed repress his spontaneous emotions. Unlike the philosophies of the East, which state or imply that the mature, "totally" conscious being is at peace, loving, and basically "good," Western dogmas have caged their adherents in a web of guilt that strengthens rather than destroys their separateness from life.

The vestiges of this oppressive Protestant morality, against which some of the existential philosophers were also revolting, are causing young men to reject Western ethics (or, at least, the way they are practiced). It is that morality which caused a California college senior to write:

> Morality is the intellect's attempt to protect itself against the animal. . . . We Americans have always fought the animal (in man) by ignoring it. Our morality has been a blindfold to wear in the daytime and a sleeping pill to take at night. I've experimented at living without masks and pills and, no kidding, it's all right. We're pretty damn fine animals when we loosen up the cinch and remove the bit.[3]

This young man states quite bluntly the attitude implicit in all youth-hippie ideas: that if human beings are subjected to authoritarian morality which treats them as evil beings divided into animal baseness and God-like consciences, they will indeed become divided, and the two halves will fight each other; but that by knowing the self and thereby unifying one's character, they can replace the self-defeating behavior which is the manifestation of psychological disunity with a unified, harmonious personality. The "unrepressed" individual, these young men believe, is a compassionately loving individual, not the basically evil character depicted by the Protestant ethic. The hippie ethic is opposed to the Protestant ethic primarily because the two conceptions of human nature are opposed.

Not only is the concept of man different in the Eastern religions but the concept of God is different also. The Western religions have continued to speak of an authoritarian God in the heavens who is the ultimate authority whose will man must obey. He is, indeed, the "father in heaven." But this whole book is about young people who could not accept the authority of their fathers on earth, or the adult society which a father represented. It is not surprising at all that they found the traditional concept of God hard to accept.*

---

* There is a strictly psychoanalytic explanation for youth's disbelief in the traditional supernatural concept of God. This is expressed most concisely by Freud in his study *Leonardo da Vinci*: "Psychoanalysis, which has taught us the intimate connection

Actually to contrast "Western religions" with "Eastern religions" would be far too complex, but fortunately this is not necessary. What reveals most about this generation is what it selectively chooses to find in Oriental thought, not necessarily the total structure of the religions themselves. For example, most hippies are attracted readily to thought on meditation, but not on reincarnation. Similarly the young turned with special interest to the sect of Buddhism known as Zen because it, in contrast to other sects, "firmly opposed the idea that the Buddhahood is something to be sought *outside* oneself or in *another* world. *Every man has a Buddha-nature, and to realize it he need only look within. Self-understanding and self-reliance are the keynote of Zen.*"[4] (Italics mine.)

Young people emphasize the aspects of Oriental thought which have to do with human behavior, and leave alone most supernatural aspects. Approaching Oriental thought in this way, they gain a philosophy that provides a meaningful alternative to their Judaeo-Christian heritage and the concept of God and the character ideals to which it has given rise.

The "divine" which young people find in Oriental thought is more in accord with their experience than the concept of God they have heard about since childhood. Oriental "deity" is not an authoritarian, supernatural symbol of power but a natural state of harmony which man himself through meditation can attain. By unifying oneself and perfecting one's awareness, one may reach the ideal state of harmony (*satori*) in which one is at peace with oneself and with the world. As young people interpret it, Oriental thought outlines goals for human fulfillment without creating a mythical being out in space. It is a meaningful religion for a college generation for whom belief in the supernatural is impossible.

J. D. Salinger's stories later published in *Franny and Zooey* were precursors of the 1960s in that they described college students' deep involvement with mysticism and religions of the Orient. It is interesting that when Christianity is mentioned in these stories, it too becomes secularized. It centers around Jesus and his character, not God and his divinity.

Most young people interpret religious thought in such a way that its message pertains to character ideals. Their interest in Oriental thought is primarily based on its psychological implications. They are searching

---

between the father complex and belief in God, has shown us that the personal God is psychologically nothing but an exalted father, and daily demonstrates to us how youthful persons lose their religious beliefs as soon as the authority of the father breaks down." In addition to this partial explanation, one must also take account of important social changes that have undermined religious belief.

for, and they find, *ideals of manhood*—not of aggressiveness, competitiveness, and college-board scores, but of gentleness, compassion, and quiet wisdom. One is encouraged not to try to impress others with one's possessions or knowledge, but to become aware of the smallness of human life and the intricacy and beauty of the natural world. Oriental philosophy cautions man to be aware of the flow of life and not to place undue importance on external possessions or prestige, which disguise the inner man. Meditation is the attempt to leave the false self and to regain one's lost harmony in the natural universe. As Hermann Hesse's *Siddhartha* indicates, one's primary goal is within oneself and not within society.

For alienated young people who had to look within themselves to find the answers the mirror of mass society could not provide, Oriental thought reinforces their individuality and helps them find these answers. They find a set of character ideals that can be a vital, motivating force in life, not a peripheral once-a-week social obligation. The contrast of Oriental character ideals with Western religious values with which the young grew up is becoming unimportant. For today there is not a choice between two systems of belief, but rather a simple realization that there are no longer deep religious beliefs in mass society.

What society can say, "Turn the other cheek," while escalating the tonnage of bombs dropped on Vietnamese villages? Who can teach their children the commandment "You shall have no other gods" when the radio announcer's voice fills the home with "Yes, you can hold your head high as you drive *this* new car into the driveway"? Who can repeat with a sense of conviction the beautiful thought, "Love thy neighbor," when every city shows how callously suburbia has ignored the residents of the urban ghetto? Who can preach, "Blessed are the meek," to a generation that has been herded by an adult society into competitive dating, competitive athletics, and competitive scholarship so that its members can "make it to the top of the ladder" in a competitive world?

I personally believe that neither gentleness nor aggressiveness alone is the answer to the question of character ideals. *But how can adults say they believe one while living the other, day after day, and not realize that somehow the two are in conflict?*

Religion in American society has come to appear so hypocritical that young people feel they cannot help gaining something by turning to other-cultural religions. The God this generation saw in adult society was a shallow one. It was a God its parents had been given by their parents, who had been raised in nineteenth-century fundamentalism. But the God this generation's parents were given in their childhood didn't fit in post-World War II American society. Most parents could not reject the religious beliefs of their childhood, but still could manage to adapt their social behavior to the secular, consumption- and prestige-oriented culture of the 1950s and 1960s. This generation saw the ambivalence of the religious values of adult society built into its parents.

To young men who perceive only the apparent hypocrisy of their parents' religious beliefs and who fail to understand its historical cause, God in adult society appears to be nothing more than an abstraction of words and a symbol of social propriety, totally removed from the secular attitudes of those who "believe" in him. Society pays weekly tribute to him, but he lost meaning and vitality as a force in adults' lives. The God young people are looking for today is the diametric opposite of this. They search for an ultimate which is the state of self-awareness and inner harmony to give their lives meaning.

Because the young people who espouse Oriental character ideals are a highly vocal and visible segment of youth culture, individual academic effort is not required in order for a young man to become aware of the relevance of the Orient. Any contact with alienated, hippie culture will introduce him to the East quite quickly. Throughout the relatively new underground and hippie newspapers are sprinkled the words *karma* and *nirvana*, Vishnu and Buddha, Lao-tse and Chuang-tzu. The San Francisco *Oracle*, once probably the most widely read of the hippie publications, is a combination of psychedelicism and Orientalism. One of the most popular issues contained a dialogue among some of the hippies' would-be gurus: Timothy Leary, whose Oriental learnings are self-evident (witness his psychedelic manual based on the Tibetan Book of the Dead); poet Allen Ginsberg, whose writings clearly reflect the East, and whose poetry readings usually begin with Oriental chants; Gary Snyder, also a poet and Zen Buddhist monk; and Alan Watts, whose academic work has all been directed toward increasing the awareness in America of Oriental systems of thought. It is these men's concern for non-Western character ideals that to a great extent explains their common popularity. The same emphasis on the Orient is present in other hippie publications.

Extensive higher education has permitted other-cultural ideals to spread in youth culture. Past the point on a youth's bookshelf where Camus' and Sartre's novels or Beckett's and Genet's plays can be found, there are books of Buddhist and Taoist teachings. The interpretive works of Watts or D. T. Suzuki generally accompany the original Oriental writings. Like the existentialism of a few years earlier, these Oriental messages have an immediacy that makes the attraction to them much greater than if the philosophies were merely of academic interest.

The influence of the Orient should not be overestimated. For most young people, Oriental thought remains an incomplete influence. It is but one source of character ideals among many that reinforce the alienated members of the generation in their conviction that better ideals of manhood can be found.

The truth is that all other nonmodern cultures also have an attraction for the young. For example, another issue of the *Oracle* dealt with the story of the American Indian, once again making American character ideals the target for criticism. As I mentioned earlier, the young are interested in primitive cultures generally, as evidenced by the popularity of primitive art objects in Greenwich Village and Haight-Ashbury, the trend of the hippie movement toward communal living, and the growing number of young American wanderers who journey to the Mediterranean countries, the Middle East, and Asia.

Involvement with the ideals of cultures other than affluent America's was a necessary step for these young people, and it is a significant factor differentiating what is happening today from the much smaller beatnik element a decade ago. The beatniks could reject the social climate in their society, but they developed no real alternative set of values. So, after dropping out, they had no choice but to drop back in. With hippies, what had been negative dissent has come to be a positive movement. This change could not have occurred without the development of another set of character ideals—whether derived from the psychedelic, the psychological, the Oriental, or a combination of them all—in contradistinction to the unacceptable set of beliefs that adult society epitomizes.

Youth and Identity

The myth of Daedalus and Icarus has long been cited as the universal model for the conflict between generations. Daedalus and his son Icarus were imprisoned in a tower on the island of Crete. A master craftsman, Daedalus constructed wings out of wax and feathers with which he and his son could escape from their cell. He instructed Icarus before their escape to be careful not to fly too high because Apollo, the sun god, might become jealous of someone entering his domain and in his fury might melt the wax and cause the wings to be destroyed. But Icarus foolishly soared too high, lost contact with his father, and, with melted wings, plunged to his death.[1]

This is the mythical model of family psychology, of youthful irreverence and parental wisdom. But it is a myth only for a world in which generations come and go but where the world itself stays the same.

What is our prison today? Has technology freed us or has it merely put us in a new cell? What are our wings today? Do we liberate ourselves from a machine age by accepting the detached, "cool," non-involved personality of mass society, or by becoming open and passionate human beings? And how do we know our gods today? Why should young men fear flying too high when no one can be sure who the gods are—if, indeed, there are any at all?

The crucial issue in the myth of Daedalus and Icarus, and the issue of paramount importance throughout this book, is that of *authority* and *identity*. Daedalus was the authority, and above him was the authority of Apollo. Icarus rebelled against both authorities and met his fate. But, as I said, this myth is for a world that does not change, for in traditional society authority is clear, unchanging, absolute. It is unquestioned. And in this firm mold of social authority, individual identities are formed.

Today we need a new model for understanding a society which is being transformed by man's inventions. What is most evident about today's young people, who have grown up in mass society, is that they have realized that traditional authority is no longer clear, that it is constantly changing, and that it is by no means absolute. Whether they looked at the authority of the government concerning Vietnam, or at the authority of the school or the church or the family, they saw authority weakened because it did not know how to cope with the rapid social change going on around it.

Look first at the family itself, which is symptomatic of the changes in society as a whole. Once the mother quietly served and supported the father; they presented a strong and united front to their children. Through parental authority was funneled the social pressure of other institutional authority, just as through Daedalus the will of Apollo was made known. But today, as divorce statistics demonstrate unmistakably, fewer and fewer children face the same absolute parental authority. Parents today are separated for most of the week. They no longer work the shop, or the store, or the farm together. Each faces alone a different set of problems. The pressures of world on the father and the pressures of home on the mother have divided many parents, emotionally if not legally, and have left a divided and ambiguous authority. And yet, when their children begin to be introspective, when they start to show a bent for psychology, parents murmur together, "Why, when we were young, we weren't so self-analytical. What's wrong with Junior?"

Nothing. Nothing at all is wrong with Junior. He is simply living today, not yesterday, in a time when parents' advice is out of touch with the world that he encounters. He is living in a world where authority is naked. He is living in a world where the pope who forbids the use of the one discovery that can prevent disastrous overpopulation is not a pope but a man, a fallible man; where the president that says defend your country by killing Vietnamese is not a president but a man, a mistaken man.

If authority today provided an absolute sense of right and wrong that worked for this generation, there would have been no casting about for character ideals, no using drugs to gain manhood, no demonstrations on campuses, no searching in Oriental thought for meaningful religious belief. *Because if authority seems absolute, a young man thinks he knows the answers. He doesn't go out looking for them.* He sits back and accepts uncritically whatever social authority tells him. But when he sees that his parents and adult society are perplexed by a changing world, when he sees that too many of their attitudes are based on a world which no longer exists, he realizes that they do not know the answers. Whether the issue is racial equality, student power, sexual ethics, or Vietnam, this generation has had to disregard authority, because authority seemed so out of touch with what was happening.

Look also at what other sources of authority are doing to weaken parental authority. Fifty years ago, most young men began work at eighteen; there were no radios; many newspapers carried mostly local news; people were less mobile. When a father authoritatively stated his opinion about a matter, there was nothing his son could turn to for other answers. But today many young people go to college and even graduate school; radios, television, and movies are everywhere; newspapers must carry international news because everything affects America today; people move constantly, especially young people. By merely opening their eyes and ears, young people today can know the opinions of a dozen different authorities. If a son today wants to question his father's opinion on, say, a political matter, he can listen to Walter Cronkite on the news. And if he wants to question *him*, he can pick up a newsmagazine. And if he wants to question that, he can turn to his college texts on economics or history or government. And if he wants to question them, he can take a look at the books that the student down the hall reads—the books that are never assigned.

In other words, with the flood of information and the opportunities that modern countries provide, young people today may question authority much more readily. They see authority as something changeable, as something relative and questionable. In terms of the myth: young people are not at all sure that Daedalus has made the best wings. Why not secure the wings with plastic instead of wax? And they are not at all sure that there really is a god whose jealous wrath will destroy them.

Either the radical theologians are right and "God is dead," or, as the youth-culture lapel button says derisively: GOD IS ALIVE. HE JUST DOESN'T WANT TO GET INVOLVED.

Since social authority is no longer automatic and absolute, neither is identity. Authority is no longer a mold, but a set of forces which have to be selectively accepted and rejected, analyzed and counterbalanced, criticized and cross-examined. And so identity is not molded into a fixed form in adolescence, but remains open to change well into the years that once were called simply "adulthood." As Paul Revere and the Raiders sing, "I've been thinking twenty-two years all about it; the closer I get to the truth, the more I doubt it."

In his comprehensive book *The Technological Society,* Jacques Ellul analyzes the ways in which man's inventions have changed the economy, the state, and man himself. Speaking of education in the technological society, Ellul says that "children are educated to become precisely what society expects of them." He concludes that, when modern young people are fully educated, any sort of social organization or behavior is possible, because what has been demanded of the young identity is a "never-ending process of adaptation."[2]

As student revolts in America, France, Germany, and Eastern Europe demonstrate, all children have not become "precisely what society expects of them." What has occurred is that *society certainly did demand constant adaptation, but it could not control that adaptation.* Because of the young's historical unrelatedness and their involvement with character ideals of other cultures, no single modern society could limit its young people's adaptation to that culture alone. For in the modern world a young man's native culture is not his destination, but the starting point on a journey to find a new identity.

This is one reason why the term "character ideals" has been used in this book, and not Freud's term "ego ideals." When Freud formulated his psychoanalytic concepts, he could assume that the ideals of manhood in upper-class Viennese society were absolute principles; that the neuroses and dreams of his patients reflected *the* basic psychology of human beings. Because of the diffusion of authority and the accelerated rate of social change that have occurred since Freud's Vienna, no such assumptions may be made today. The modern young man does not have one father behind whom stand united the ideals of church, state, academia, youth culture, and society. On the contrary, he has many fathers, many sets of ego ideals, many contradictory versions of what adulthood should mean. Since authority in a rapidly changing mass society appears more relative and questionable than in a traditional society, identity remains in flux.

This generation alone has grown up in the global village. People whom the older generations called "foreigners" are this generation's neighbors.* By the media, by his long education, by his need to question authority, indeed by his total experience, a young man today is forced to become aware of what other generations could ignore. And the fact that seems self-evident but which is nevertheless overlooked by adults is that *what a young man is aware of, his identity must be consonant with*.

Earlier generations were aware of a very limited cultural world that supported a very fixed hierarchy of authority. Consequently almost every young man developed a culturally limited and quite permanent identity. The less conflict there was seen in authority, the less conflict existed visibly in identity. Authority had not been fragmented and weakened by accelerating social change, so neither were young men's identities fragmented and weakened. They kept the traditionally rigid concept of self that characterized most members of slowly changing societies.

But for the postwar generation things *are* changing rapidly, there *is* conflict and fragmentation in authority, and identity *does* remain open and flexible well into "adulthood." In a previous chapter I approached this constantly changing identity in terms of three steps: (1) realizing the meaninglessness of the social definition of one's identity; (2) searching in one's alienation for new ideals and values; and (3) finding a self-determined definition of oneself. The postwar generation of college students contains many young people in whose life histories this process occurs not once but over and over again.

How does a son of a Midwestern real-estate dealer come to be reading Oriental philosophy in a fishing village in Hawaii? How does the son of a New York financier come to be risking jail by resisting the draft? How does a New Jersey high-school student, after four years of honor grades, come to be dropping acid with dropouts in Los Angeles? How does a Chicago lawyer's son come to be living in a hippie commune in northern Maine? How do any of today's young people come to be so far removed from the values of adult society without experiencing

---

* The word "foreigner" has never entered youth culture. It was so out of place in young people's experience that the word died. I have never heard anyone in the postwar generation use the word, despite the fact that their parent's generation are quite at home with it.

repeated, intense periods of change, without looking repeatedly for new selves because their old selves are no longer consonant with their growing awareness?

The college generation is filled with young people who began adolescence believing in God but ended adolescence in agnosticism; who began, as children ought, thinking that drugs were totally bad, but realized later that they often had a purpose; who in high school thought the United States was the champion of the world, only to realize in college that their country was often just the opposite; who in just about every sphere of life—psychology, politics, religion—had to adapt themselves to the diametric opposite of their childhood beliefs. It is quite understandable that their identities never became rigidly set, for they have had to change their beliefs more radically during their youth than any generation before them.

Robert Lifton, who over the years has had quite intimate contact with many Japanese and Chinese young people, has found striking examples of this identity in flux. He has written about the life history of one young man who before the age of thirty had been: a proper son of an upper-class Chinese family, a student rebelling against traditional culture, and ardent Marxist active in the Communist movement; then, because of participation in a thought-reform program which achieved the opposite of its goal, an "anti-Communist" writer; a convert to Protestantism—and still, at the age of thirty, seemed on the verge of more changes.[3]

This changeable identity characterizes youth in America and Europe in even greater numbers. Lifton explains this in terms of *"historical dislocation,* a break in the sense of connection which men have felt with past symbols—symbols revolving around family, ideology, state, and the life cycle in general."[4] Lifton feels that what has disappeared are "clearly defined criteria of what is right and wrong transmitted within a particular culture by parents to their children."[5] He concludes that the life cycle itself no longer fits the old pattern because the transitions which mark the cycle—"the *rites de passage* surrounding birth, entry into adulthood, marriage, and death"—seem insufficient, even meaningless. And because of the shallowness of these rites, man today "often seeks to improvise new ones with whatever contemporary materials he has available, including . . . drugs."[6]

Lifton says that modern life is creating a new kind of man, a "protean man" who never finds a fixed permanent identity because the world in which he finds himself is changing so rapidly. When college students today read about protean man, they find the picture of their experience drawn with amazing clarity. In trying to find a specific set of character ideals which had meaning for them, the young were searching for some sort of fixity and permanence. But, aware of conflicting ideals, they were unable to accept any definite identity, and refused to accept any of the traditional definitions of who they were supposed to be.

You might remind a hippie in Los Angeles that he is from the upper class, the son of a fine New England family, a graduate of a prep school where he was in the best "academic track," a former student at a prestigious college, an American. But for him, for this protean man, these definitions mean very little.

The need for an identity consonant with the young awareness is affecting postwar college students not just in America but in many other countries as well. As the young's recent activism in many cities on both sides of the Atlantic demonstrates, the necessity of searching for a sense of self that fits in this shrinking world is a factor to be reckoned with in national affairs. Because these young people are growing up not in a traditional village but in a global village, they are searching not for a traditional identity but for a global identity.

These young people are aware that the future conflicts of the world are not going to be determined, as national leaders still suppose, solely by international military or political struggle, but also by a psychological struggle—a search for a global identity that disregards nationality. It is this struggle of opposing character ideals or personality types that is the key to understanding the elements of today's youth which I have been analyzing. It is also the key to understanding future generations, who will be part of this struggle even more completely than the postwar generation.

A professor of sociology at the University of Pennsylvania, Philip Rieff, has written that three sets of character ideals have dominated successive historical periods in Western civilization:

> First, the ideal of the *political man*, formed and handed down to us from classical antiquity; second, the ideal of the *religious man*, formed and handed down to us from Judaism through Christianity, and dominant in the civilization of authority that preceded the Enlightenment; third, the ideal of the *economic man*, the very model of our liberal civilization, formed and handed down to us in the Enlightenment.

But today, Professor Rieff concludes, these ideals have given way to new ones revolving around *the psychological man*, "a child not of nature but of technology."[7] Psychology became the basis for character ideals because it was man's mind itself, not just his politics, religion, or economics, that was the target of the technological society. We should not be surprised that the real children of technology, the postwar generation, are most involved with psychological man and his ideals. Finally a generation of college students has realized what all men must realize in a technological society: that, as Bertrand Russell put it, "it is by its effects outside economics and politics, at least as much by effects inside them, that a social system must be judged."[8]

The psychological conflict of character ideals, and the ensuing search for a global identity, has become more crucial because other conflict has become less important. The conflict of economic systems seems peripheral to American young people, for they know well that the differences in economic structure between one bloc and another are steadily decreasing. Both industrial Communist and capitalist countries are being reduced to the same dependence on their technological complex. As Paul Goodman, youth's sentinel in the adult world, states in *Like a Conquered Province*, "It should be obvious by now that the vital conflict today is not between one bloc and another bloc, nor between Left and Right, but between a world-wide dehumanized system of things and human decency and perhaps survival."* Goodman comments with insight that strangely "only the young seem to recognize this—in remarkably identical language from Berkeley or Prague or Warsaw or Madrid."[9]

Unconcerned about the psychological dimension which has become so important to their children, many adults misunderstand youth's reaction to this social change. They often assume that weakening allegiance to American capitalist ideals of man and society must mean that young people are attracted to Communist ideals. But adults' deep-set fear of Communism has hidden the truth from them. It is the supremacy of technological values, common to both the United States and the Soviet Union, the unwillingness of communist and capitalist adult societies

---

* It would be of considerable comfort, no doubt, to some, to think that Goodman is alone. But he is not. Erich Fromm, for example, writes that "the alternative is not capitalism or communism but bureaucratization or humanism."[10] From another perspective, John Kenneth Galbraith writes of the United States and the Soviet Union that "both systems are subject to the imperatives of industrialization. This for both means planning. And while each uses different techniques for dealing with the individual who contracts out of the planning, planning in all cases means setting aside the market mechanism in favor of the control of prices and belief for what serves the goals of the industrial mechanism. Instead of contrast leading to implacable conflict, a more evident economic tendency is convergence."[11]

alike to recognize the social and psychological side effects of unrestrained mechanization, which this generation is reacting against with such conviction.

These conditions have caused the beginning of what I refer to as the search for a global identity. It is the disregard for traditional loyalties and accepted character ideals and the consequent search for ideals of manhood. This struggle is not bounded by national borders. Student activism in Buenos Aires, Berkeley, Prague, Warsaw, Madrid, Tokyo, Berlin, and Paris lends support to the view that it is becoming worldwide.[12] Even in China, where the government has tried to control rapid cultural change by attempting to institutionalize youthful alienation, groups resembling nomadic "hippies" have been reported to be wandering the countryside.[13]

The beginning of the search for a global identity is unmistakable proof that all the previous ways of defining oneself have been broken down by modern life. No future generation will be able to re-create the old beliefs in permanence and absoluteness. Religion, nationality, family, social class, race, occupation—nothing offers a fixed identity to the alienated young, who are as close to Buddhism as to Methodism, as close to the conspicuous opulence of Beverly Hills as to the angry poverty of Watts. All that is left are their minds, surrounded by the maze of machinery that mass society has created. In such a world, where each man is in isolation in the cross-currents of modern life, it is not surprising that the members of a single college generation have taken a number of radically different paths toward the hazy world of adulthood.

I have been struck by something in alienated youth groups that has received very little notice from adults. Whether the group is of hippies or of blacks or of draft-resisters, its members call each other "brother." Letters from the New England Draft Resistance are addressed: "Dear Brother." When the genius of soul James Brown talks to his black audiences he calls them "soul brothers." Members of hippie communes call themselves "brothers and sisters," not the old collegiate "guys and gals."

Gone completely is the word "comrade," from the radical groups of the 1930s. Gone too is the word "buddy," carried over from army language. The young people today who recognize the meaninglessness of old definitions of self, of old concepts of loyalty and authority and belief, must search for a new concept of family and community. They must call men brother not because they have the same "dad" as father, or because they believe in the same God as father, or even because they have the same fatherland, but because they share the young awareness of being symbolically fatherless. Orphaned by a world of technology, they find in the poetic phrase "the family of man" a very deep and meaningful allegiance.

Blindly obeying the symbols of fatherhood did not provide an identity for those with the young awareness. Only through allying itself with the causes that lead to brotherhood did this generation find its manhood.

A Strange Vibration

All across the nation
Such a strange vibration. . . .
There's a whole generation
With a new explanation.

—Scott McKenzie

Only quite recently did the beginning of a search for identity consonant with the global village become discernible. Analyses of the young generation of the 1950s consistently pointed out the passivity, caution, and conformity of the college generation. As Clark Kerr, then president of the University of California at Berkeley, said near the close of the decade, students wouldn't cause anybody any trouble, they were too well behaved. A few years later Mr. Kerr's campus was shut down by the Free Speech Movement, which had the support of thousands of students.

"Passivity is the last word we expect to use in connection with a generation of college students," wrote one contributor to a symposium on youth in a 1957 issue of *The Nation*, "but it is the only word that applies to the American university student of the past few years."[1] That article, composed of a number of essays by university professors across the nation, was entitled "The Careful Young Men" and revealed that no strong current in the youth community could be seen. A similar article in 1967, however, had a strikingly different message. Called

"The Gentle Desperadoes" by *The Nation*, the class of 1967 revealed "a highly visible, highly vocal, generally intelligent" segment of the student population that was clearly exerting an "influence both horizontally upon their contemporaries and vertically upon their elders."[2]

This group, which has dared to look for an identity consonant with the young awareness, is indeed affecting society. But rather than absorbing this influence, rather than liberalizing the demands for a homogenized personality structure within American society, adult society's reaction to this psychological challenge is one of intolerance. Traditional American culture, by socially rejecting youth's character ideals, has created a culture within a culture. Entire villages of hippies have appeared in the countryside. Cities are finding entire sections absorbed almost exclusively by hippie residents. A syndicated newspaper organization spanning the nation provides these separated communities with cultural cohesion. Drug procurement and purchase forms a network that connects most major American cities. Stores and restaurants catering wholly to hippie buyers can be found in any major urban scene.

As always, when a gap between men appears and communication deadens, conflict between the two factions begins. Restaurants in parts of California have put up "No Hippies" signs. (It's the clothes and hair now, not solely the color of skin, that identifies the undesirables.) Vigilante committees of "concerned adults" have been formed to fend off the hippie menace. Citizens' committees in Hawaii, which has begun to receive a large number of nomadic young people from the mainland, have held discussions on "how to harass the hippies."[3] Police in urban areas and scenic rural areas have begun to stop young men to frisk them and ask for IDs merely because the car is old, faces are unshaven, or clothes are sloppy. Police and narcotics squads are cracking down on drug-users, both on and off campus, to the point of planting informers within the student and dropout communities. Mayors of cities with sizable youth populations have harassed hippies and their magazines to the extent that ACLU lawyers have had to come in to protect the rights of the young people involved. A mutual antagonism has developed between young people—activists, hippies, and students—and police. One of the basic tenets of underground newspapers is an anti-police line. Papers such as the *Berkeley Barb* or the *Los Angeles Free Press* devote much of their space to diatribes against law-enforcers.

Attempts to enforce uniformity in reaction to behavioral deviance are certain only to aggravate the conflicts by worsening communication. And communication is obviously bad enough. Magazines and newspapers delayed making a solid attempt to understand the new youth movement until the effect of the youth groups could no longer be denied, and then, unfortunately, the articles were one-sided and confusing. The media did not mention that hippie communities during the summer of 1967 had lower crime rates than the "straight" areas of the cities. But all the media were waiting zealously to use what disturbance there was in order to conclude that "The Hippie Movement Is Dead" or that there was "Trouble in Hippieland." It was almost as if adult society were trying to say: we told you you couldn't do it.

It is hard for the media, of course, to treat with fairness youth groups who challenge the very manner in which they operate. *Time* made one of the boldest attempts to understand the new character of youth by giving "the hippie philosophy" a cover story. Although the article was commendable for finally acknowledging that a hippie culture existed, it only reflected the lack of understanding of youth culture that typifies most adults. The *Time* article showed that the media would contradict themselves not only in different articles but even within a single one. The writer felt secure as long as he was talking about catchy phrases or strange clothes or psychedelic stores, but as soon as he had to mention his subject, the hippie philosophy, he contradicted himself.

The article stated confidently that the hippies' professed aim "is nothing less than the subversion of Western society by 'flower power' and force of example."[4] Yet a few pages later the author concluded that hippies have no desire to reform the world or redirect it to new goals. He just couldn't decide what was happening, apparently. He first said that the cultural challenge of the hippies "sounds like a pipe dream" and that "it conveys the unreality that permeates hippiedom."[5] Yet later on the same page he acknowledged that "perhaps the most striking thing about the hippie phenomenon is the way it has touched the imagination of the 'straight' society that gave it birth."

With articles such as this as their only source of knowledge it is small wonder that adults blindly criticize the young groups. And as young people themselves are pushed farther out by the unreasonableness of society, as they become more isolated in their own youth culture, their understanding, too, diminishes. They become as hardened to the condition of their society as their society is to them.

Young people today are experiencing the results of the observation that sociologist Riesman made about the time they were born: "While society may punish people more or less for what they do, it lacks the interest or psychological capacity to find out what they are."[6] What psychological knowledge society gained, it used to fit the individual better to its own needs. Because today's generation is psychologically oriented, it finds the traditional criteria on which society bases its standards and goals one-dimensional.* Consequently members of this generation have found the means for the expression of traditional conflict between societies—political and economic ideologies backed up by military force—failing to encompass their central concerns. Hippie newspapers ask: Does the degree to which a society has exploited the wonders of the atom for destructive purposes correspond at all to the degree to which it has explored the wonders of human psychology, its potential and development? Does the measure of the budget spent for armaments and military exploits reflect the measure of individual fulfillment and mental health of that society's citizens? Mass society has made young people wonder if there is any reason to suppose that the country that might "win" an economic, political, military struggle would also be the country with the most fulfilling set of character ideals. All indications, in fact, lead the young to the opposite conclusion.

Until the last third of the twentieth century, concerns such as religious dogmatism, political loyalties, and economic insecurity precluded a concern for the inner man. But today young people's involvement with psychological character and identity has made the question of the inner man central, and the focal issue for future conflicts. Jung, in discussing modern man's determination to look within himself, many years ago said that man

> wants to live with every side of himself—to know what he is. That is why he casts history aside. He wants to break with tradition so that he can experiment with his life and determine what value and meaning things have in themselves, apart from traditional presuppositions. Modern youth gives us astonishing examples of this attitude.[7]

Freed from the binding commitments and allegiances that tradition requires, young men increasingly find their values and meaning in character ideals quite alien to their own culture, whether in the writings of psychologists or in the philosophies of other cultures. Although it was their nation that made hunger and fear of external threats unnecessary considerations, their nation does not automatically thereby claim their aspirations for a fulfilling life. By giving young people the bounty and

---

* "One-dimensional" expresses my meaning well—an awareness of the political and economic dimensions of man but an exclusion of the psychological dimension. For a more complete and scholarly explanation of the term, see Herbert Marcuse's *One-Dimensional Man*.

the knowledge to ask the questions "Who am I?" and "What do I believe in?" with a culturally unbounded perspective, the state has relinquished its complete sovereignty over their allegiance.

These alienated young people are a growing element in society. Adults who acquaint themselves with what psychologists have to say about youth often find consolation in looking at statistics. The "trouble" —those who break with tradition—seems to be localized in a small minority. In a *Time* article saluting the "under-twenty-five generation," a psychologist said that of the college-student group only 1 in 10 deviate from the expected path of professional training. "Few of these men and women," he said of this generation, "have any doubt that they will one day be part of our society. They wonder where they will fit, but not about whether."[8] But a few months later some of the media carried figures that were *double* that 10 per cent and other media carried articles that mentioned *half* that estimate. The truth is that these writers, and the adult public, have not really known the true extent of the young's critical attitudes and alienation. There have been two reasons for this: they first misunderstood the size of the alienated segment of youth, and then they misunderstood the dynamic effect of this segment.

The Size. The adult writers who have described both the nature and the extent of youth's estrangement from society are always outside the youth culture they attempt to analyze. For the most part, the analysts of youth culture are either professional writers, quite learned in the art of knowing what will sell; or they are academicians who view youth through the windows of their ivory tower; or they are psychiatrists who see young people on the therapeutic couch. The social positions of these men limit their information. Their knowledge of youth's attitudes is confined to observation of young people who are *visibly* different. They have no way of knowing the degree to which these same attitudes are present in the lives of those who do not visit psychiatrists, who do not choose to live in the hippie communities of our nation, who do not holler to professional magazine writers, "Hey, look! I'm different." These writers' statistical estimates of alienated young people must be limited to only a fraction of the actual number. To be alienated does not primarily mean that you have to be sitting on the curb, barefoot, at the top of the Strip in Los Angeles with beads around your neck and a joint hanging from your mouth. To be alienated is to be dissatisfied with the kind of personality and life experience that this culture permits and expects. With this definition of social alienation, it is clear to members of youth culture that the number of alienated young people is much higher than the estimates behind which adult society hides from the truth.

The Dynamic Effect. Not only the size of the group but the kind of people that constitute it can easily be misunderstood. The young people of the 1950s were alienated but fearful, and fearful alienation results in conformity. Economic insecurity and the Joseph McCarthy era made the young unwilling to stick their necks out. Their alienation was shared by only a handful of people, they thought, and so they remained totally inactive in student affairs and social issues. As one of the college students of the 1950s writes about himself and his generation: "We mostly assumed that our discontents were the result of personal maladjustments rather than societal ones. Even when we suspected that established institutions were unnecessarily hierarchic, authoritarian, and repressive, it seldom occurred to us that they could be changed."[9] Members of that generation did not speak out; there were no audiences. They did not band together; there seemingly were no partners.

Today's young people are convinced that only the fearful hide behind apathy and cynicism. Because of this, the tenor of youth culture is radically different. The earlier alienated young people took the first step, quietly rejecting the conventional mores of American society; today's generation is taking the second, actively searching, sometimes in vain but often with success, for other character ideals that fit its conception of what manhood should be. These young people are not rebels without a cause. They have an audience and know their partners because a large part of the postwar generation shares their alienation and their need for a more fulfilling way of life.

Now there are too many taking part in this psychological rebellion for the alienated to remain either silent or fearful. Their influence has become disproportionately great because they are often the actively intelligent members of youth culture. These social "anomalies"—the critics, the demonstrators, the hippies, the new breed of student leaders (recognizable in places as disparate as Iowa and Stanford)—are by no means unintelligent misfits. They are the young people who once would have striven with enthusiasm, and success, to be this nation's leaders. Despite the fact that this group comprises only a minority of the generation, it is a social force much greater than its numbers indicate.

When we realize the size and the dynamic effect of the alienated group, the increase in its numbers can be better understood. While in the 1950s this minority was but 3 to 5 per cent, it became by the mid-1960s a solid 15 per cent of the college generation. As we approach

1970, their numbers have swelled to 25 per cent. If society does not respond to the criticisms of the young, it can be estimated that by 1975 many more of the college generation will be sharing many of the alienated attitudes that today are mistakenly attributed to only a small and insignificant dropout fringe.

If society can grasp the meaning of a group of alienated and articulate young men of this size, it can begin to understand the magnitude the search for a global identity will attain in the future. Our nation will contain a vast reservoir of capable young men who, although they became citizens of the United States automatically at birth, will have virtually no attraction or allegiance to the character ideals of their society.

The Times They Are
A-Changin'

In the first verse of this song, Bob Dylan coaxes those
who are blocking "the new road" to get moving. If
they don't start swimming, he warns them, they'll "sink like
a stone." As challengers of the power structure
have said throughout history, what is today will be
gone tomorrow. And those who are first
now will later be last.

Alienation has caused the goals and corresponding behavior of different parts of this generation to diverge greatly. Within previous generations there was, to be sure, also a divergence in final behavior. But this was not because the original goals were radically different. The question then was "Can the goals be attained?" not "Are the prescribed goals worth attaining?" As the challenge of the former question diminished, a concern for the latter grew. Because acceptable character ideals are no longer prescribed by economic and political necessities, the goals and ideals themselves diverge widely within youth culture.

Without crossing the border into the realm of the clinically ill, we have seen all the forms of alienation and have witnessed the full spectrum of behavioral reactions to the Western way of life. It is necessary to understand, of course, first, that the spectrum is a continuum. The classification of individuals into behavioral types is arbitrary and is done only for purposes of description. Second, words can ably describe objects but not processes, and they tend to degrade the latter into terms of the former. The process of alienation is not an object;

it is not a uniform condition. It is the experience of reacting to the social and psychological manipulation of mass society, which today affects everyone, although to different degrees and in different ways.

The traditionalists. This group supports the institutions and the character ideals of Western society, and its members orient their lives toward the pursuit of established social goals. They have adopted the framework of attitudes and values represented by the older generations and find that framework compatible with the world as they see it. This is the group of young people who accept what marriage has come to be; who do not dream of questioning, much less disputing, the validity of their nation's foreign policy; who do not consider adult society to be one-dimensional and unfulfilling but consider *themselves* to be inadequately measuring up to the challenging image of mass society's ideal personality. Any inner doubt or feeling of unfulfillment, these traditionalist young people immediately consider a personality shortcoming that must be hidden. That society (which seems monolithic and absolute) could be changed, or that they as individuals should not have to be subjected to the mechanized patterns of Western life, is never seriously considered by the traditionalists.

The cynics. This group is aware of the incompleteness of the accepted adult way of life and mistrusts mass society, but its members do not feel sufficiently removed from the prevailing system to be impelled to find alternative goals. Cynical young people have accepted the unparalleled value of doubt. Their contact with adult society has taught them that a philosophy of disbelief is the safest way to live. They are knowledgeable and alienated enough to discard some of the clearly fallacious notions about American life and the world situation. The cynics are the young people who enjoy satirizing the businessman with three-piece suit and briefcase; who have contact with their parents primarily through arguments about the car and financial matters; who sometimes use drugs, but only socially; who ridicule *both* the administration's Vietnam policy *and* their fellow students' activism; and who have had a sufficient number of their childhood beliefs destroyed to make them apprehensive about embracing any cause, either of adult society or of youth culture. Occasionally these young people identify themselves with the social aspects of hippiedom by dressing with cultivated sloppiness and by avoiding the traditional college functions which the traditionalists attend. Cynical young people stay in college; they are practical and want the money a degree will make available. They are as a group indecisive and apathetic about everything, everything but their sarcasm. They don't think society has fooled them, but, in a way, it has. Society has convinced the cynics that a detached and sarcastic way of life is the best one they could achieve.

The activists. Members of this group have a variety of goals and ideologies they wish to further, their end being to infuse adult society with their convictions. Their dissent is political, but it is rooted in psychological criticisms of adult society's hypocrisy. The individuals of this group find the inequities of adult society so unacceptable that they actively engage in existing programs or create their own movements and campus organizations in order to alter various aspects of the system. These people are the ones who are intellectually (not merely academically) motivated, for they are searching for viable alternatives to the system that warrants their criticisms. They are politically active as well as politically alienated. They form the ranks of civil rights workers and anti-war marchers, campus political leaders, workers in Vietnam Summer projects, and a multitude of other less-publicized groups dedicated to helping the underprivileged, such as Head Start, VISTA, Upward Bound, and campus social-service projects. It was these young people who formed the first enthusiastic wave of Peace Corps Volunteers. The most vociferous activists question the capacity of the American political and economic system to deal with the problems of the modern world and, in their own disorganized way, attempt to spread their ideas. The activists stay in society in order to gain the influence and power to change the existing order.

The Hippies. This group is dissatisfied with adult society for psychological reasons in addition to the political. The hippies function outside of any socially recognized institution because they abhor organizations. Sometimes, because of pressure from the Selective Service, they are found superficially involved in a college set-up. These individuals are young men who use drugs extensively for psychological purposes and as *rites de passage*; who have been influenced by Oriental philosophies and their character ideals; and who are preoccupied with their minds, often to the point of passivity as far as activism is concerned. Their lives are individualistic, and they feel that others will escape from the hassles of modern life when they realize that the depersonalizing forces in society are becoming still more pervasive. To sustain their self-image, the hippies interact frequently with straight people and enjoy contrasting themselves to people who have not broken away from the socially patterned frustrations. Any form of authority is anathema to these psychological dropouts. The same disorganization and "leaderlessness" which plagues the New Left activists is even more present in hippie communities and is, in fact, their credo. Hippies pity traditionalists; blame cynics for having sold out because they, like adult society, are missing the joy of deep and spontaneous involvement in human relations and in life; and criticize those activists who have let themselves become just as oriented around money, prestige, and power as the members of the society they are trying to change.

The Other-Culturists. This group has rejected adult society completely and has adopted a way of life associated with other cultures. It believes the American way of life is on the way out and that Western character ideals have very little to offer. It is past the point of having to interact with the society of which it was once a part and, for the most part, is occupied with attaining the meditative state of Oriental philosophies. Other-culturists feel that modern man has lost the awareness of his place in nature and will never gain the Cosmic Consciousness which gives life meaning if he does not first reject his role in society. Many feel they are beginning a new civilization which, at the downfall of this one, will begin a new phase in the historical process.

It is not hard to see that as we progress from one extreme to the other, from the traditionalists to the other-culturists, the degree of alienation increases. As the young's criticism of adult society's values deepens, and as their awareness of the unwillingness of adult society to respond to accepted means of dissent sharpens, this generation finds itself being pushed away from the traditionalist extreme toward the opposite end of the spectrum. We have only to look at the change of distribution in this generation in order to conclude that the process of alienation is gaining momentum.

The traditionalists, who were in the great majority in preceding generations, lost ground steadily during the 1950s to the cynics. By the early 1960s, the number of cynical young had grown so large that some began to try to change the obvious shortcomings of adult society. At that time, however, still only a fraction of dissenters had become activists. By the mid-1960s the public had become aware of the swelling ranks of the activists, both in socially recognized programs and in their own endeavors. Because the inertia of adult society concerning civil rights and the Vietnam war revealed that the problems were rooted beneath the political structure in the minds of men, hippies appeared and received wide publicity. Only those most closely in tune with subsequent developments in alienated communities recognized the first other-culturists before their numbers grew, toward the end of the decade.

The generation's alienation from the way of life in adult society is steadily growing and is affecting every element of youth culture. The older generations do not understand why or how it is increasing and, by their avoidance or intolerance, accentuate the young's feelings of generational isolation.

For a long time adult society has been telling its young people about the "challenge of youth"—the challenge of meeting society's needs, no matter what those needs come to be. All that society recognizes is that, in order "to enter history, each generation of young persons must find an identity consonant with its own childhood and consonant with an ideological promise in the perceptible historical process." In other words, society has recognized only, and therefore emphasized only, that the young should mold themselves to fit an existing social niche. "But," psychologist Erikson continues,

> in youth the tables of childhood dependence slowly begin to turn: it is no longer exclusively for the old to teach the young the meaning of life. . . . *It is the young who, by their responses and their actions, tell the old whether life as represented by their elders and as presented to the young has meaning.* [Italics mine.][1]

Members of the postwar generation, by their responses and actions in every sphere of life, are telling conventional society that life as represented by their elders does not have meaning for them, and that meeting the demands of their parents' society is a meaningless challenge—a Pyrrhic victory. Adult society for an increasing number of young people is not, and with its present values and character ideals cannot be, the environment in which they can find a meaningful challenge.

Such a challenge, a *rite de passage*, is necessary in order for a youth to become a man. Although this society has not provided it, no generation can wait idly on the threshold of adulthood. In response to the need for and absence of such a challenge, young men have had to find their own. A few are considered acceptable by adult society; most are unacceptable. But all the newly discovered *rites de passage* of this generation have in common the fact that adult society does not understand them for what they are—attempts to gain full manhood.

In effect, the young have stated their own challenge, a challenge *from* youth. They challenge adults to help them, or let them, establish meaningful character ideals as the primary concern of modern culture, so that future generations may find value in becoming adults in their society. *But since adult society has concentrated exclusively on the*

political and economic necessities, it is unwilling to accept or acknowl-
edge the psychological challenge of its alienated youth.

For the postwar generation of college students, and for those that follow it, the psychological challenge is the next frontier. One cannot help hoping for international cooperation rather than violence, racial harmony rather than conflict, economic justice rather than inequity, democratic development rather than totalitarianism, population control rather than explosion, and human fulfillment rather than mechanization. But these goals will not be attained unless the young awareness spreads—that is, unless the old awareness gains an understanding of the cultural and psychological obstacles that must be surmounted. It is the young awareness which can successfully take these hopes and make them truths, because each goal depends on men's abilities to "travel with their minds." Each goal requires that men develop an awareness that is expansive, mobile, empathic, and that men's identities be formed, not rigidly in the mold of local and traditional authority, but flexibly in the context of the world-wide historical forces Western technology has unleashed. Unless this generation successfully infuses adult society with the psychological perspectives of the young awareness, the next generation will be the loser.

It cannot be denied that there are among young people much bitterness due to frustration, much cynicism because of their unrelatedness to adult society, and much apathy resulting from the absence of all credible beliefs. But do such bitterness, cynicism, and apathy have to be a part of growing up in mass society? I think not. They are rather a warning sign to this society that the idealism of young people is not necessarily the possession of the society that nurtured them. It is a reminder that it is the challenge *of* youth to achieve society's manhood only if the challenge *from* youth to adult society is accepted.

House of Mirrors: II

The implications of youth's alienation are significant when viewed in an international context. The young people of the affluent countries will be the leaders of the world powers in the next few decades and can be examined as a group in order to understand some aspects of the future.

Already it is clear to American young people who have been in Europe that they have much in common with their European counterparts. Student activism and alienation on both sides of the Atlantic bear a striking resemblance. European youth culture has yet to establish the cultural predominance that the American one has achieved,* but, as affluence and higher education extend to a greater percentage of the population, young people in Europe will increasingly join the ranks of those who have not moved on to adult society.

The over-all pattern of alienation characterizing American youth seems to be developing in the affluent northern European countries as

* As of 1966, the percentage of young people between the ages of twenty and twenty-four in the United States enrolled in colleges and universities was 43. In comparison, the percentage in Russia is 24; France, 16; Sweden, 11; Germany, 7.5; Britain, 7.

well. The rapid social change caused by technology is having similar effects on youth's relationship to adult society, regardless of the particular country's religious, political, and cultural background. This international phenomenon is further evidence of the search for a global identity and re-emphasizes an idea that has been implicit throughout this book.

Alienated college students in modern countries have in common their view of the world as a "House of Mirrors." Because mass communications have since birth made them intimately aware of other cultures, and because their own culture is changing so rapidly that it has lost all trace of absoluteness or fixity, sensitive young people today cannot help looking into mirrors besides that of their own culture. The traditionalist has accepted *his own* culture's reflection of him as the only or the most valid self-image; the other-culturist has accepted *another* culture's as his reference. But the vast majority of young people are caught between these two extremes, caught in the psychological puzzle of the global village and trying to piece together a global identity out of the multiple and conflicting self-images which they are told represent them.

With the confusing relativism of living in the House of Mirrors, it becomes tempting for the young to create their own mirror, their own social values and character ideals based not on the culture of any nation but on the needs and aspirations of an age group. It is indeed inviting to call one's organization the Youth International Party, no matter how presumptuous the name may be. Although the actual basis for such a party does not yet exist, mainly because other countries do not have the affluence and mass higher education that America has, the fact is that young people throughout the modern nations feel much more bonded to one another than ever before.

Again, it is Erik Erikson who has pointed out what most adults have failed to realize: that the young in modern countries today have a need for "a new, a fraternal conscience," and "a more universal identity."[1] This is why young dissenters are less concerned with national opinion—what their parents' society thinks—and are so aware of international opinion. When demonstrators at the Democratic Convention in Chicago chanted, "The whole world is watching!" they were saying in effect: "We are dissenters in our country, and our country condemns us. But this time the whole world is watching, and in its eyes it is not youth but adult society which is being judged guilty."

It is the young alone who, guided by their fraternal conscience and global identity, are the jurors in this new international courtroom. They constitute, as Robert Lifton puts it, "a human vanguard" because they indicate "the kinds of psychological experience and identity shift" of which adult society is but dimly aware.[2]

Naturally, as the influence of past conditions and cultural differences becomes less relevant for the youth of the Western industrial nations, the influence of the present world situation becomes much more important to them. The mass media enhance this, of course, by creating the global village. Nuclear weapons further emphasize it by making any international event of utmost relevance to everyone.

Even the young people of the Soviet Union now have many things in common with European and American youth. A candid book on the unrest of Soviet young people, entitled *The View from Lenin Hills*, reveals that outspoken criticism and deep alienation characterize the Soviet college elite. Written by William Taubman, a Columbia University graduate student participating in an exchange program to Moscow University, the book chronicles his intimate contact with and perceptive observations of the new generation in the USSR.

"Soviet leaders, I am convinced, have misunderstood and underestimated the mood and potential of the new Soviet generation, just as we in the United States have," wrote twenty-five-year-old Taubman.

> They, I think, have been taken in by their own propaganda. We have been misled by their propaganda and our own. We both are in grave danger or miscalculating the influence of young Soviets on the future of their own society and its relations with the rest of the world. Both of us would do well to look objectively at these young people who will shape the Soviet future and with whom we will have an urgent need to communicate.[3]

The picture of Communist young people in *The View from Lenin Hills* gives the young American reader an amazing parallel to his own youth culture. Soviet adult society tries to blame youth's dissent on "corrupting" influences from other cultures and on ideas spread by subversive writers and artists. Soviet parents, like American parents, search for any explanation of their sons' dissent except the true one: that the young are responding to a changing world. Soviet government officials, too, pretend that the alienated young people are few and exhort their fellow adults to "struggle for the mind of every young person."[4]

The Soviet postwar generation responds indignantly to social control and manipulation, as do its American counterparts. "What do you know about youth?" demanded one Moscow University student of a party official. "What right do you have to condemn us?"

"Where have you been for the last thirty years?" another asked. "Have you forgotten what happened after the war?"

The Soviet Union is running into the same problems that the United States has been dealing with. Old ways of thinking that were deeply ingrained in today's adults amid the insecurity of war and poverty cannot stand up in a world of rapid technological change. As one Communist professor of economics explained at a discussion Taubman attended, "There is no *Communist* way to run a factory any more than there is a *Communist* way of putting a car together." Taubman says that Soviet young people, like American, "are fascinated by the theory, attacked in the Soviet press, that all industrial societies have common problems of modernization, technology, and management, the solutions to which have little to do with ideology."[5]

Soviet adults are learning from their sons the same lesson American adults are: social change brought about by unrestrained technology is independent of ideology. Advanced industrial societies are *mass* societies first, and Communist or capitalist only an increasingly distant second.

Adult society in both the Soviet Union and the United States is trying to hide social reality. It has unsuccessfully attempted to cover cultures in the midst of rapid transformation with an overlay of staid political, economic, and social ideas. As the rate of change accelerates, adults' version of their society bears less and less resemblance to the actual experience of their children. Fortunately, the members of the college generations in both countries are questioning this façade. Taubman writes:

> If young Soviets knew young America's battle cry, they would shout it to their own party leaders: "Tell it like it is!" Like many young Americans, they are disturbed by the gap between reality and certain versions of it. They want to know the whole truth, for better or for worse, and they fear that for too long they have not had it. They are asking their leaders to level with them:[6]

But college students in all modern nations are realizing that their old leaders *can't* level with them because they are too tied to the past. And as a consequence, while adult societies in different countries feel animosity and mistrust toward one another, youth cultures in different countries feel a deep rapport.

Student demonstrations provide an excellent illustration of this international generation gap. When Russia and the Warsaw Pact nations invaded Czechoslovakia in August 1968, Americans were furious at the actions of the Communist aggressors. When American parents read of hundreds of Czech students bravely staging a sit-in in defiance of the Russian troops, they were thrilled. They heard of young Czechs in Wenceslas Square in Prague who refused to move even when Russians fired machine guns over their heads and Russian tanks rolled nearby. "What fine, courageous young men," American parents told each other, "standing up to the Communists like that."

But when their own sons, American students, staged a sit-in in front of the Selective Service induction center in Oakland, California, and refused to move even when police began using their clubs, or when their own sons refused to disperse in front of the Pentagon when armed troops threw tear gas and clubbed with their rifle butts, there were no cheers from American parents. To them, these demonstrators were not courageous; they were good-for-nothing rebels, hippies, and radicals.

Now imagine, on the other hand, what Soviet parents must have thought of these two incidents: *exactly the opposite.* They probably thought the Czech students were foolish and immature for supporting "counterrevolutionary forces," and the American students were fine, courageous young men because they tried to halt the functioning of "the militaristic institutions of American imperialism."

This shows the difference between adult society and youth culture, between the old and the young awareness. Soviet and American parents consider these two incidents wholly separate events. One was clearly good, and the other clearly bad. Both sets of parents are so tied to the past that they see youth's actions not in terms of the actual world situation but in terms of the ideologies of their own formative years. Because of this, the old Soviets and old Americans have to conveniently sidestep the fact that the young Czechs were chanting both "Russians, get out of Czechoslovakia!" *and* "Americans, get out of Vietnam!"[7] It is a chant of the young awareness, and so they must ignore it.

The young alone, Czech and American students, realize that each demonstration was quite closely related to the other. Each was directed at stopping a superpower from overcoming by sheer military might another country; each demonstrated a disregard for old political ideology and a concentration on the new circumstances of the postwar period; and in each case it was the young generation that found the freedom of action and the courage to stand up against policies which older generations in their countries resisted more passively, if at all.

It is interesting to speculate what the students at Moscow University whom Taubman described thought of these student sit-ins. The Soviet postwar young people have but vague memories of the Stalinist period. Their early adolescence was spent under the leadership of the less repressive Nikita Khrushchev. They have had relatively more access to information from the West, and their college education has diverged somewhat more freely from the party line. It is my bet that a good number of them, in their personal attitudes if not in their public behavior, identified with their fellow young people around the world, not with the ideological, repressive tradition of their adult society.

Men are fascinated by what has greatest relevance to their lives or, at least, *seems* to have. Factions of adult society are still fascinated by new supersonic million-dollar fighter planes. Aware college students in America, as well as in Czechoslovakia, France, England, Germany, and Russia, couldn't care less. The situation for all groups of modern youth is parallel: they are looking to other cultures and among themselves for the guidance which their rigid adult societies cannot give them.

Although the cultural differences grounded in adult society are losing their relevance for the young, I do not by any means suggest that the differences are insignificant. There are still many intellectual disagreements that divide American and Russian college students, and even a few that divide American and European. What is most heartening in all these youth cultures, however, is the emotional tendency to draw toward rather than withdraw from each other. The young are inclined to find cultural similarities, while adults seem so bound to the past that they are predisposed to find only cultural differences. Very rarely does one realize a truth unless one already has some emotional commitment to it. And it is in youth culture of such places as Berkeley, Paris, Berlin, London, Prague, Tokyo, that this commitment is present in abundance.

The initial response to this development might be elation. As the cold war drags on, almost everyone looks forward to two young generations on different sides of the Atlantic and of the "Iron Curtain" that will be able to trust each other more than the present older generations have been able to. But there are two major problems that might leave this wish unfulfilled unless they are recognized and solved. The problems can be solved only by American adults and American youth, and in their solution each generation has a challenge.

The fortunate development of international rapport between youth cultures was indirectly caused by the young's alienation from adult society. But the effects within our own society of adults' unwillingness to change have not been so fortunate. For the mutual trust which is so important in a democratic country has been lost between young and old, just as it has been lost between blacks and whites, and between hawks and doves. If adults react to generation differences by condemning youth, by attributing youth's deep dissent (as did Hubert Humphrey) to their "self-indulgence" rather than to accelerating social change, mistrust and division within America will grow. The nation as a whole will be left less capable rather than more capable of establishing peace with other countries because of the generation gap. Adults must realize that in a changing world their sons are going to find their own answers and that what the young need is adult society's trust and understanding, not its condemnation. Adults must find the ability to continue learning long after the age when adults in the past could omnisciently begin teaching.

The task for young people is even greater because they are also trying to gain manhood. They have to find solutions to their identities as well as to the problems facing society. Despite their growing alienation, young people must choose to grow up the hard way. They must find manhood in their society, not out of it. Criticisms of adult society which lead alienated young people to drop out are grounded in the same insights that could improve adult society. Although self-awareness is surely part of manhood, sharing oneself and the strength of one's awareness with society is also part of being a man.

The members of the postwar generation who experience alienation are the ones who can attack the roots of the social problems that cause it. If they retreat into traditional thinking and behavior, or if they withdraw from their society, the only fuel for the engines of social change will be wasted. The traditionalists and cynics must realize that they have been like clay in the mold of mass society, and that their approach to the problems which face the postwar generation will prolong rather than solve them. The activists must continually examine their motives and methods in order to insure that their profound indictment of American society be tempered by an equally profound understanding of it. The hippies and other-culturists must apply their insight, intellectual ability, and freedom to the social process—either personally, artistically, or politically—in order to improve the social circumstances that forced them to drop out.

And together youth can provide a corps of activists who, acting compassionately because of their young awareness rather than rebelliously because of their failure to find it, could guide America toward human as well as technological goals. For what is needed is not violent revolts which bring our society to a standstill, but capable young people who will resolutely lead their generation and the following ones to humane political goals and mature character ideals. Then, perhaps, those with the young awareness will survive and flourish and come to be leaders rather than, as now, being driven in alienation to the outskirts of an aging society.

Epilogue

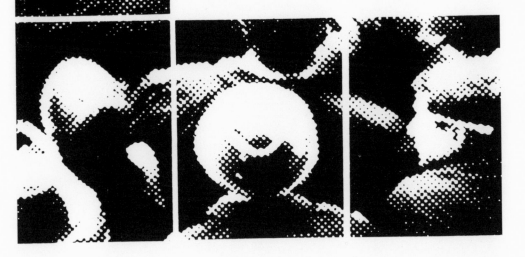

Within You

Some pharisees asked Jesus when the Kingdom of God would come. His answer was: "The Kingdom of God does not come in such a way as to be seen. No one will say, 'Look, here it is!' or, 'There it is!'; because the Kingdom of God is within you."

—Luke 17: 20-21

Young people whose identities mass society has not destroyed become aware that alienation has within itself the seed of its own transformation. The cynics were alienated *socially* because of their distrust of mass society; the activists were alienated *politically* by the hypocritical values of adult society; the hippies were alienated *psychologically* by the socially patterned frustrations of modern society. The most alienated hippies and other-culturists epitomized the alienation which the others felt to a lesser degree, for they were openly alienated *spiritually* by the absence of meaningful character ideals.

A search for meaningful character ideals has always been part of religion; but today it *is*, or must be, religion. A God of wrath or mercy, life after death in heaven or hell, baptism by submersion or sprinkling —religion has had to remove its clumsy vestments and bare the ultimate question: *for what character ideals should men strive*? Because adult society seems, with cowardice, to have avoided this question and let the needs of mass society answer it, members of this generation have had to search within themselves and in other religious traditions for their ideals.

Until recently most men directed their search for ultimate meaning to the supernatural, to some being up there or out there who was separate from this world. God was a being in space who pulled strings like a master puppeteer, or was the omnipotent judge in the cosmic courtroom. To believe in him was to find ultimate concern in a being external to the human condition. To believe in God was to accept absolute rights and wrongs, and young people are painfully aware that the pressures and opportunities of modern life are so radically different that new moral questions exist today for which the answers must be relative. To believe in God was to accept that authority had answers for everything, but the young learned that no one had viable answers to the questions of their lives. And to believe in God was to accept that there was already some kind of divine justice on earth, but the young awareness made young people so aware of their world that they were forced to conclude that God's justice had forgotten about a lot of human beings (which means he is not omniscient), or that his justice could be applied only to some lives, not to others (which means he is not omnipotent), or that his justice does not care about some people (which means he is not love). Perhaps this generation concluded that a God like this was not worth saving.

The postwar generation's rejection of traditional religion is unmistakable. The ultimate meaning for young people cannot be *a being* somewhere up there. The ultimate meaning must be *Being itself*. Today's young people direct their spiritual need not to the supernatural but to the natural: to themselves, to other men, and to nature. In everything that explodes from youth culture this generation is spreading its belief that, if one is to find ultimate meaning in life, it will be in the natural, in Being itself, in what is most deeply and profoundly and uniquely human. The young are telling their society that religion cannot survive in the form of a mythical heavenly figure. No longer can man afford piously to love God while he fearfully avoids his fellow man.

In order for religion to have meaning in the modern world, it must be transformed, and in young people the transformation has begun. The alienated young believe in a religion of interpersonal relationships. They consider success in terms of personal relations, not in terms of material wealth, social prestige, or spiritual fervor. Throughout this book we have seen the extreme emphasis members of this generation place on open communication between people. With Camus, they have realized that what is human and solely human is the most meaningful part of life. And the young have a psychological approach to life because it helps them realize the potential meaning of human relations.

This emphasis on personal relations above other facets of "success" is nothing esoteric, nothing radical. It is a natural, human reaction to being brought up in a mass society. A powerful writer and one of America's outstanding child psychologists, Bruno Bettelheim, a man whose work on German concentration camps General Eisenhower made required reading for all military-government officers in Europe, writes:

> Just as democracy requires a more educated and moral population than do more primitive forms of society, so modern man requires a more highly developed emotional sensitivity so as not to succumb to temptations inherent in a machine age. The more mechanized and fragmented the world around us, the more we must develop the humanity of human relations. The more we live in a mass society, the better we must know how to have intimate relations.[1]

This, it seems to me, is what this generation—the children of technology, not of nature—is trying to do. If mass society tends to destroy what is unique in a young person, he attempts to preserve his uniqueness in his personal life. He tries to find a deeper feeling of relatedness to one person or a few people because of the relatedness he has lost to his community as a whole.

The emphasis in youth culture on human relations reflects not only modern psychology but modern theology as well. Many of the exciting theologians today are also attempting to transform religion, and their ideas are closely attuned to those of young people. Joseph Fletcher (*Situation Ethics*), Paul Tillich (*The Courage to Be*, for example), Bishop John A. T. Robinson (*Honest to God*) are some of the most widely read and most highly respected theologians in youth culture. These writers have paralleled the thinking of youth. That which has ultimate meaning in human experience, they conclude, can be called "God," and the ultimate meaning in human experience is the capacity to love. These theologians bring "God," the concept representing man's ultimate concern, down from heaven to earth. Man's ultimate concern is not a distant God but the ever-present goal of realizing one's potential for loving others.

We have been called the Now Generation for every reason but the right one: "now" means "love." Joseph Fletcher interprets Christianity in a way that has meaning for today's young:

> The Christian ethic is a love ethic primarily, not a hope ethic. . . .
> This means it is for the present, here and now. By faith we live in the
> past, by hope we live in the future, but by love we live in the *present*.[2]

Members of this generation have made "love" their password. It is
most clearly the ethic of the hippies but it is also, much more subtly,
the ethic of youth culture as a whole. By emphasizing that Love is God,
rather than merely that God is Love, youth reinterprets the Biblical
phrase in order to stress compassion for what is human rather than faith
in what is divine. "He who does not love does not know God" (I John
4:8) could well be the scriptural basis for youth's attitudes. By living
by this thought, rather than its converse (which traditional religion
seems to do), young people have established their own religion. They
find their God, their ultimate concern, through love, not their love
through God.

In almost every sphere of activity the love ethic is manifested. How
can adults fail to see the implicit criticism on placards that proclaim:
MAKE LOVE, NOT WAR? There have always been pacifists, although never
so many as today, but there have never been signs with those words
until this generation. For young people are reacting against a society that
has devalued human relations, that has subordinated them to acquisitiveness and competitiveness, and that has resulted in greater affluence
and greater aloneness.

Young people who are attracted to Oriental religions are simply
carrying the ideas of their generation a little further. By accepting as
their goal the achievement of harmony within themselves and with the
world, they are stressing that the ultimate concern of their lives is to be
found right here. Their God is within them, within each man; it is part
of human, earthly, mortal life.

The young awareness is unable to accept that men who cannot find
peace within themselves will ever find peace with other men; that men
who cannot work on the problems of their own minds will ever work
on the problems of the world; and that men who cannot communicate
with other men will ever communicate with life. For all we can ever
know of the meaning of life is what we know of ourselves, what we know
of other men, and what we know of nature itself. Is it so strange, ask
alienated young people, that the age of divided selves, of impersonal
relationships, and of separation from nature, is also the age of absurdity
or "the death of God"? All man's avenues for finding meaning or finding
God have been shut off by the effects of living in a mass society.

This is the subtlest message from the young who complete the process of alienation. Young men who move beyond traditionalism and cynicism are dissenting because their society has become so involved with the inventions of man that they have forgotten the creations of God. If we want to know a philosopher, we read his books; an artist, we inspect his paintings; an architect, we explore his buildings. So too, if we hope to find religious meaning, we should try to discover our inner selves and our capacity to love, which is the only God.

This message is subtle only because of the ears to which it is directed —ears that pick up a mile away a murmur about a stock rise or about a change in hemlines, but which cannot hear in the blazing hippie song "All You Need Is Love" the same humanistic theme that pervades Christianity. The message is the young's exclamation mark for their realization that "the essence of life is human relations!" The message is that the essence of life is love, and that the way to know God—that is, the way to find meaning in life—is to love.

No group of young men better demonstrates the new religion of youth than the Beatles. British television personality David Frost had George Harrison and John Lennon appear on his London television program on September 29, 1967. They began to talk about Maharishi Mahesh Yogi and transcendental meditation, but soon they were simply talking about themselves.

> HARRISON: Through Christianity, how I was taught it, they told me to believe in Jesus and in God and all that. They didn't actually show me any way of experiencing God or Jesus, so the whole point of to believe in something without actually seeing it—well, it's you know, it's no good. You've got to actually experience the thing. You know, if there's a God, we must see him; and that's the point in—of—the whole thing: it's no good to believe in something, you know, just hallucinations. . . .
> LENNON: Yes, well, that thing about the "Kingdom of Heaven is within you," you know, that's all it means, to have a peep inside, you know—
> HARRISON: And to contact it—
> LENNON: There's no big scene there, or some old fellow. . . .

Selected Bibliography

The following books are intended to provide a number of different perspectives on the young awareness. Paperback publisher is listed whenever possible.

Baez, Joan. *Daybreak*. New York: Dial Press, 1968.

Butz, Otto (ed.). *To Make a Difference: A Student Look at America: Its Values, Its Society, and Its System of Education*. New York: Harper and Row, 1967.

Erikson, Erik H. *The Challenge of Youth*. New York: Bantam Books, 1965.

Friedenberg, Edgar Z. *Coming of Age in America*. New York: Vintage Books, 1963.

Jencks, Christopher. "Is It All Dr. Spock's Fault?" *New York Times Magazine*, March 3, 1968.

Keniston, Kenneth. *Young Radicals: Notes on Committed Youth*.

New York: Harcourt, Brace and World, 1968.

Kornbluth, Jesse. *Notes from the New Underground*. New York: The Viking Press, 1968.

Kozol, Jonathan. *Death at an Early Age*. Boston: Houghton Mifflin, 1967.

McLuhan, Marshall, and Fiore, Quentin. *Peace and War in the Global Village*. New York: Bantam Books, 1968.

Salinger, J. D. *Franny and Zooey*. New York: Bantam Books, 1964.

Taubman, William. *The View from Lenin Hills*. New York: Harcourt, Brace and World, 1968.

Wakefield, Dan. *Supernation at Peace and War*. Boston: Little Brown, 1968.

Reference Notes

Youth and History

1. Alistair Cooke, *Generation on Trial: USA v. Alger Hiss* (New York: Knopf, 1950), p. 1.
2. Daniel Bell, *The End of Ideology* (New York: Macmillan, 1959), pp. 373ff.
3. From a speech by Paul Goodman at the annual meeting of the National Association of College and University Chaplains, Boston University, April 3–6, 1967.

The Dangling Conversation

1. T. S. Eliot, "The Love Song of J. Alfred Prufrock," *The Complete Plays and Poems 1909–1950* (New York: Harcourt, Brace, 1952), p. 5.
2. Jack Newfield in *Evergreen Review*, March 1968, p. 25.
3. Martin Esslin, *Theatre of the Absurd* (New York: Doubleday Anchor Books, 1961), p. 7.

4. Albert Camus, *The Myth of Sisyphus* (New York: Knopf and Vintage Books, 1955), p. 7.
5. Ibid., pp. 16, 21.
6. Ibid., p. 38.
7. Ibid., p. 22.
8. Ibid., p. 47.
9. Ibid., p. 46.
10. Ibid., p. 66.

Youth and Mass Society

1. David Riesman, *The Lonely Crowd* (New Haven, Conn.: Yale University Press, 1950; paperback, 1961), p. 256.
2. David Riesman makes this same point in his introduction to *The Lonely Crowd*, when he says that he and his associates "were convinced that the older social sciences—history, political science, economics—gave far too little weight to the understanding of social change that might be gleaned from a better grasp of

psychoanalytic psychology" (p. xxii).

Let the Hurt Creep On Thru

1. Marshall McLuhan, *Understanding Media* (New York: McGraw-Hill, 1964; paperback, 1965), p. 166.
2. Ibid., p. 225.
3. Ibid., p. 157.
4. Kenneth Keniston in *Commentary* 29, June 1960, pp. 486–89.
5. Erik H. Erikson, *Identity and the Life Cycle* (New York: International Universities Press, 1959), p. 46.
6. McLuhan, op. cit., p. 157.
7. Connell Persico, "Live and Let Live," in Otto Butz, ed., *To Make a Difference: A Student Look at America* (New York: Harper, 1967), p. 110.

Mechanical Rape

1. McLuhan, op. cit.
2. Charles Frederick Reed, et al., *Psychopathology: A Source Book* (Cambridge, Mass.: Harvard University Press, 1958), Chapter 23.
3. The survey was taken among Harvard undergraduates in February 1968. Approximately 2000 questionnaires were analyzed. Members of all classes responded. Results were projected from the random sample, and I believe they would obtain for any other small, highly selective college located in or near a big city.
4. The same trend is also becoming evident in Britain, according to this report. *Science*, Vol. 159, March 15, 1968, p. 1213.
5. Erik H. Erikson, *Insight and Responsibility* (New York: Norton, 1964), pp. 104–105.

No Satisfaction

1. Jacques Ellul, *The Technological Society* (New York: Knopf and Vintage Books, 1964), p. 378.

Youth and Politics

1. Kenneth Keniston, *Young Radicals: Notes on Committed Youth* (New York: Harcourt, Brace, 1968), p. 81.
2. Riesman, op. cit., p. 256.
3. Erich Fromm, *Escape from Freedom* (New York: Holt, 1941; Avon paperback, 1965), p. 80.
4. Erik Erikson, *Childhood and Society* (New York: Norton, 1964), p. 314.
5. *Saturday Review*, July 1, 1967, p. 40.
6. Ibid.
7. Irving Louis Horowitz, *Three Worlds of Development* (New York: Oxford University Press, 1966), pp. 189–90.

The Old Road Is Aging

1. *Ramparts*, December 1967, p. 34.
2. Albert Camus, *Notebooks 1942–1951* (New York: Knopf, 1963), p. 214.

Mr. Businessman

1. William H. Whyte, *The Organization Man* (New York: Simon and Schuster, 1956; Doubleday Anchor Books, 1957), p. 71.
2. *Center Diary 18*, published by the Center for the Study of Democratic Institutions, p. 28.
3. *Newsweek*, January 27, 1969.
4. John Kenneth Galbraith, *The New Industrial State* (Boston: Houghton Mifflin, 1968), pp. 201–202.
5. Ibid., p. 210.
6. Ibid.
7. In Erik H. Erikson, ed., *Youth: Change and Challenge* (New York: Basic Books, 1963), p. 79.

Preachers of Equality

1. Cf. Jonathan Kozol's *Death at an Early Age* (Boston: Houghton Mifflin, 1967).

One Push of the Button

1. Ruth Benedict, *Patterns of Culture* (Boston: Houghton Mifflin, 1934; paperback, 1961), p. 257.
2. Gunnar Myrdal, *Beyond the Welfare State* (New Haven, Conn.: Yale University Press, 1960; paperback), p. 179.
3. *United Nations Demographic Yearbook, 1965*, p. 103.
4. Keniston, *Young Radicals*, p. 252.
5. Gabriel Marcel, *Man against Mass Society* (Chicago: Regnery, paperback, 1962), p. 94.
6. C. Wright Mills, *White Collar* (New York: Oxford University Press, 1951; paperback, 1956), p. 347.
7. James M. Gillespie and Gordon W. Allport, "Youth's Outlook on the Future."

A Fading Dream

1. Arthur M. Schlesinger, Jr., *The Bitter Heritage* (Boston: Houghton Mifflin; New York: Fawcett paperback, 1966), p. 127.
2. *The Atlantic*, March 1968, p. 57.
3. Ibid., p. 59.

Youth and Psychology

1. Herbert Marcuse, *Eros and Civilization* (Boston: Beacon, 1955; New York: Vintage Books, 1962), p. xvii.
2. Riesman, op. cit., p. 251.
3. Marcuse, op. cit., p. xvii.
4. Colin Wilson, *The Outsider* (Boston: Houghton Mifflin,1956; New York: Dell, 1967), p. 154.

What Did They Put in Your Head?

1. Christopher Jencks, "Is It All Dr. Spock's Fault?" *New York Times Magazine*, March 3, 1968.
2. Erich Fromm, *Man for Himself* (New York: Holt, 1947; Fawcett paperback), p. 19.

3. Galbraith, op. cit., pp. 270–71.
4. Ibid., p. 273.
5. Max Weber, *The Protestant Ethic and the Spirit of Capitalism* (New York: Scribner's, 1948; paperback), p. 118.
6. Ibid., p. 53.
7. Fromm, *Man for Himself*, p. 73.

They All Look Just the Same

1. Fromm, *Man for Himself*, p. 77.
2. McLuhan, op. cit., p. 129.
3. Riesman, op. cit., p. 269.
4. Galbraith stresses the same need when he criticizes the assumption that "all men should work a standard number of hours a week . . . none may work less." He further criticizes other assumptions: that all men have the same preference for the acquisition of wealth; that all have the same capacity and desire for leisure; and that all should be treated alike. "None of this is necessary," Galbraith concludes. "The employed person should be allowed a much wider set of options than at present as between work and goods on the one hand and leisure on the other" (op. cit., pp. 366–367).
5. Ibid., p. 265.
6. Kenneth Keniston, *The Uncommitted* (New York: Harcourt, Brace, 1965), p. 363.
7. Benedict, op. cit., p. 254.

Continue to Pretend

1. Eda J. LeShan, *The Conspiracy against Childhood* (New York: Atheneum, 1967), p. 26.
2. Cf. Kauffman's "Youth and the Peace Corps" in Erikson's *Youth: Change and Challenge*, p. 155.

Know Who You Are

1. *Look*, June 13, 1967, p. 23.
2. Erikson, *Identity and the Life Cycle*, p. 100.

Youth and Manhood

Now a Man

1. Elizabeth M. Thomas, *The Harmless People* (New York: Knopf and Vintage Books, 1959), p. 31.
2. Riesman makes a similar point when he concludes that "the current divorce rate is, in part, an index of the new demands made upon marriage . . . these demands not only begin high, in the choice of a mate, but as Margaret Mead has observed, include the expectation that each partner grow and develop at the same rate."
3. Rebecca S. Vreeland in a paper delivered at the American College Health Association, Washington, D.C., March 30, 1967.

Go Ask Alice

1. *Time*, August 30, 1968, p. 44.

Give a Damn

1. *Science*, Vol. 159, February 9, 1968, pp. 607–11.
2. In Erich Fromm, et al., *Zen Buddhism and Psychoanalysis* (New York: Grove Press, 1963), p. 5.
3. Karen Horney, *Our Inner Conflicts* (New York: Norton, 1945), pp. 241–42; Ronald Laing, *Politics of Experience* (New York: Pantheon, 1967), p. 48; Erich Fromm, *Escape from Freedom*, p. 286.

The Neon Gods

1. Carl Jung, *Modern Man in Search of a Soul* (New York: Harcourt, Brace, 1933; Harvest paperback, 1955), p. 215.
2. William Barrett in *Irrational Man* (New York: Doubleday Anchor Books, 1958), p. 9, stresses the difference between existentialism and traditional philosophy when he writes that "the very themes of Existentialism were something of a scandal to the detached sobriety of Anglo-American philosophy. Such matters as anxiety, death, the conflict between the bogus and the genuine self, the faceless man of the masses, the experience of the death of God are scarcely the themes of analytic philosophy. Yet they are the themes of life."
3. Louis W. Cartwright, "The New Hero," in Butz, ed., op. cit., p. 14.
4. William T. De Bary, et al., eds., *Sources of Japanese Tradition* (New York: Columbia University Press, 1958), p. 232.

Youth and Identity

1. I am grateful to Dr. George W. Goethals for showing me the poignancy of the Icarian myth as a means for contrasting the traditional issue of authority and identity with the modern situation.
2. Ellul, op. cit., p. 348.
3. Robert J. Lifton, "Protean Man," *Partisan Review*, Winter 1968, p. 14.
4. Ibid., p. 16.
5. Ibid., p. 19.
6. Ibid., p. 26.
7. Philip Rieff, *Freud, the Mind of the Moralist*, as reprinted in Gordon Wright and Arthur Mejia, Jr., *An Age of Controversy* (New York: Dodd, Mead, paperback, 1963), p. 420.
8. Bertrand Russell, *Roads to Freedom* (New York: Barnes and Noble, paperback, 1966), p. 212.
9. Paul Goodman, *Like a Conquered Province* (New York: Random House, 1967), p. ix.
10. Erich Fromm, *Beyond the Chains of Illusion* (New York: Dutton, paperback, 1959), p. 196.
11. Galbraith, op. cit., p. 332.
12. *The New York Times*, March 26, 1968; and *Saturday Review*, August 17, 1968, pp. 41–47.

13. As reported by Robert J. Lifton in a lecture at Harvard University, March 20, 1968.

A Strange Vibration

1. *The Nation*, March 9, 1957, p. 108.
2. *The Nation*, June 19, 1967, p. 78.
3. *Maui News*, May 13, 1967.
4. *Time*, "The Hippies," July 7, 1967, p. 18.
5. Ibid.
6. Riesman, op. cit., pp. 251–52.
7. Jung, op. cit., p. 238.
8. *Time*, January 16, 1967, p. 19.
9. Jencks, op. cit.

The Times They Are
A-Changin'

1. Erik H. Erikson, "A Memorandum on Identity and Negro Youth," *Journal of Social Issues* 20:41, October 1964.

House of Mirrors: II

1. Erikson, *Childhood and Society*, pp. 275, 315–16.

2. Robert J. Lifton, *Thought Reform and the Psychology of Totalism* (New York: Norton, 1961), p. 469.
3. William Taubman, *The View from Lenin Hills* (New York: Coward McCann, 1967), pp. 238–39.
4. Ibid., p. 239.
5. Ibid., p. 244.
6. Ibid., pp. 241–42.
7. As reported by an on-the-scene newsman for the *Montreal Gazette* in the *Chicago Tribune*, August 28, 1968, p. 2.

Epilogue

Within You

1. Bruno Bettelheim, *The Informed Heart* (New York: The Free Press, 1960), p. 100.
2. Joseph Fletcher, *Situation Ethics* (Philadelphia: Westminster Press, 1966), p. 142.